USES OF THE FORENSIC SCIENCES

USES OF THE FORENSIC SCIENCES

The proceedings of the Conference
held in Glasgow in April 1986

Edited by
BRIAN CADDY

1987

SCOTTISH ACADEMIC PRESS
EDINBURGH AND LONDON

Published by
Scottish Academic Press Ltd
33 Montgomery Street
Edinburgh EH7 5JX

SBN 7073 0516 0

Typeset by Pindar (Scotland) Limited
Printed in Great Britain by Lindsay & Co Ltd, Edinburgh

CONTENTS

An Introduction to the Conference vii
B. CADDY

FORENSIC SCIENCE

"What am I Bid" 3
I. E. DONEY

Statistics — Do they have a Role to Play in the Interpretation of Evidence? 8
I. W. EVETT

Can Forensic Science Survive as a Non-Medical Discipline? 14
J. A. J. FERRIS

The Investigation of Fatal Fires 23
D. J. X. HALLIDAY

The Rainbow Warrior Incident 28
M. LAWTON

The Organisation of Forensic Sciences in Switzerland 38
J. MATHYER

Kilroy Was Here! 46
W. J. RODGER

Fire Bugs — The Role of Bacteria and Fungi in Spontaneous Heat Generation 51
R. E. H. SKELTON

Blood, Sweat and Tears 57
P. H. WHITEHEAD

LEGAL

The Solicitor and Forensic Science 65
A. R. BROWNLIE

The Place of the Expert in Criminal Court Proceedings with Special Reference to Recent Proposals for Change 70
C. GOODWIN JONES

The Expert in the Adversarial Process 80
M. HILL

Forensic Medicine — An Independent Science? 89
LORD MORTON

Proof of Fact in Criminal Trials 93
M. STONE

FORENSIC MEDICINE

Post-Mortem Interval by Microwave Thermography 101
L. M. AL-ALOUSI and R. A. ANDERSON

Value of Forensic Psychiatry in a Court of Law 116
R. N. ANTEBI

The Air India Jumbo Jet Disaster Kalishna — Injury Analysis 121
I. R. HILL

Handmaidens 146
W. D. S. MACLAY

Forensic Medicine — How Will It Develop? 154
A. A. WATSON

POLICE

Interpol Today 163
R. G. KENDALL

Can Technology Replace Detective Skills? 167
B. D. K. PRICE

"First Catch Your Hare" 177
A. K. SLOAN

AN INTRODUCTION TO THE CONFERENCE

B. Caddy

Forensic Science Unit, University of Strathclyde,
204 George Street, Glasgow, G1 1XW

The Forensic Science Unit was established in 1966 under the direction of Dr Francis Fish and it lays claim to the only official academic chair in Forensic Science in the United Kingdom. This is presently held by Professor W. J. Tilstone who is presently director of the Forensic Science Laboratory in Adelaide, South Australia. However, the university has a much longer connection with Forensic Science. Prior to becoming a university this institution was known as the Royal College of Science and Technology and before that as Anderson's College and Anderson's University after the Professor of Natural Philosophy, Professor Anderson. One of the students at that time was a certain Henry Faulds born in 1843. He qualified as a doctor and was sent as a missionary by the Scottish Presbyterian Church to Japan where, apart from his professional commitments, he studied the fingerprints of both Japanese and non-Japanese peoples and of monkeys. The driving force behind this study appears to have been an attempt to discredit Darwin's Evolutionary Theory. However, in October 1880 he published in the scientific journal, *Nature* (1) a paper entitled "On the Skinfurrows of the Hand" in which he detailed methods of taking and classifying fingerprints but also describing how they might be used in criminal and paternity cases. This paper preceded that of Sir William Herschel by one month. We like to think that our Unit continues in the tradition of Henry Faulds in its logical and practical approach to the Forensic Sciences.

A recent report by the Royal Society (2) under the chairmanship of Dr W. F. Bodmer, FRS points out how badly informed is our society on scientific matters. In particular, the report states that "there is clearly a strong case for Parliamentarians in particular, to have a much better understanding of science and its relevance to their responsibilities than they now have". Another group highlighted as having little knowledge of science are the Civil Servants. Again, I quote, "Better understanding of science by government and the higher levels of the Civil Service should also lead to better policies for science". What is relevant to science in general must also apply to the forensic sciences. How good are we as scientists, lawyers, medics, policemen and others involved in the legal process at convincing those in authority of the need for a highly competent and active service?

It is perhaps no coincidence that the lack of appreciation of the Forensic Sciences by parliamentarians and administrative Civil Servants occurs at a time in the United Kingdom when pressure is being placed upon the Forensic Sciences to look towards cost effectiveness of such services. This has resulted in a series of policy options recently commented upon by Dr W. J. Rodger in his Firth Memorial Lecture to the Forensic Science Society (3). As suggested in that lecture decisions are being made by non-scientifically trained minds on what constitutes acceptable scientific ability for the analysis of samples and for the presentation of any such findings to the Courts of Law. This is a dangerous path to tread, for what may initially be considered an acceptable ability often becomes a minimum acceptability. Some of this problem may arise from the fact that administrators employ external highly qualified scientists of international repute to assess the Forensic Sciences. For all their expertise one must ask "What do they know about Forensic Science?" If I could quote again from Dr Rodger's Firth Memorial Lecture, "There are Scientists and Forensic Scientists, the one only truly becomes the other after many years of experience". If one could draw a parallel: who, for example, would expect the General Medical Council to accept the opinions of the Royal Society of Chemistry on their performance? Whilst one recognises that such experts may have some role to play, are there no sufficiently qualified forensic scientists of international standing to be employed in this role, or is it that those responsible feel that no forensic scientist could divorce himself sufficiently from the service to make an impartial review? Alternatively, might an experienced forensic scientist be more aware of the problems facing the forensic sciences and any report would make it more restrictive to those in authority to decide upon their policy options? It is with some pride that I can report that Scotland has not taken this pathway but has called upon all those involved in the legal process, namely the forensic scientists, the lawyers and the policemen, to assess its requirements.

The Forensic Scientist, in the United Kingdom, is presently under pressure; he is underfinanced especially in terms of personnel, although in Scotland there is the additional problem of accommodation and equipment; he is overworked in terms of caseload; he is under pressure as a witness and the turnover of staff has begun to accelerate especially for the more able scientists. As with higher education, this Government expects more and more from its Forensic Sciences for less and less investment, a path of development which will only lead to complete demoralisation and a second-rate service. In spite of this the forensic sciences have a glamorous image in society although the public as well as many lawyers do not always distinguish between forensic science and medicine. In the light of recent cases in the United Kingdom, the media have portrayed the Forensic Scientists as incompetents and that is a belief held by some sections of our society and which requires to be redressed.

How may this be achieved? Perhaps one indicator of the direction in which this can be resolved is seen from those august bodies representing the legal and medical professions, the General Medical Council and the Law Societies. These societies are statutory bodies, membership of which is essential to the practising of that particular profession. These societies represent professions and offer advice to their members in terms of conditions of employment and their general welfare. Such societies have a code of practice and are responsible for maintaining the standard of performance of their members to the extent that they can impose disciplinary measures. Such societies are routinely consulted by legislators and those in positions of power and authority. One may ask just how much consultation was conducted with the Forensic Scientist in the writing of the new Criminal Evidence Act and how much of his advice was accepted? It is time that there was a statutory body in the United Kingdom which represents the Forensic Sciences and the forensic science profession. Who better to fulfil this role than the Forensic Science Society, the organisation which has the largest membership of Forensic

Scientists and which is international in outlook. Whilst the Courts will always be the ultimate arbiter on what constitutes expertise, we might hope that qualifications of the Forensic Science Society would become the means by which the Courts would reach their decisions.

How good are we at communicating our own speciality to others within the legal process and those outwith the Courts? For example, has the introduction of civilian scenes of crimes officers imposed a barrier between the investigating officer and the scientist? At a recent meeting of the Council of the Forensic Science Society it saddened me when the reason given for the resignation from the Society by a senior police officer was the irrelevance of contributions to the *Journal of the Forensic Science Society* for the pursuance of this officer's profession. This may of course be true, but the explanation for this can only be that there are insufficient articles on topics relevant to this officer's work being submitted to the journal by his colleagues. This also represents a very narrow view of the role of the police officer who surely should be interested in all the aspects of the legal process. He should also be in the business of communication. None of us in the forensic sciences can relinquish our responsibility to communicate the uses of the forensic sciences.

While there are no easy solutions to our problems, communication of these problems to the various branches within our domain is important. Equally if not more important is that we make society aware of our function. Society must be made aware of "The Uses of the Forensic Sciences" through such conferences as the present one. We each have that same responsibility of communicating our worth. This will require an interaction with the media something with which we have to come to terms. I quote again from the Royal Society Report, "Mechanisms need to be found for improving the contact with (Forensic) Scientists and the understanding of science, not only by science journalists but also, and perhaps even more so, by journalists as a whole". Only by such means can the superficiality of some media reports be suppressed, understanding of journalistic problems be appreciated and a climate of trust be established. I would like to think that this conference is one way in which we can make a beginning.

References

1. Faulds, H. On the skinfurrows of the hand. *Nature*, 1880; 22: 605.

2. *The Public Understanding of Science*, Report of a Royal Society *ad hoc* Group endorsed by the Council of the Royal Society. ISBN 085403 2576.

3. Rodger, W. J. Forensic Science — policy option. *Journal of the Forensic Science Society*, 1986; 26: 69–78.

FORENSIC SCIENCE

WHAT AM I BID?

I. E. Doney

The purpose of this short paper is not to provide any academic information on the Uses of the Forensic Sciences but to put the case for a possible new customer.

In considering the workload of any forensic laboratory it goes without saying that the biggest customer must be the police. Then probably comes the defence and then a very small, an almost insignificantly small, portion of private people — private investigators for instance — who use the forensic sciences for various purposes.

The reason for this latter group being small is almost certainly because the general public are not aware of what the forensic sciences can offer them or if they are aware, they do not know how they can be contacted.

This paper will refer to one small part of the small group — the world of the antiques collector. Its purpose is to suggest that the world of fine arts and antiques could benefit much more than it does already from the services of the forensic sciences, if the public were more fully aware of their capabilities.

It is well known that all forensic laboratories have at some time or other been engaged in the identification of works of art, documents, metals, clothing but mostly in connection with forgeries or police work. There must be a place, too, for satisfying the enquiring collector who may want his modest treasure authenticated and who is prepared to pay to have it done!

Most human beings are collectors at heart. To go through a lifetime and collect nothing must be a rare occurrence. Some people collect books or collect stamps, some coins, some collect porcelain or silver and some collect works of art. In acquiring some group of objects they gradually acquire specialist knowledge and devote much of their leisure time to the study of them.

Acquiring some rare piece to add to a collection is the thrill of the game and the envy of fellow collectors.

The fascination of bidding for some unusual lot in the auction rooms and salerooms is captivating and unending. A collector's collection is never complete. However, it is obvious that the authenticity of the piece must be beyond question.

To whom does the bidder turn for advice if he suspects a raw deal or wonders if he has made a foolish purchase?

Usually he will turn to another collector equally or more authoritative or he will go to some reputable house where someone with experience will give an opinion.

Sadly, what he will sometimes do is go to the not so reputable authority. The antiques business abounds with shrewd dealers with a flair for making a quick profit. They can easily beguile the innocent owner by under-valuing an object or deploring its authenticity, then offering a small price in order to make a large profit later on.

In the field of antiques this is, after all, a feature of a few of the traders and merely considered good business, certainly not dishonesty.

This paper poses the question — can forensic science help the private collector better than the dealer? It is already used in the field of forged treasures, so why not towards the public at large. The inherent honesty of the scientist and his impartial opinion based on scientific fact to back it up would surely appeal to the collector, the purchaser and the auctioneer alike. The scientific equipment available to the forensic scientist is evidence enough that he is far better serviced than the average fine arts dealer, to make authentic pronouncements.

The annals of forensic science reveal many examples of how it has already helped in this field and a few spring to mind at once.

In the famous Wheatley/Palmer case certain pictures were reputed to have been painted by the nineteenth-century painter Palmer. Forensic evidence showed discrepancies between scrapings of paint from some of the pictures and those available at the time Palmer lived: an easy exercise for the forensic scientists but errors in the paintings had been missed by art dealers all over the world.

In a paper to the International Association of Forensic Sciences meeting in Bergen some years ago, Dr Julius Grant told how he had been asked to authenticate an impressionist painting. He had compared the signature on similar paintings by the same artist in various art galleries and museums. He had compared scrapings of paints and canvas and had declared the picture genuine in a painstaking and time consuming investigation. He was astonished later to find his decision challenged by a celebrated art dealer who picked up the painting, took it to a window and declared it a fake in what seemed only a few moments. Dr Grant with his usual modesty declared "I suppose we shall never know which one of us was right!"

Another example concerns the famous painting by Velazquez in the early seventeenth century known as the Rokeby "Venus" (1). For some time people used to think the Cupid on the picture was an eighteenth-century addition. Scientists used a tiny hypodermic syringe to take out a complete "biopsy" or section of the picture showing all layers from back to front. Samples were taken from the blue ribbon worn by Cupid and from the green drapery adorning Venus. Both revealed a mixture of two pigments, azurite and smalts. It was known that azurite was hardly ever used after 1650 whilst smalts was first used in about 1600. This was strong evidence that both parts of the picture were painted at the time of Velazquez and suggested it was genuine.

Delegates who attended the recent Australian Forensic Science meeting in Melbourne in February 1986 heard Hermann Metz and Peter Ross describe their investigations into the authenticity of certain pictures by early Australian artists which are fetching high prices in the slick auction rooms of today (2). They felt that whilst non-destructive examinations such as "soft" X-rays and visible microspectrophotometry had their place in investigations, nevertheless it was also frequently necessary to use needle biopsy techniques to establish the various layers of paints applied to pictures. Additions to original pictures could thus more easily be distinguished.

In a different vein, the well-known story of Van Meegeren shows how he set out to foil both the art expert and the scientist at the same time. Lanee Salway tells the story in his book *Forgers* (3). Born in 1889 Van Meegeren began life as a painter but when his work deteriorated he blamed the art critics. He decided he would get his own back on them by painting a Vermeer and duping the experts.

He had to try to deceive the scientists too so he bought old canvases and wiped off the pictures and paint. Then he ground up natural pigments by hand so that the particles would look irregular under the microscope.

It took him seven months to paint "The Disciples of Emmaus" by Vermeer! He then announced the picture had come from a Dutch family and he wanted to sell it!

Various art experts inspected it and declared it genuine and it was bought by a Rotterdam museum for £52,000, in those days (1937) no mean sum. Hans Van Meegeren was delighted. He could now expose the experts! Instead, however, he decided to extend his skills and painted five more spurious Vermeers. By this time the Second World War had begun and the German leader Herman Goering bought "The lady taken in adultery" by Vermeer, faked by Van Meegeren. After the war it was discovered and Van Meegeren was charged as a traitor accused of selling art treasures to the enemy. He at once confessed it was a fake. But he had done his work too well! No one would believe him — all the experts testified the pictures were genuine Vermeers!

Eventually the judge ordered him to paint another Vermeer to fool the experts. He painted "Christ teaching in the temple" and the charge was changed from treason to forgery.

Modern forensic scientists could have exposed him in a few moments.

Moving next to the field of books and documents. The work of the document examiner is little known outside his forensic setting. He could be of immense help to the simple collector of treasured books or documents seeking authenticity for his bid if he only knew how to contact him.

The case of the forged Hitler diaries illustrates this point exceedingly well. There were so many mistakes in the diaries that, in retrospect, it is difficult to appreciate how they attracted so much publicity. It is even more surprising that a University historian (and the analogy with the art dealer is obvious) was apparently asked to check the authenticity of the Hitler diaries before the forensic scientists became involved. When they eventually did come on to the scene the project collapsed at once.

It is reported that simple scientific examination of the paper used in the diaries showed that the firm making the paper had not been in existence before 1955. Sometimes the German eagle's head was facing the wrong way! Typed labels on documents purporting to be several years apart, e.g. Diary 1931 and Diary 1935 for instance, had all been typed on the same typewriter at the same time. It is obvious that any normal typewriter would show tell-tale wear-and-tear marks as the years go by.

Another mistake was discovered on examining the ink. When an ink stroke is made on paper, time causes the chloride ions in the ink to migrate to the periphery of the stroke. The rate of migration can be estimated. In the case of the forged diaries it was shown that the ink could not have been applied as long ago as fifty years.

In discussing the uses of the forensic sciences it is easy to see how the collector and indeed any reputable auction rooms and salerooms could benefit from the expertise and facilities of the forensic laboratories if there were more publicity given to let the public know they are there.

Collectors of silver and precious metals have sometimes found that a fake hallmark has been found on some object. A Georgian date with a rare silversmith's mark found on the bottom of a cream jug may be authentic but the jug as a whole is a fraud. In such cases the whole circular base complete with genuine hallmark has been inset into the base of another jug or article. The forensic scientist could demonstrate this in a similar way that he matches up striations on bullets and other metal objects showing that the base was not part of the original jug. A silver dealer might recognise it too but would lack the facilities to prove it to some unbelieving customer.

Further on the subject of metals a frequent note on the auctioneer's catalogue reads "hallmark indistinct". Years of polishing have worn down the precise letters. They are often still there but imperceptible to the naked eye or the collector's hand magnifying lens. They can easily be revealed by the modern techniques of forensic science laboratories. Partly obscured signatures on pictures can also be identified whilst the use of ESDA techniques for impression marks on documents are everyday procedures in most laboratories.

It could be argued that many of these procedures are also available to the antique trade. Collectors, however, sometimes have an unjustified mistrust of the trade but would have faith in some impartial investigator giving a scientific opinion on his possessions.

Antique pistols and firearms of various types are popular lots in the salerooms of the world nowadays. Some of the articles described as "restored" turn out to be more restored than original. Ballistic experts, used to matching up precise items of firearms and justifying their findings in courts of law, would be able to assist the collector in a manner quite beyond the aesthetic opinion of a casual dealer.

The forensic scientists have not sold themselves to the public or the trade in this field. They have demonstrated but not exploited their expertise. There is surely a place for extending the use of the forensic sciences and attracting other customers to their laboratories.

Scientists who are matching up particles of glass every day of their lives, matching up paints, examining marks on metals and vehicles, with sophisticated scientific equipment, must surely be equally good at examining differences in works of art. The document examiner, the car crash expert, the chemical analyst and toxicologist are already there if the enquiring collector only knew how to approach them.

It goes without saying that all procedures must be non-destructive and the lay person might feel that some treasured piece of porcelain, for instance, could not be analysed without risk.

This is the field in which the scanning electron microscope and Energy Dispersive X-ray Fluorescence Spectrophotometer come into their own. Changes in crystalline forms, inconsistencies in colours and changes in pigments would assist in establishing whether parts of a treasure were incomplete or added to.

Then again fine cracks can provide material such as minerals, grit and stone used in the original manufacture without making the procedure destructive. Some decorative flower added to an article as "restoration", however cleverly done, could hardly escape such scientific scrutiny. The shrewd art dealer may be able to detect it too but would not have the proof at his fingertips in the way that the scientist would. The forensic scientist could defend his findings in court whereas the dealer could only give his opinion from experience. However good that may be, it lacks scientific appraisal and for the simple collector it lacks scientific appeal too. It is clear that this expertise is available but untapped.

It may be felt that any one laboratory would not be expert on all facilities for all investigations and the enquiring collector would be dissuaded from contacting them. However, the local laboratory would be the starting point and would know the people to contact in another area. Alternatively there could be a centrally known establishment where items could be assessed and then referred to the appropriate expert.

How would the public, the auctioneers, the salerooms get to know about this use of the forensic sciences? How could they enquire how to clarify an indistinct signature on a picture, an indentation on a book, a rubbed mark on metal? How could they verify the rare penny, the rare stamp, the forgery?

It would have to begin like everything else by publicity. There would have to be notifications to auctioneers, both national and local, to probate experts, salerooms and trade magazines. The two sides are there. They need to be brought together.

This paper began by posing a possible question from the lay consumer public — can the uses of the forensic sciences be extended to the world of fine arts? The scientist can ponder over the answer. Who knows? Perhaps one day the salerooms and even the private customer could bring an added, even lucrative, source of income to impecunious laboratories.

References

1. Harrison, W. *Forgery Detection.*

2. Metz, H. and Ross, P. *The Examination of a Questioned Oil Painting.* State Forensic Science Laboratory, Melbourne, Australia.

3. Salway, L. *Forgers.* Harmondsworth: Kestrel Books, 1979.

STATISTICS — DO THEY HAVE A ROLE TO PLAY IN THE INTERPRETATION OF EVIDENCE?

I. W. Evett

Introduction

The title of this paper appears to have its origin not far from the source of an editorial in the *Journal of the Forensic Science Society* entitled "Away with the Fuzz" (1). Its theme was that statisticians were making nuisances of themselves by dabbling in forensic science. Indeed, the final sally of the editorial was "away with the statistical fuzz!"

Before discussing the problems which might underlie such attitudes and addressing the question in the title, it would be best for us to have similar ideas about what the word "statistics" is supposed to mean. The *Concise Oxford English Dictionary* (COED) gives two definitions:

1. Numerical facts systematically collected.
2. Science of collecting, classifying and using statistics.

A forensic scientist who attests in court that the blood group of a stain associated with the crime scene is the same as the blood group of the defendant will be expected to give some indication of the extent to which the blood group occurs in the population at large. The forensic science literature contains many articles giving the relative frequencies of blood phenotypes — indeed part 2 of Volume 25 of the *Journal of the Forensic Science Society* (2, 3) was largely given over to two important articles on the subject — but what are these data but statistics? They certainly satisfy the first of the COED definitions.

Of course, there is no particular reason for singling out blood from all the other evidence types. There is ample evidence that forensic scientists of all disciplines recognise the value of relevant background data collections. So whether we like it or not, we are stuck with statistics: certainly according to the first COED definition. The question in the title should not be "*do* they have a role to play in the interpretation of evidence?" but "*what is* the role they should play in the interpretation of evidence?" If we accept that we should gather statistics in accordance with the first COED definition then surely we should accept that the collection, classification and usage should be carried out scientifically. In other words we accept the need for statistics as a science, according to the second COED definition. So when we talk about the role of statistics it is inevitable that we must not just talk about the accumulation of data as an isolated exercise but also about the ways in which those data will be used.

Whereas it is accepted generally that statistics are relevant to interpreting evidence there are considerable problems in applying them in casework because in the individual case there will be, in addition to the hard facts and statistics, other features which may defy quantification. This is the main reason why statistics as a science has not made much impact upon the day-to-day practices of the operational scientist. The problems of using statistics will be explored in a little detail because then it becomes possible to point the way towards future developments: this will clarify the role, not just of statistics as numerical facts, but also of statistics as a scientific discipline operating within the requirements and restrictions of forensic science.

Data

Forensic scientists now have to deal with data of a complexity hardly dreamed of twenty years ago. The amount of information which can be extracted from tiny scraps of paint, glass, fibres, etc. is both exciting and daunting at the same time. Modern techniques increase the scientist's potential for establishing differences in those cases where the trace material in fact originated from a source other than the control: something which is of benefit to all parties in the legal process. However, in those cases where the data from the trace material and the control material are not clearly distinguishable, the modern-day scientist has a bigger problem than his predecessors faced. The problem exists at two levels: there is the task of handling the data generated in the individual case efficiently, and this is no small task because, depending on the nature and extent of the trace material, there might easily be a hundred or more separate numbers to appraise critically; and there is the task of relating the individual case data to whatever background data there are available to assist in interpretation.

Collecting background data which are going to be relevant to forensic science casework presents many problems. Nevertheless, the number of such collections has grown over the years and it is quite exciting to see the ingenuity which the collectors have exercised. One can go back almost twenty years to the survey by Pearson, May and Dabbs (4) of paint and glass in suits handed in to a dry cleaners. And then most recently the study reported in this year's *Forensic Science Society Journal* by Walsh and Buckleton (5) of glass on footpaths in Auckland.

Transfer/Persistence Mechanisms

The data interpretation problem cannot be handled in isolation from other important casework features. It is necessary for the scientist to ask himself questions of the type "Is it reasonable to expect this quantity of fibres/glass/paint, etc. to have been found on the suspect if he (or she) had committed the crime?" Such a question has to be addressed in the light of the perceived circumstances of the crime and the events leading up to the suspect's apprehension; and in the light of what is known about the mechanisms of transference and persistence of the relevant material.

There are several examples in the literature which have expanded our knowledge in this area. The work of Pounds and Smalldon (6, 7) at the Central Research Establishment in the 1970s represented some impressive trail blazing.

Imponderables

However, notwithstanding the knowledge we might have of background data collections and transfer/persistence mechanisms it is inevitable that in the individual case there will be details of the circumstances which will be completely unknown. Whereas we might have good information about the trajectory of glass fragments from a smashed window, in the individual case we might have no knowledge about how close the criminal actually was to the scene window or how hard he hit it.

Alternatives

In addition to the other problems which the forensic scientist faces he must also be able to review the interpretation in the light of changing perceived circumstances relating to the crime. Thus, a scientist dealing with a glass transfer case might initially, in the absence of other information, relate his casework data to a background population of a general nature: yet later the explanation might be put to him that the glass on the suspect's clothes came, not from the crime scene, but a more specific alternative source such as a milk bottle.

The Way Ahead

The foregoing place formidable demands upon any attempt to introduce mathematical treatments of the interpretation problem. In general, if we reduce the circumstances to a frame of reference which is sufficiently simple for a mathematically tractable analysis then we end up with a model which is inadequate to cope with the complexity of real life casework. The constraints within which an objective purely numerical treatment can operate mean that there will probably always be need for subjective input in the form of the judgment of an experienced scientist.

This state of affairs is not, however, peculiar to forensic science and considerable progress has been made over recent years in areas as diverse as geological exploration and medical diagnosis in building computer-based systems which provide judgemental aids by combining objective, statistics-based, information with the subjective opinions of experts.

Figure 1 shows the main components of the interpretative problem and the elements for its solution.

Inference

A simple system which enabled the combination of objective and subjective components was devised two years ago at the Home Office Central Research Establishment. This was for the admittedly rather restricted problem of deciding whether a given hair originated from a dog or a cat. A purely mathematical routine is applied to measurements carried out on the hair and the result is used to modify the operator's own subjective view based on the other unquantified features. The theoretical basis is a statistical discipline known as Bayesian inference. It is becoming widely recognised among those who are interested in the application of statistical methods to the interpretation of scientific evidence that Bayesian inference promises to be a valuable tool: those who were present at the section on evaluation of evidence at Oxford may recall that a high proportion of the papers contained at least an element of the Bayesian philosophy. Bayesian methods provide the potential for combining casework and background data effectively; for taking account of transfer/persistence mechanisms; for helping the scientist to identify the most relevant range of questions to be addressed in an individual case; and of course, for combining subjective judgments with numerical results derived directly from data.

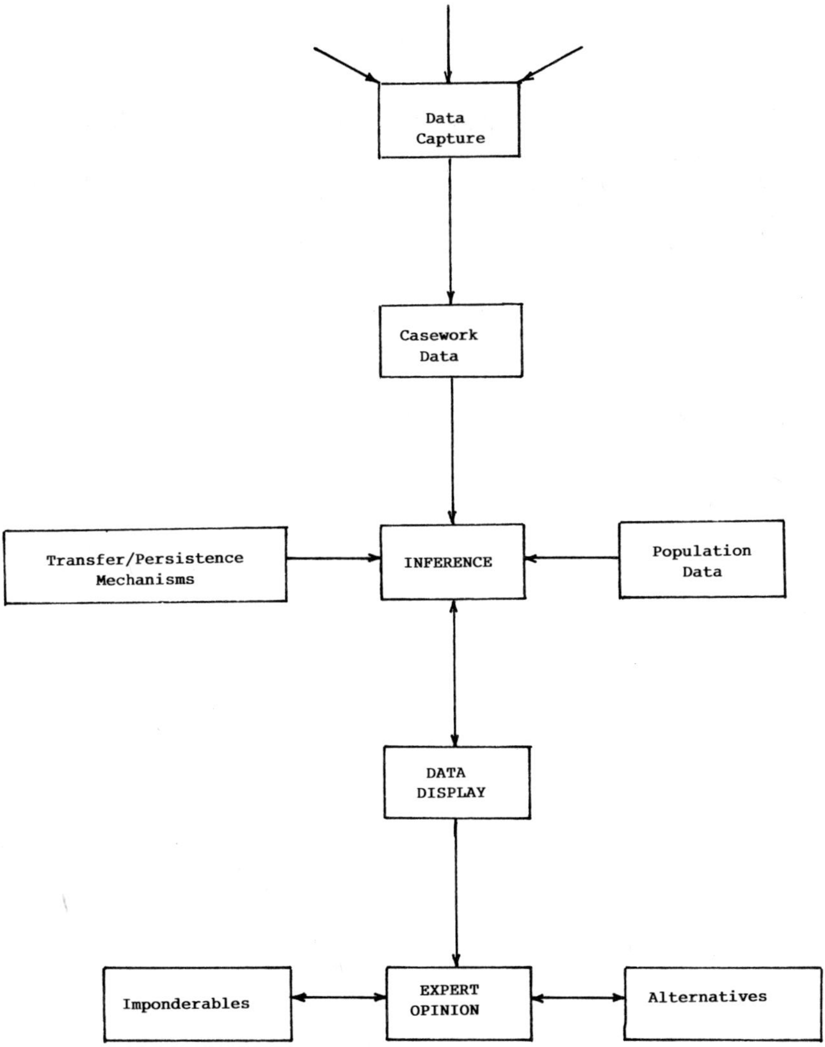

Figure 1. A diagrammatic representation of the interpretative problem.

The mathematics of statistical treatments which could ultimately provide such aids to interpretation will inevitably be complex and will make demands on computing power which would not have been feasible in the past. However, the potential now exists for developing such facilities and embedding them into routines which are easy to use. It is not necessary to turn the forensic scientist into a high-powered mathematician: he need only be prepared to come to terms with the underlying concepts.

The routines would be highly interactive so that the scientist could explore the data structures derived in his case and carry out calculations of evidential value under whatever different sets of circumstances need to be addressed. He could also investigate the sensitivity of the calculations to the various assumptions that would have been made and to the various items of subjective input which he has provided.

For such an inferential system to be of most use it would need to be coupled with facilities for handling the data efficiently and also for creating an effective interface with the scientist.

Data Capture

As new analytical techniques become available so it becomes important for us to have methods for bringing together in an individual case all of the data from several different instrumental systems efficiently and cheaply. This would bring benefits not just in efficiency but also in quality assurance. The industry is converging towards standards which will progressively render data transfer to a central focus an integral feature of our work.

Data Display

Modern developments in computing, in particular the use of colour and graphics, offer the potential for assisting the forensic scientist by displaying complex bodies of data in comprehensible visual patterns. Computer packages which produce bar charts, spreadsheets, scattergrams and graphs at the terminal are being used now in many fields because they can provide useful judgemental aids.

Such software could enable the forensic scientist to explore visually relationships within his casework data; between the casework data and whatever background data is available; and to interact with the interpretive routines within the computer.

Conclusion

In response to the question in the title the answer is "yes" on two counts. Firstly, statistics as numerical facts are widely recognised by scientists and courts as being of crucial importance to the interpretation of evidential value.

Secondly, statistics as a science, coupled with the power that is available in modern computers, offers the means of assisting the scientist to find his way through the maze of data sets and imponderables. The fuzz will still be there — it will always be there — but the scientist will be far better equipped to deal with it and to derive the estimates which are going to be of most value in shedding light on the case which he is assisting to investigate. This will lead to greater effectiveness for forensic science and will significantly benefit the investigative and legal processes.

References

1. Editorial. Away with the Fuzz. *Journal of the Forensic Science Society*, 1979; 19: 157–158.

2. Steadman, R. Blood Group Frequencies of Immigrant and Indigenous Populations from South East England. *Journal of the Forensic Science Society*, 1985; 25: 95–134.

3. Rothwell, T. J. The Frequency of Occurrence of Various Human Blood Groups in the United Kingdom, with observations on their Regional Variation. *Journal of the Forensic Science Society*, 1985; 25: 135–144.

4. Pearson, E. F., May, R. W. and Dabbs, M. D. G. Glass and Paint Fragments Found in Men's Outer Clothing — Report of a Survey. *Journal of Forensic Sciences*, 1971; 16: 283–300.

5. Walsh, K. A. J. and Buckleton, J. S. On the Problem of Assessing the Evidential Value of Glass Fragments Embedded in Footwear. *Journal of the Forensic Science Society*, 1985; 26: 55–60.

6. Pounds, C. A. and Smalldon, K. W. The Distribution of Glass Fragments in Front of a Broken Window and the Transfer of Fragments to Individuals Standing Nearby. *Journal of the Forensic Science Society*, 1978; 18: 197–203.

7. Pounds, C. A. and Smalldon, K. W. The transfer of fibres between clothing materials during simulated contacts and their persistence during wear, Part III. A preliminary investigation of the mechanisms involved. *Journal of the Forensic Science Society*, 1982; 22: 301–308.

CAN FORENSIC SCIENCE SURVIVE AS A NON-MEDICAL DISCIPLINE?

J. A. J. Ferris

The historical evolution of the forensic sciences, with the formation of multiple sub-specialties including almost every subject known to man capable of supporting the designation science, has in large part been dictated by the evolution of science itself. At the turn of the century it became apparent that contemporary scientific techniques could be used to support the police in their criminal investigative roles. Until that time the principal scientific input into crime investigation had been from university departments of forensic medicine and pathology, but it soon became apparent that almost all branches of the newly developing scientific revolution could be applied to the field of crime investigation. The general philosophy that appeared to develop was that any scientific technique which could be applied to such work could be absorbed into this new, ever-expanding community of forensic science.

As we approach the end of the twentieth century, the increasing rate of discovery in basic biology, bio-engineering and computer science has inundated the forensic community with a wide array of innovations. Consequently, the public and the judicial system demand a second-to-none forensic science service that takes full advantage of every expensive new technology. How is it going to be possible to fulfil these expectations in the face of continuing limitations on funds and resources?

There appears to be a growing concern among many administrators, who are constantly being pressured to trim budgets, that forensic science is being driven by technical and commercial imperatives not always linked to improvements in crime investigation or useful evidence. The attitudes of governments that pay for these new technologies are crucial. Government is becoming more involved in deciding which innovations to encourage, where to allow such developments to take place and are viewing with very great suspicion the high-priced items being requested by the forensic science laboratory service such as the mass spectrometer-gas chromatograph (MSGC), liquid scintillation counters and lasers.

It is apparent that the only way to reconcile these rising expectations for forensic science services within the limited resources available is by collaboration between laboratory professionals in all fields of forensic science in the cost-effective use of laboratory facilities.

It is the belief of the author that forensic scientists from all disciplines should be prepared to pool their expertise, to review major innovations and to advise and cooperate with both government and industry. There is no doubt that the engine driving forensic science into the twenty-first century is in real danger of running out of fuel. Without a constant refill of pounds or dollars, it will be impossible for forensic science to keep pace with the development of the rest of the scientific community. If a significant gap develops between these two communities, it will become increasingly difficult to recruit top quality scientists into our laboratories.

It is difficult at present to persuade new graduates from universities to accept standards of pay and promotion no longer comparable with industry. If we are unable to offer such new recruits an opportunity to take part in innovative research and development then they will be rapidly disillusioned and flee the system. The immediate consequence of this will be a reduction in standards of scientific evidence and a rapid realisation that forensic science has become no more than a second-class laboratory support system presenting barely credible evidence in court. It is suggested that general morale in the forensic community is already suffering as a direct consequence of budget cut-backs on training and recruitment.

How to maintain a high quality of forensic laboratory service in the face of constraints on funding will continue to be a critical issue until the end of this century. One obvious approach is to pool professional and technological resources into larger laboratory communities. It is apparent, however, that if we look at the funding support available to the various branches of forensic science and forensic pathology that the direct budgets available to the traditional forensic science laboratories far exceed those available to the field of forensic pathology. However, if we look beyond these traditional budgets and barriers, we see that the forensic pathology community in large part operates out of large university-based clinical laboratories. If we consider forensic pathology as simply representing a division of the whole field of laboratory medicine and then compare the relative financial resources available indirectly to forensic pathologists, the fiscal picture is completely altered.

In the city of Vancouver in British Columbia there are four principal hospitals associated with the University of British Columbia medical school. Vancouver General Hospital used to be the largest hospital in Canada and one of the largest hospitals in the Commonwealth. Today, as a result of specialisation in some areas of clinical medicine and decentralisation in others, this hospital in terms of its overall size, has lost some of its past glory but not its reputation. The University Chairman of Pathology oversees not only the operation of this huge department but also all of the academic and research activities involving the whole of laboratory medicine in this hospital group. The laboratory budget for Vancouver General Hospital is approximately $15 million but the laboratory budget for the entire group is approximately $40 million. In addition to this direct funding, over $6 million of research grant money is placed on an annual basis at the disposal of the laboratory staff in this group. Since most of the pathologists in the group have university appointments and since these hospitals have a long traditional association with the University, there is a general understanding that up to 25 per cent of the time of all members of the University Department of Pathology may be devoted to academic pursuits. In a straw poll of several colleagues, it would be reasonable to suggest that approximately 10 per cent of the time of all of the pathologists is devoted to research and development. If this is the case, then not only is there a $6 million research budget but there is an additional "hidden component" of $4 million also applied directly to research and development.

Working within this large department of pathology with its own specialty laboratories whose location is dictated only by logistical convenience enables one to draw upon almost any resource component of this network to support the activities of the forensic pathology service.

Toronto, in Ontario, boasts one of the largest and most efficient forensic science laboratories in the world. Directed by Mr Doug Lucas, a staff of approximately 110 forensic scientists working in a beautiful, modern laboratory facility operate with a budget of approximately $6 million. Mr Lucas estimates that between 2 per cent and 3 per cent of this budget is directed to research and development. As with almost all of our government funded but non-university affiliated forensic science laboratories, the "hidden component" of the budget for research and development is negligible. This means that in the largest and most innovative forensic science laboratory in Canada less than $150,000 a year is devoted to research and development. The funding that is available is spent on developing techniques invented by others. This is the process of technology transfer and is not innovative research.

It is misleading, however, to suggest that such apparent disparities in budgets for research and development between medical laboratories and forensic science laboratories occur only in Canada. Such differences in funding are typical throughout the Western world. Consider, however, the very considerable shortfall in funding not only for research and development but for routine forensic science in the Third World where governments everywhere are attempting to divert what funds they have available to them to medical care and medical laboratories. It is a political fact of life that health care will always take priority over the forensic sciences for funds. If we can accept this fact and learn to live with it then the solution to some of our budgetary problems may become more apparent.

At present, the forensic science laboratory services can be divided into several groupings. Much of forensic biology is human biology. Toxicology is really a form of laboratory-based applied pharmacology. Forensic serology and immunology, which in many laboratories are now distinct from forensic biology, are unashamedly direct developments from laboratory medicine.

Techniques such as the enzyme-linked immunosorbant assays (ELISA) have been successfully applied in many clinical immunological laboratories for almost fifteen years (1, 2). Only within the last three or four years has this technique been successfully applied in the field of forensic science (3). Much of contemporary forensic science applicable to the investigation of human body fluids is based upon medical laboratory techniques which have been developed in teaching hospitals, used in clinical laboratories and then by a process of technology transfer taken up by the forensic science community and applied to the very special circumstances of forensic science.

No one would suggest that the nature of the samples submitted to forensic science laboratories is in any way directly comparable to the type of material routinely investigated in a medical laboratory. Nevertheless, the problems in the area of body fluid and body fluid stain examination are relatively constant, namely sample deterioration with age, sample size, drying, distortion and decomposition. There is no real reason, however, why the particular problems associated with forensic science field work cannot be applied at an early stage during the research and development of a new clinical technique. There is no reason why medical research laboratories could not be developing forensic procedures in parallel with the procedures required for patient care and diagnosis.

The ELISA technique as it develops in forensic immunology offers an opportunity to add an invaluable parameter to the area of body fluid identification. The major disadvantage, however, seems to be the cost of purchasing fully automated equipment such as dispensers and spectrophotometers. Although some success has been demonstrated with manual techniques, (4) such automated procedures, if available, are going to allow for the more cost-effective use of immunoglobin allo-typing. Such automated equipment is available in many clinical laboratories.

Often the difference between medical and forensic laboratories is one of philosophy rather than substance. Several years ago, as a result of toxicological analysis done on blood samples taken from the body of a young infant dying in the cardiac unit at the Sick Children's Hospital in Toronto, a series of deaths by Digoxin poisoning were uncovered. Over the course of the following 18 months very considerable research was carried out by the forensic toxicologists developing techniques for the identification of Digoxin in fluids and tissues taken from infants' bodies, many of which had been embalmed and most of which were decomposed. Fatal or toxic levels of Digoxin were identified in many of the samples.

A young nurse was arrested and charged with murder; however, the charge against her was dismissed at a preliminary hearing. It became apparent that the police investigation and arrest had been precipitate and inappropriate. The public outcry was such that a major judicial inquiry was held and the forensic toxicologists were obliged to produce all of their analyses involving not only the results of their investigations of the deaths of the children in question, but also the details of all of their experimental studies.

During this inquiry, a report was published identifying a Digoxin-like immunoreactive substance (DLIS) found in newly born infants and in premature babies (5). The press immediately linked this new finding with the Toronto inquiry and suspicion was cast that the results of the forensic toxicology investigations were incorrect and that in some of the cases of apparent murder no crime had been committed. The real tragedy of this case is not that the forensic toxicology results were wrong nor that the work on the identification of DLIS was misleading, but that these two major investigations had proceeded in parallel, independently and largely unknown to each other. It was only after several months of confused press reporting, inappropriate interviews on television and claims by one scientist that there never had been a murder, that the medical laboratory researchers working on DLIS were made fully aware of the forensic implications of their findings and were able to direct their research to determining the possible significance of DLIS in the Sick Children's Hospital Digoxin case.

In retrospect, of course, we now know that Digoxin-like immunoreactive substance could not have accounted for the findings of such high levels of Digoxin in some of the murdered infants in Sick Children's Hospital. But the whole experience for those involved was unpleasant, uncomfortable and largely unnecessary. As long as the forensic science community continues to function largely isolated from laboratory medicine, such confusions and misunderstandings will continue to arise.

In the area of forensic toxicology the pattern of work of the forensic toxicologist is often dictated by the pressures of the judicial system. Most forensic toxicology laboratories are concerned primarily with the detection of crime by the identification of restricted drugs or by the identification of toxic or fatal levels of drugs. Coroners, however, involved in the investigation of death and in particular in the investigation of human factors associated with unnatural deaths, may not be directly concerned with the identification either of restricted drugs or toxic levels of drugs. It may become important to identify drugs in therapeutic or below therapeutic levels. Many forensic toxicology laboratories are unable or are unwilling to take the time to analyse for drugs in concentrations that may have no criminal significance.

In September 1985 a twin engine Beach aircraft with a party of seven Chicago police officers on a hunting trip in northern Quebec near the Labrador border was making a final approach to land at the small airport at the town of Schefferville. Within two minutes of the pilot's last communication with the control tower, the plane crashed and burst into flames killing all seven passengers plus the pilot.

An investigation immediately commenced at the scene which involved examination of the aircraft and recovery of the bodies. Post-mortem examinations were performed at the hospital at Schefferville. Blood and urine samples were taken for toxicology from the pilot and blood samples were taken from all of the passengers. These samples were sent to the provincial forensic science laboratory in Montreal where toxicological analysis failed to reveal any evidence of significant poisons or carbon monoxide.

At this stage of the investigation it was discovered that the pilot had a long history of asthma but he had managed to conceal this medical problem from his aviation medical examiners. Because of the possibility that an asthmatic attack may have been a factor in the accident and because it was known that he had been taking Salbutamol in the form of an inhaler, the forensic laboratory was asked to look for evidence of Salbutamol in the tissue samples. This particular forensic science laboratory did not have the techniques available to detect therapeutic levels of Salbutamol and arrangements were made for the blood and urine to be sent to the Civil Aviation Medical Toxicology Laboratory in Toronto.

Analysis of the urine sample from the pilot showed traces of the drug but since this substance is excreted extremely slowly from the body and since none was detected in his blood, it was thought highly unlikely that he had been using his inhaler at the time of the accident. However, as part of the screening procedures in the aviation medical laboratory, fatal levels of hydrogen cyanide but low levels of carboxyhaemoglobin were detected in the pilot and three of the passengers. Traces of cannabinoids were also detected in the pilot's urine. None of these tests forms part of the routine screening procedures in the forensic science laboratory but all of these results were extremely important in the interpretation of the circumstances of the accident.

In the province of British Columbia, the segregation of forensic toxicology services into criminal and non-criminal is now almost complete. The Royal Canadian Mounted Police (R.C.M.P.) Crime Laboratory is concerned almost exclusively with toxicology tests as part of an investigation of criminal activity. The British Columbia Coroners Service, however, requires an extensive and speedy toxicology service. As a result a separate provincial forensic science laboratory has been established funded directly by the Coroner's Office with the resulting duplication in equipment, staffing and the attendant problems of quality control associated with any division of responsibilities.

The Department of Clinical Toxicology at Vancouver General Hospital is one of the largest and best equipped toxicology laboratories in the country and yet its responsibility is almost exclusively in the area of clinical toxicology, research and development. It was in this laboratory that the Digoxin-like immunoreactive substance was identified. There is almost no exchange of information, samples or expertise between any of these three laboratories. Each of the laboratories considers itself expert and of course, the quality of results produced by the laboratories is comparable.

Unfortunately, quality of service is often assessed by the consumer not on the basis of accuracy or reproducibility of results, but on the rapidity with which results are produced. For example, the average turnaround time for toxicology screening in the R.C.M.P. Crime Laboratory is six weeks. The average turnaround time in the Coroner's toxicology laboratory is ten to fourteen days. The average turnaround time for toxicology screening in the hospital toxicology laboratory is six hours for a preliminary result with a full final follow-up report within twelve to twenty-four hours of the sample being received.

The reasons for the significant disparity in turnaround time between the three laboratory services is a reflection, not of the quality of staff or equipment, but a combination of the pressures and expectations of their role and therefore directly reflects the overall budgeting. No forensic toxicologist in this room will deny that with adequate financing he would be able to compete in terms of turnaround time and quality with any clinical laboratory anywhere in the world. However, realistically this funding is not available and will not be available.

This point may be illustrated by giving the particular example of the application of DNA fingerprinting to forensic science. DNA genetic fingerprinting is a technique whereby the hereditary genetic material DNA is isolated and identified from any given animal or human tissue source. The DNA molecule is then cut into fragments by a simple process of restriction enzyme digestion and the resulting fragments can be detected by hybridisation with radioactive or fluorescent probes. The correct identification of the source of tissues, such as bloodstains, hairs, skin, semen or indeed any tissue containing DNA will provide the forensic scientist with a tool which has potential advantages beyond our wildest dreams.

The use of DNA analysis will revolutionise identification procedures in forensic immunology resulting in certainty as to the origin of tissue, provided material from a suspected source is available for comparison purposes. In the past twelve months a series of papers have appeared in which a simple Southern blot technique has allowed for the positive identification of blood samples using a variety of human DNA probes (6, 7). Jeffreys *et al.* (7) have calculated that the probability that DNA fragments from any two unrelated individuals are identical when a two enzyme and probe system is used is considerably less than 5×10^{-19}. These techniques have recently withstood the rigours of the British legal system and were upheld as valid in a case of disputed paternity (8).

Clearly the next step is to apply these procedures to the identification of body fluid stains. In a preliminary communication shortly to be published we, in Vancouver, have outlined a simple DNA dot blot system to differentiate human males and females as well as humans from other animals by the examination of dried bloodstains of varying ages (10). This work was performed in the Molecular Probe Laboratory in the University Department of

Pathology in Vancouver where a wide variety of probes are routinely being used to assist with the identification of genetic abnormalities in children.

In order to independently develop a single DNA laboratory the forensic science community would be required to invest over $250,000 in equipment and facilities alone. Such a laboratory would require minimum staffing by two technologists specially trained in these procedures since once an analysis has been initiated, it cannot be stopped halfway to allow for holidays or sick leave. However, we have identified the cost of sharing this laboratory with a research development programme for forensic science. We believe that while recognising that some of the hardware cannot be time shared efficiently in the light of the different functional requirements of forensic science, it would still be possible to provide an initial full-time forensic science recombinant DNA service for a capital investment of less than $40,000. An additional annual operating budget of approximately $25,000 to include salaries, benefits, materials and supplies would be required. Presented with these financial options the best hope for the development of the DNA probe in forensic science is either to contract with existing medical laboratories to carry out the research and development and ultimately provide the routine service or to arrange for a sharing of facilities and training of forensic scientists within such a medical genetic laboratory.

The reintegration of medical laboratory services into forensic science can only be to the long-term advantage of the science of crime investigation. The technical and administrative problems associated with such a reorientation of thinking are not insurmountable. The basic problems are the biases that have developed between the medical and non-medical branches of forensic science.

The traditional view is that forensic science conducted within a medical laboratory setting must be under the control of the forensic pathologist. This is not true. Forensic pathologists, in their efforts to find kudos and status, have insisted on financial and administrative independence from other branches of laboratory medicine and as a result have found themselves isolated and deprived of funding. The forensic pathologist must also reintegrate himself with his clinical laboratory colleagues. Status is not achieved by independence. Reputation is best based on quality of work.

Similarly, the recognition that medical scientists are presently paid more than non-medical laboratory scientists should not be used as an excuse to inhibit the reintegration of the human biological forensic sciences.

Professor Bill Tilstone is currently Head of the Forensic Science Laboratory Service in Adelaide in South Australia. He coordinates all branches of forensic science, including forensic pathology. Such an establishment is only successful when each of the individual disciplines strives for excellence in an environment of adequate funding and where interdisciplinary rivalry operates as a force to promote quality and not destroy reputations. Salaries are based on the market value of the individuals. As you are probably aware, Professor Tilstone as Director of the Service does not receive the top salary within the system.

At the beginning of this discourse the question was posed, "Can forensic science survive outside a non-medical discipline?" Basically it all depends on how we divide and classify forensic science. Clearly the future of the human biological sciences may well be within the environment of university medical laboratories. However, the very nature of forensic science and the need to present evidence in a reliable and understandable way will always make us different.

It can be argued that the non-biological sciences can be appropriately grouped together in separate institutions. Furthermore, we should be much more prepared to contract our research and development to university departments where we can encourage early application of these techniques to the field of forensic science. This is best done by having forensic personnel located within these various academic disciplines.

It may be that we within the field of forensic science and medicine are no longer the best people to determine our own future. When it comes to a question of introducing a new technology into forensic science, perhaps such projects should be studied by a multi-disciplinary group including representatives of the judicial system, the police, forensic scientists, universities and the private sector. Decisions should be made with the full awareness of resource implications, department goals and the complex needs that the technological advances must serve.

It is perhaps not wrong to relate cost benefit analysis to demands for capital equipment in a system that is not a revenue generator but is subject to global budgeting. Efficient forensic laboratory services in the next few years must implement technology changes by cost-effective means. This may involve some reorientation of laboratory services, some decentralisation of research and development and a sharing of expertise across traditional scientific boundaries.

It is particularly important that forensic scientists, politicians and representatives of the justice system should take part in this decision making in order to ensure the best possible cost–benefit ratio for the application of forensic science to crime investigation.

We must not attempt to absorb all new scientific techniques into the forensic science world. Similarly, we cannot afford to neglect new development because of fiscal restraint.

This balance between maintenance of services and research and development will continue to be attacked by the late twentieth-century disease of fiscal restraint. Our best therapy for this contemporary disease involves the reorganisation of our traditional laboratory boundaries and the acceptance of the fact that forensic science laboratory funding will not be major political priority in most of the world in the foreseeable future.

References

1. Avarmeas, S. Coupling of enzymes to proteins with glutaraldehyde. Use of conjugate for detection of antigens and antibodies. *Immunochemistry*, 1969; 6: 43–52.

2. Engvall, E. and Perlman, P. Enzyme linked immunosorbent assay (ELISA). Quantitative assay of immunoglobin G. *Immunochemistry*, 1971; 8: 871–874.

3. Newall, P. Advantages of monoclonal antiserum and ELISA in the identification of Gm(3) in dried blood stains. *Forensic Science International*, 1983; 23: 44.

4. Newall, P. An enzyme linked immunosorbent assay (ELISA) for the identification of Km(3) in dried blood stains. *Canadian Society of Forensic Sciences Journal*, 1985; 18: 78–85.

5. Pudek, M. R., Secombe, D. W. and Whitfield, M. F. Digoxin like immunoreactivity in premature and full term infants not receiving Digoxin therapy. *New England Journal of Medicine*, 1983; 308: 904–905.

6. Jeffreys, A. J., Wilson, V. and Thein, S. L. Hypervariable minisatellites regions in human DNA. *Nature*, 1985; 314: 67–73.

7. Jeffreys, A. J., Wilson, V. and Thein, S. L. Individual specific fingerprints of human DNA. *Nature*, 1985; 316: 76–79.

8. Jeffreys, A. J., Brookfield, J. F. Y. and Semeonoff, R. Positive identification of an immigration test-case using DNA fingerprints. *Nature*, 1985; 317: 818–819.

9. Gill, P., Jeffreys, A. J. and Werett, D. J. Forensic application of DNA fingerprints. *Nature*, 1985; 318: 577–579.

10. Tyler, M. G., Kirby, L. T., Wood, S., Darius, S. and Ferris, J. A. J. Human blood stain identification and sex determination using recombinant DNA techniques. *Forensic Science International* (submitted publication).

THE INVESTIGATION OF FATAL FIRES

D. J. X. Halliday

Introduction

This is intended to be an overview of the way in which the investigation of fatal fires is carried out in the Metropolitan Police District (M.P.D.) and will touch upon some aspects of these investigations that are not normally encountered in the examination of other types of fire.

Fatal Fires in London

Approximately 150 people a year die as a result of fatal fires within the M.P.D.; this figure amounts to about 17 per cent of all the fire fatalities in the United Kingdom as can be seen in Table 1. London also has a high percentage of those fires which claim five or more lives at any one time.

TABLE 1

Fire Fatalities, 1981–1983

	1981	*1982*	*1983*
United Kingdom	975	905	893
Greater London	—	149	153
Number of fires where 5 or more died			
United Kingdom	3	3	5
Greater London	2	1	3

The figures illustrate the problem faced by police officers and coroners; any of these fires could have been deliberately started in order to conceal or commit an act of murder. A number of arrangements used to exist outside London for the investigation of these fires; in some areas the scene was jointly investigated by scenes of crime officers (S.O.C.O.'s) and Fire Brigade investigators, in other areas the responsibility rested solely with the Fire Brigade, the police role being essentially passive until such time as the fire was found to be suspicious. The amount of technical assistance provided by the regional forensic science laboratories appeared to be limited to visiting only fires of extreme importance or providing an analytical service for other investigators. Such a situation is not totally satisfactory since the role of the scientist is often regarded as that of a technical consultant and that person is prevented from examining the best evidence available which is of course the scene. Recent Home Office guidelines (1, 2) have remedied this, and far greater emphasis has been placed upon the attendance of forensic scientists at fire scenes.

The Metropolitan Police Forensic Science Laboratory has always perceived a demand for the examination of fire scenes by a forensic scientist and the Fire Investigation Unit (F.I.U.) was set up some $9\frac{1}{2}$ years ago to provide this service. The eight full-time members of the Unit work in pairs using two vans equipped with lighting, excavation equipment, packaging materials and other items necessary to carry out a full scene examination.

It is greatly to our advantage that, compared with other police force areas, the M.P.D. is geographically very small and the Laboratory is centrally located. With transport and equipment readily available the F.I.U. can respond to calls rapidly, attending most scenes within the hour.

The investigation of fatal fires is accorded the highest priority by the Unit and we attend the scenes of all such fires of which we are informed. Through general orders, police officers and SOCO's are aware that we automatically attend such fires and that we should be contacted as soon as one takes place. From the fire investigator's point of view there are distinct advantages in an early examination of the scene, since disturbance by other interested parties is kept to a minimum and the body is likely to be still *in situ*. Through a 24-hour call-out system a member of the Unit is always available to examine such scenes and to provide a report on the fire to the police officer.

The advantages to the police are apparent in this arrangement, as with current economic, and hence manpower, restrictions the sooner the officer knows that a fire is accidental the less time and money is wasted upon a major investigation. Conversely if the fire is deliberate the officer can be assured that any subsequent prosecution can be backed up by properly presented forensic evidence. Ultimately we all wish to avoid the necessity of having to examine a months-old fire after a belated allegation of foul play is made.

The Fire Scene

The responsibility for calling the F.I.U. out to fires generally rests with the SOCO who must also make arrangements for other support services, including a photographer, to attend. The Forensic Intelligence Officers (F.I.O.'s) will also be informed, but they are primarily concerned with suspicious deaths and may or may not visit the scene depending on the circumstances (Figure 1).

At the scene of the fire the body will often have been recovered by the Fire Brigade during the course of fire fighting so that resuscitation can be attempted, but where the body is still *in situ* there is a great deal of pressure, particularly from coroner's officers, for it to be removed as quickly as possible. More often than not little evidence of significance is lost if the body is taken away but arguably the risk of losing evidence far outweighs other considerations and wherever possible no disturbance should be permitted until the fire investigator is present. Such an arrangement relies, of course, on the rapid attendance of the investigator.

The investigator's first responsibility upon arriving at the scene is to make a proper record of the condition in which it has been found. Photographs, written and taped notes, and even video may prove useful. The importance of taking notes and photographs at this stage cannot be over-emphasised since the movement or clearance of items at the scene may destroy evidence that later proves to be vital. The condition of the body and its clothing can be of particular significance and the note-taking should extend to cover these aspects. Prior to its removal the body should be moved carefully away from the

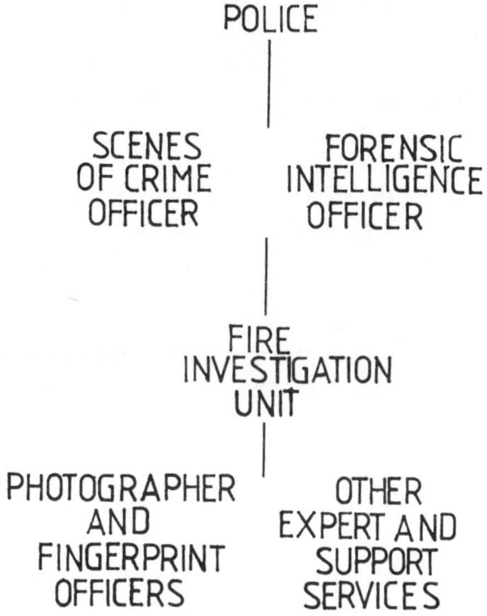

Figure. 1 Inter-relationship of all those involved in fire investigation.

area in which it was found so that materials beneath it can be examined. The condition of these materials is often indicative of the stage of the fire at which the victim collapsed.

When the body is moved a visual examination may reveal wounds, disturbance of the clothing, containers or unusual damage caused by the fire. It is also possible that the smell of a flammable liquid will be apparent. In many cases the question of sampling and examination of individual items may arise and this must be treated as a matter of checks and balances. Differing circumstances at individual scenes may make certain aspects of the forensic evidence more important than others, and the fire investigator should be prepared to accept a compromise if the overall investigation will benefit. Other experts at the scene, particularly biologists, may be concerned with patterns of bloodstaining for example, and often their sampling procedures must take priority over the fire investigation.

The fire investigator should take clothing, containers and other items relating to the fire itself as his own exhibits, since this avoids any subsequent problems should the continuity of these items be questioned in Court. Other items of a forensic nature should be taken by the SOCO or F.I.O. and it is important that the investigator works closely with them and discusses fully the implications of each item taken.

Problems that arise can often be resolved by the attendance of other experts at the scene. These are available from the Laboratory or support services in the M.P.D. and the investigator may find himself working with fingerprint officers or accident investigators. All of these people can make a valuable contribution to the overall picture at the fire. Similarly, outside bodies such as the gas and electricity boards can be useful sources of advice and should be relied upon for information that is outside the fire investigator's own range of expertise.

Once the body has been removed from the scene the "where, how and when" of the fire should be established by excavation, reconstruction, examination of burning patterns and careful consideration of possible sources of ignition. Since many fatal fires are accidental, the scientist must assess the condition of the scene before the fire, and the habits of the victim, in resolving the "how". A careful examination of other rooms in the house for instance may reveal smoking habits, the use of candles for lighting or religious purposes, abuse of the electrical system or even evidence of previous fires!

At the end of the scene examination the police officer will want an opinion as to the cause or possible causes of the fire. This is provided in the M.P.D. in the form of a preliminary report and is given to the officer as soon as the fire investigation is complete. The preliminary report will not be substantially modified later, other than to eliminate certain possibilities after the laboratory examination or testing of exhibits that have been taken. This necessarily means that some preliminary reports are vague as to the exact cause of the fire; however, they may serve to assure the police officer that the fire was not deliberately started and that therefore no prolonged or expensive police investigation is necessary.

And so to Court . . .

The most important part of the fire investigator's work is undoubtedly his or her attendance at Court to give evidence on the findings at the scene. It may be felt that this article has placed undue emphasis on the necessity of making a detailed record during the examination of the fire; however, it may well be that some seemingly irrelevant detail assumes a new importance in hindsight. For example, an anomalously high cyanide level in the victim's blood sample may be explained by his proximity to certain types of fabric or padding material. The investigator could also be asked to comment on a hypothetical sequence of events that may require a knowledge of what was present in other parts of the building not affected by the fire.

There is one thing that every fire investigator can be sure of: any sin of omission will be found out, usually after an awkward question from a member of the public in the coroner's court!

Conclusion

In summary the requirements for a regular, efficient and successful investigation of fatal fires may be detailed as follows:

1. The availability of a fully equipped specialist unit for fire investigation.
2. Scene examination should be carried out by forensic scientists who are experienced fire investigators since it may be necessary to present the evidence from both the scene and the laboratory examinations in a Court of Law.
3. Minimal disturbance of the scene and body by others before the investigation starts (consistent, of course, with the Fire Brigade's mandate to preserve life and extinguish the fire).

4. A system of communication that minimises the time it takes to call such a unit out to the scene of a fire.
5. The ready availability of other support services at the scene if required.
6. The provision of information regarding the cause of the fire to the police officer dealing with the incident at the earliest possible opportunity.

References

1. Fire Service Circular No. 9, 1985.
2. Home Office Circular No. 71, 1985.

THE RAINBOW WARRIOR INCIDENT

M. Lawton

For a small country like New Zealand the bombing of the *Rainbow Warrior* was without precedent. It was the deliberate sabotage of a vessel in our waters which was directed by agents of a foreign government with whom we were on friendly terms. The case initiated a large, intense and expensive enquiry headed by Superintendent Galbraith, a police officer formerly from Glasgow. The author's role is that of the scientist in charge of the forensic section in Auckland and she therefore assumed an early involvement in the enquiry and together with three other members of that section and specialists from outside the section spent the five months following the bombing, carrying out a large and diverse number of forensic examinations in relation to many aspects of the case. Communication between the police team and the scientists was generally excellent, one police exhibits officer being the main liaison. The police also held daily conferences which were frequently attended by the author when results and discussion of the direction of further lines of investigation were relayed.

Before proceeding with the details of the scientific examinations a few minutes will be taken to give the summary of facts which were delivered by the Solicitor General at the depositions hearing. It was prepared following an indication from the Defendants' solicitor that they were prepared to plead guilty to manslaughter, the solicitor having had access to statements from prosecution witnesses beforehand. While that outcome was well accepted by those involved in the investigation it was of course a grave disappointment to the journalists who had gathered from all corners of the earth to cover the story in the specially restored old High Court building. It left little for them to report although some journalists briefly turned their attention to an enterprising street vendor on an opposite corner who had Swiss passports for sale.

The summary of facts is as follows:

All charges arise from the scuppering and disabling of the *Rainbow Warrior* at Marsden Wharf in the Port of Auckland on the 10th of July last. Shortly before midnight on that night two high explosive devices which had clearly been attached to the hull of that vessel at some time previously, detonated within the space of two to four minutes. The force of the explosions were such as to cause a hole eight feet by six feet to the ship below the waterline at the engineroom, and extensively damage the stern and propeller assembly. As a result the vessel sank within minutes with the loss of the life of Fernando Pereira who was drowned in circumstances which will be described later. It is alleged that the two defendants, both of whom are now stated to be serving commissioned officers in the French Armed Forces, arrived in New Zealand on the 22nd of June and once here took steps in furtherance of a predetermined plan to ensure that the much publicised intended voyage of the *Rainbow Warrior* to French territorial waters would not in fact eventuate. For such an action to succeed it was fundamental that the vessel had to be extensively disabled so as to prevent her being repaired and manned in sufficient time to enable the voyage to be undertaken. To achieve the mission the two Defendants, as will be detailed later, were associated with other members of the French Security Forces who travelled to this country in furtherance of the action and who also played significant roles in the scuttling of the ship and the death of Mr Pereira.

The first step in New Zealand of the undertaking was the arrival here of a young woman known as Frederique Bonlieu. She was clearly sent ahead of the main party to gather intelligence, in particular of what was happening amongst Greenpeace members, and pass information back so that further steps could be taken. She arrived in Auckland on the 23rd of April last, travelling on a French passport with a false identity. Prior to her arrival a member of the Greenpeace movement had received a letter from a mutual friend noting the possibility of Bonlieu's visit to this country. She was therefore accepted by the Greenpeace members and indeed from the time of her arrival, partook of their hospitality and friendship until her departure from New Zealand on the 24th of May. During her stay with the Greenpeace organisation she learnt of, and reported on, the movements of the *Rainbow Warrior* and that organisation's future plans involving the vessel.

Two days after Bonlieu's departure from New Zealand a group initiated the chartering of a 38-foot sloop, the *Ouvea* in Noumea. Charter arrangements were completed by the end of May and on the 13th of June the vessel left Noumea with four persons aboard, these persons subsequently arriving in New Zealand under the names of Raymond Velche, Jean Michel Berthelo, Eric Audrenc and Xavier Jean Maniguet. Subsequently, their correct identities were revealed as Roland Velche, Jean Michel Barcelo, Gerald Andries, all of whom are members of the Direction Generale Des Services Exterieur (that is the French External Security Service), and Maniguet who is a doctor and a reservist in the French Navy.

Enquiries made by the New Zealand police officers subsequent to the events on the 10th of July have established that Andries purchased a Zodiac inflatable dinghy and a Yamaha outboard from a marine supplier in London on the 29th of May, i.e. five days after Bonlieu left New Zealand. It is the Crown's contention that the *Ouvea* was the means by which the equipment and explosives necessary to carry out the sinking of the *Rainbow Warrior* were brought to New Zealand.

On the 22nd of June, the *Ouvea* arrived in Parengarenga on the northern tip of New Zealand. On that day the Defendants arrived by plane at Auckland. They travelled on Swiss passports in the name of Mr and Mrs Turenge. The passports have been established to be expert forgeries and it is now acknowledged that their identities and all other material particulars were false.

Subsequent to the 22nd of June the *Ouvea* moved down the coast to Whangarei from where, according to its log, it left New Zealand waters on the 9th of July.

Between the dates of its arrival and departure meetings took place between crew members and the Defendants at which it is the Crown's contention the Zodiac dinghy and the Yamaha motor were handed over to the Defendants and, no doubt, relevant information on the *Rainbow Warrior* was exchanged. Crew members also liaised with another Frenchman using the name, Jean Louise Dormand, who in turn reported regularly to Paris. During this period the Defendants also made visits to the waterfront area of Auckland, and more particularly to the Marsden Wharf, subsequent to the arrival there of the *Rainbow Warrior* on the 7th of July.

The *Rainbow Warrior* from the time of its arrival in the port of Auckland remained berthed at Marsden Wharf. It had a crew, including its captain, of 13 of whom approximately 10 usually slept aboard. It was open to the public during much of its stay.

On the evening of the 10th a party was held on board to celebrate a birthday and there was a meeting of Greenpeace Fleet Skippers. Shortly before the explosions about 30 persons were aboard, and at the time of the first explosion 12 persons, including the captain, remained aboard the ship. Some of them had retired to bed in the crew accommodation located on the main deck above the engineroom and at the same level immediately aft of it.

At about 11.50 p.m. the first explosion occurred causing the damage on the starboard side at the level of the engineroom. No warning had been given. The reaction of the captain on seeing the massive inrush of water flooding that compartment was to give the order to abandon ship. A number of the crew were in the accommodation area, including the deceased. All of them except the deceased made good their escape. The evidence available indicates that he, after the first explosion and about the time the order to abandon ship had been given, went to his cabin in the aft accommodation to retrieve his photographic equipment. The evidence suggests that he was there when the second explosion at the stern of the vessel occurred and there was a discernible but limited increase in the inrush of water. There is no evidence that he sustained injuries as a direct result of either explosion. He died from drowning.

There is no doubt that the placing of the explosives and their detonation was carried out by persons trained and expert in underwater warfare. Despite extensive police enquiries, no person has been located who observed any untoward activity in or about the vessel or the wharves that night. Clearly, however, the activities were likely to have been carried out by a number of persons. The Crown's investigations do not establish the Defendants' role in this affair as other than in support of those who actually placed the explosives. As part of their support role the Defendants were responsible for the picking up and removing from the scene one of those responsible for the placement of the explosive devices. This recovery was made after the devices had been placed and the timers had been set, when one of the persons responsible for the placements then made his way in the Zodiac from the wharves at Hobson Bay and a rendezvous with the Defendants. Subsequent to the night's events a search led to the discovery under Ngapipi Bridge, of the Yamaha outboard motor which had been brought by Andries weeks earlier in London. The Zodiac dinghy was left abandoned at the recovery point.

The identities of those who actually placed the devices had not been established.

During the night of the 10th the Defendants claim to have driven to Thames and certainly by the morning of the 11th they were in Hamilton where they telephoned their contact in Paris and altered their plane reservations to ensure the earliest possible departure from the country.

They were, however, interviewed by the police on the 12th July and denied all knowledge of the *Ouvea*, its crew members and the scheme to sink the *Rainbow Warrior*. They were arrested on the 15th July and have been in custody since that date.

How were the couple known by the name of Turange first implicated? There has been in New Zealand for a few years a strong neighbourhood watch movement and on the night of the bombing, watch was being kept over Okahu bay in Auckland to prevent vandalism to any of the boats moored there. A Zodiac dinghy was seen to come ashore and was met by a campervan. These actions, late at night, were apparently enough to arouse the suspicions of the persons on watch who noted the registration number of the campervan and called the police. The police arrived shortly but not before the campervan had departed leaving the Zodiac abandoned. However, the registration number of the van had been noted and following the explosion it was an easy matter to trace the van and find that it had been hired out to Alain and Sophie Turange. Not such an easy matter to detain them, however, as there is currently no terrorism act or provision to detain a suspect without laying a charge under New Zealand law. They were therefore released, although not until after many hours of voluntary questioning. They denied any involvement in the bombing or indeed with the Zodiac and simply stated that they gave a lift to an unknown fisherman who had flagged them down. However, general enquiries and information received by the police was not in accordance with that story and it was with some relief that intelligence from Europe was soon to confirm that the passports held by the Turange couple were false. This gave the enquiry team the reason that they needed to lay a charge and re-arrest the couple within hours of them leaving the country.

No forensic involvement began until the morning of the 12th July when a small group of scientists including the author strolled down the few hundred yards from our laboratory to where the damaged boat lay listing on her side. Marsden Wharf is part of Downtown Auckland and a very busy area. Forensic examinations in New Zealand are carried out by a very small section of the Government Department known as the Department of Scientific and Industrial Research. Although not part of the Police Department the work is almost exclusively carried out on their behalf. We have limited experience with criminal explosions of any kind in New Zealand and this was obviously not an ordinary bomb scene with most of the potential evidence under water. Our normal work of assisting in a meticulous search of the scene was not possible and was to be carried out by police and naval divers who set up a grid and searched the seabed for several weeks.

Our work was initially confined to the other areas of the investigation, the vehicle and the boat searches, inspection of items recovered from the seabed and consultation with the police on scientific enquiries.

With so many potential exhibits from a wide variety of sources all the items were catalogued on a microcomputer. This allowed them to be cross-referenced and sorted in a number of fields. Cross-referencing was a vital part of the work, trying to relate boat to campervan to ropes to paint, etc.

Over the following few days many vehicles were searched, in particular the campervan, samples were collected and scores of sightings of French men and women were reported by the general public. The fact that New Zealanders were so observant or possibly just inquisitive was a prime factor in establishing the movements of the agents leading up to or after the bombing.

On 16th July the police requested that a scientist accompany a police team to Norfolk Islands to examine the yacht *Ouvea*. Following the well-publicised reports of the bombing and ensuing enquiry, customs officials had remembered the irregular movements of the yacht *Ouvea* and its crew when it had arrived in New Zealand a short time before. Now it had arrived in the Norfolk Islands, a small outpost under Australian law. With no powers of detainment on Norfolk Island the New Zealand police were only able to search the boat and briefly interview the crew before allowing the boat and the crew to depart. One amongst many samples taken was a swab from beneath the right side cabin sole boards. This was the only swab of many taken from the vehicles, the *Ouvea* and the *Warrior*, on which explosive material was positively identified. Identifying the explosive material could not be carried out on the spot, however, which would have given the New Zealand Police Department grounds to detain the *Ouvea* crew. It was days later after the *Ouvea* had mysteriously disappeared that the swab was examined and the presence of nitrocellulose, a trace of ethylene glycon dinitrate and either TNT or PETN were detected. We had not at that time developed instrumental techniques to confirm these results and considered it prudent to send a scientist with considerable experience in gas/liquid and high-performance liquid chromatography to the Royal Armament Research and Development Establishment at Fort Halstead in Kent. Here, he confirmed that the swab from the *Ouvea* contained EGDN and TNT.

A second major discovery on the *Ouvea* was the presence of a large number of maps which were fingerprinted by the police. One map was later to show the presence of a fingerprint from Dominique Prieur. This was detected by ninhydrin. More exciting from a scientific point of view was the presence on another map of another fingerprint belonging to Alain Mafart which was detected by laser, this being the first time that laser has been used in a case in Auckland. A third connection was contributed by the maps on one of which was found the address of the Greenpeace Auckland headquarters. It was a map given to Bonlieu by one of the Greenpeace members.

One of the first items for examination in Auckland was the Zodiac dinghy. Partly covering it was a blue canvas boat cover and attached to the front of the boat was a padlock and chain. No identification was found. A serial number which should have been present on a metal plate had been removed. In addition, the Zodiac should have had a second number inscribed in the timber of the boat itself under the transom plate but no sign of this ever having been present was found. The cover had a black circle situated centrally at both ends. On closer inspection they were obviously not an integral part of the design and were easily removed with organic solvents. Underneath the black circles were the figures 21. Some smears of fresh blood were present on the Zodiac pontoons and on the cover. There was sufficient blood from both areas to determine that they were human blood, they were from different persons and that one set of blood grouping factors was common to about 5 per cent of the population while the other blood was common to 6·5 per cent of the population. Neither area of blood could have come from either of the couple known as Turange. Attached to the front of the Zodiac was a set of ropes which ended in two clasps which will be referred to below.

Meanwhile a number of items had been recovered from the Auckland harbour. Among them was a Yamaha outboard motor which was found by a police diver while tracing a direct line from the *Rainbow Warrior* to the bay where the Zodiac was abandoned. This item still had a serial number and was eventually traced to an outlet in London where the purchaser of the motor and a Zodiac was identified as a young Frenchman, later known to be one of the *Ouvea* crew. To help prove the connection between the Zodiac and the motor, casts were taken of the marks made by the motor on the transom plate of the Zodiac and on a test piece of plywood. The plywood of which the transom was constructed was easily split and the marks were therefore indistinct. It appeared unlikely from the series of marks that a motor had been mounted on that transom more than a few times, the class characteristics of the markings were from a Yamaha 3 or 4 hp two-stroke engine manufactured before 1983. An analysis of the petrol/oil two-stroke mixture in the Yamaha indicated that the petrol was New Zealand super grade mixed with an oil which was not of New Zealand origin.

The week after the bombing an oxygen bottle was recovered from the harbour, close to where the Zodiac was abandoned. This was followed by a second bottle found further upstream two weeks later. Both bottles were small and white with markings clearly stamped around the necks. They also had a blue company logo which read in part "Compagnie Francaise ... Produits Oxygene" and the valve in each case was marked "Fenzy Paris". Each bottle weighted 2·6 kg and floated in water. One bottle had its valve open so that any residual gas in the bottle would have mixed with the atmosphere. However, upon analysis of the contents which were sucked out under vacuum, an oxygen level of 30 per cent was determined. As normal air has an oxygen content of about 20 per cent the contents of the bottle was very likely oxygen. A suggestion that the bottles could have been used for refrigeration was disproved by showing the absence of freon. On the second oxygen bottle the valve was closed and an oxygen level of 90 per cent was obtained which was entirely consistent with an original filling of oxygen. The possible use of these bottles were in re-breathing diving equipment for shallow diving, no air bubbles being evident with this type of apparatus.

The only other feature of interest about the bottles was that the second one to be located was covered with a black material. This turned out to be constructed from a pair of tights. The waist band had been torn away as had the greater part of one leg and the lower part of the other leg. Part of the crotch seam had been darned. Enquiries indicated that the garment was made in France.

One other item from the harbour caused a great amount of excitement for a few days. It was found close to the *Warrior* and looked at first sight like an army water bottle. However, the presence of a detonating cap meant that it was treated with extreme caution. A gamma-ray photograph gave some insight into its function. A sample of its main contents was identified as potassium superoxide, a chemical which in the presence of moisture is capable of giving off a vast amount of oxygen. Its most notable use is in breathing apparatus. Interesting as all this was, a second bottle was soon found which proved to be, as far as the bombing was concerned, an innocent red herring.

Another aspect of the scientific investigation was to see if a relationship was present between the suspects and certain labels found in the rubbish bin in their motel room. The labels referred to inflatable dinghies and accessories and the suspects vehemently denied any knowledge of them. The labels were wrapped up in a white paper towel along with a tampon, its holder and wrapper. An identical white paper towel had also been found in the campervan but the piece in the bin did not physically fit with this. The tampon, however, although not bloodied, had been used, and an extract was of vaginal epithelial cells which gave a grouping reaction consistent with the ABO type of Sophie Turange. Two small pubic hairs were attached to the sticky side of the labels. These were later compared with hairs lifted from items taken for laundering from Sophie Turange in prison and could have come from the same origin. In addition the writing on the tampon was in French only. New Zealand imports tampons which have French and English writing on them but none which have French writing only so even the tampon had French connections.

A number of ropes were examined throughout the course of the investigation, some from the seabed and some not. One of the ropes which caused the most headache was the one which was attached to the bow of the Zodiac. In all, this consisted of a thick rope joined to a length of finer rope which had a karibena on each end. The thicker length of rope was nylon and was approximately 3000 millimetres in length. The free end of each of the three strands of this rope were twisted back on themselves to form a sealed end. The finer rope was of vegetable fibre and was 2600 millimetres long. The join to the thick rope which was by a hitch was equidistant from both ends of the finer rope. The finer rope was spliced at both ends for a distance of 140 millimetres to attach the karibenas. The ropes themselves were quite dirty and under microscopic examination appeared to have a vast variety of miscellaneous debris and paint embedded in them. The reason for the interest in this collection of ropes was the fact that sightings had been reported of a Zodiac boat being towed by a campervan, the boat being towed in an unusual manner. Any New Zealander would have put an inflated boat of that size on a full trailer while this boat was trailed on two wheels at the back only, the front being pulled up off the ground against the back window of the campervan. This procedure being totally illegal in New Zealand meant this strange sight caught the attention of a number of people. The wheels which were described were offered by the manufacturers as an optional extra. Assuming therefore that the rope was used to attach the Zodiac to the campervan it would have been helpful to confirm this connection. After an extremely intensive examination of the ropes which plainly showed that one of the karibenas and two areas on the rope were smeared with mid-blue metallic paint we failed to identify the blue paint as coming from either of the campervans or any of the other vehicles known to have been used in the operation.

Also present on the finer rope 870 millimetres from one karibena was an area which had a fawn/grey appearance. It was composed of silver-coloured aluminium paint particles which appeared to have lost their binder. One of the rental vehicles which was examined, a Holden Commodore station wagon, known to have been rented by Velch, possibly accompanied by Dr Maniguet was of silver metallic and had around the back door areas, silver metallic paint with the same decomposed appearance as the material on the rope. That is far from proving scientifically that the car and the rope had been in contact. Despite not being able to positively link any particular vehicle to the ropes the distance between the two areas of blue paint were the approximate width of a vehicle and it is very likely that the rope was attached to the boat for the purpose of towing.

A further possible connection was made between the Holden Commodore and the other items that were examined, by comparison of a very slight smear of blue green metallic paint found on the rear right upright of the station wagon with the Yamaha outboard motor. Both paints were consistent by the analytical methods used. Again, the paint wasn't necessarily from that particular outboard.

The Commodore was also connected with the motor by an eye witness report of an incident which occurred before the bombing. Two forestry workers at the Topuni Forest north of Auckland were cutting trees when a campervan parked nearby. Shortly after the van left and within a few minutes a Holden Commodore parked in the same spot. The car moved around the site several times to avoid falling trees and eventually the forestry workers went over to talk to them. The two people in the Commodore said that they were waiting for their friends and when they were told that they had missed them were obviously upset. The forestry workers observed two outboards, and a canvas bag in the back of the car. The car and the campervan eventually met at a clearing a few miles further on where it was observed by a witness that a number of items including a motor were handed over. Because of their uneasy manner the forestry workers inscribed the registration number of the Commodore in dust on their truck where it remained until it was examined by the police some time later.

Now for the *Rainbow Warrior* itself, the items removed from it, and the salvage carried out. The amount of debris which was dredged up from the seabed by divers looking for any signs of an explosive mechanism was enormous. It was all sorted, labelled and sealed in heat-sealed plastic bags. Anything that could in any way have been connected with the case was forwarded for laboratory examination and those items which appeared unconnected were mounted on boards for a cursory examination to ensure that nothing was missed.

The police quickly called in the navy after the explosion and it was their job to search the sunken starboard aft cabin in the middle of the night to find the drowned body of Fernando Pereira. The navy took charge of the salvage operation and began the job of sealing the 2 × 2·5 metre hole in the starboard side midships and the other area of extensive damage in the area of the stern gland. The eleven-man team spent 557 hours diving over the next 35 days until huge plates were secured in place and the boat was raised and towed to the naval dry dock across the harbour to be thoroughly examined.

While the navy crew were repairing the boat police divers were working alongside sifting the seabed. Apart from the damage in the hull considerable damage had also been made to a concrete stringer of the wharf. Another red herring was to be found there. This one was a bent piece of metal pipe which had managed to balance itself nicely on a crossbeam. One possible theory, later discounted, was that the explosive material was attached to the pipe which was in turn secured to the crossbeam, the explosive being suspended out over the water close to the boat. The copper/nickel pipe was an unusual alloy and the Greenpeace crew had no recollection of a similar pipe in the *Warrior*. However, when a full inspection of the ship was possible later, identical piping was found under the engineroom floor, which wouldn't have been observed by the crew.

Most prominent amongst the debris were a large number of pieces of webbing belt and also ropes. The largest was a yellow webbing contraption consisting of four separate belts joined by a blue karibena. The karibena was broken and, although the belts were in generally good condition, there were areas of blackening and local damage. The eight ends of the webbing pieces had been hand sewn. Six ends were doubled over and sewn with nylon 2-ply thread. The sewing was in the shape of a rectangle with a join across one diagonal. The remaining two ends were doubled over twice and the sewing was in the shape of a small rectangle only. It appeared that two persons had constructed the webbing.

Other webbing belts were attached to rope loops, each of which was held by twine whipping which would have required a needle to secure it. Some of the belts and ropes had obviously been close to the explosion centre. The twines used for whipping the rope were all 16-ply waxed polyester. A large needle and twine had been recovered from the campervan which had been hired by Prieur and Mafart but the thread in that case was 12-ply waxed nylon. The thread on all the pieces of webbing found was 3-ply nylon.

There were also a large number of pieces of metal brass collected from the seabed by the sunken ship. They had the appearance of being close to the explosion centre but they were not part of the ship itself. It is possible that those pieces could have been part of an explosive device but their origin could not be determined.

Eventually the *Rainbow Warrior* was raised and helped by support from huge floats it was pulled to the navy base across Auckland harbour and positioned in the dry dock to allow at last a full inspection of the damaged hull.

The ship was damaged in two separate areas, firstly the starboard midships and secondly in the immediate area of the stern post and propeller.

The seat of the explosion appeared to be at frame 32, and half a metre above the bilge keel which put it under the water. The explosion was caused by man-made devices on the outside of the hull.

The reasons for those conclusions were that the ship's side had been dished inwards, indicating that the force was from the outside. There was extended indentation of the ship's side plating around the area of the hole and the side plating was ripped. Those characteristics are typical effects of an explosion in water against a metal air-filled structure, the force of the water enhancing the explosive force.

Inside the ship's engineroom was chaos and there was evidence of large heavy metal objects having been thrown across the room. Although the size of the hole and the other damage was considerable the amount of the explosive was estimated as only between 5 and 10 kilos, the effect being enhanced because of the force of the water.

The stern explosion was very close to the centre line of the ship just above the rope guard next to the stern post. This explosion was also man made.

Again the hull plating had been dished in and the two upper ice guards had been bent upwards after their welds had fractured. The force of the explosion pushed the propeller blades and caused them to be displaced downwards. A complete fracture occurred at the base and a partial fracture occurred at the top of the propeller. Again the charge weight of the explosive was in the range of 5 to 10 kilos. The media and some of the books produced on the bombing have perpetuated the idea of limpet mines being used to attach the explosives. However with the charge weight mentioned, which is a lot less than initial estimates, the magnetic fixings of the limpet mine would have to be considerable and would have been heavy and difficult for divers to swim with. Despite a thorough search of the seabed no magnets were recovered to support the idea of limpet mines. In addition the complex array of webbing and ropes indicate that they were probably used to attach the devices.

On the keel of the *Rainbow Warrior* approximately half way between the two seats of explosion was an F clamp. Attached to it were more karibenas similar to those on the yellow webbing contraption. Also present were a rope loop whipped with twine and a frayed length of rope. The twine was the same as that on the other recovered ropes. The purpose of the F clamp and ropes is likely to have been to provide guidance in the pitch black of the harbour, particularly to ensure that the explosive on the hull was placed at the correct site. A search of the inside of the engineroom failed to reveal any clue to the nature of the explosive device. A piece of anti-saboteur material was recovered from the engineroom (a mouse trap), but that alas was of no effect.

Lack of space does not permit a discussion of the many other items examined, the clothing searches or fibre comparisons. Nor does it permit description of the soil or vegetation samples examined by specialists from the Botany and Geological Survey Divisions of the DSIR whose analyses assisted in tracing the movements of certain items and persons.

To conclude, as is normally the case, scientific evidence was only a part of the overall investigation, an investigation which continued long after the sentence was passed. The New Zealand Police Department sent officers to several countries as well as making the most extensive enquiries in New Zealand. Added to that, the public response for assistance with the enquiry was enormous and there's no doubt that luck was involved in making the initial connection between the bombing and the campervan and hence the two agents.

THE ORGANISATION OF FORENSIC SCIENCES IN SWITZERLAND

J. Mathyer

Before discussing the organisation of Forensic Sciences in Switzerland, it is necessary to be reminded of some particularities of that country. Switzerland has a population of a little over 6·5 million inhabitants, speaking four "National Languages", German, French, Italian and Romantsch. Three of the national languages, German, French and Italian are what are referred to as "Official Languages" and are spoken in the Swiss Parliament (National Council) or in the Federal Courts.

To digress, German is one of the national and/or official languages but, in fact, the German which is spoken in the German part of Switzerland is not exactly the same as the one which is spoken in Germany. In practice they speak German dialects which vary from one part of the country to another. As an example, the Swiss German dialect spoken in Zürich is not the same as the one spoken in Basle or Bern. However, the written word is the same German as in Germany or in Austria. Romantsch is not a dialect, but a real language, with a literature and newspapers. It is a language of Latin origin (as is French, Italian, Spanish and Rumanian) spoken in the Canton of Grisons which has a population of 40,000.

Switzerland is a Confederation of 23 Cantons, three of which are divided into "half-cantons", Appenzell, Basle and Unterwald. This makes 26 states, each of which has its own criminal police. In addition the Confederation maintains a Federal Police Force whose roles are restricted to problems of state security but also include counterfeit money, drug trafficking, terrorism and cases involving explosion, etc. The Swiss Confederation does not maintain any Central, or National, forensic science laboratory but, since 1942, a unique Federal Penal Code has resulted in 26 Codes of Penal Procedure, one for each Canton. Such a system explains why there is no police organisation and administration in a particular Canton which is exactly the same as that of its closest neighbour.

In order to assess the organisations in each Canton it was necessary for the author to send a list of questions, in both French and German, to the chiefs of police of all the Cantons and half-Cantons, and also to the chiefs of police of the most important cities: Zürich, Bern and Lausanne. The latter are cities in which separate criminal police organisations exist, in addition to those of the Canton. For the town of Geneva, there is only one police administration which is common to both the Canton and the Town; the same is true for Basle-Town (Basel-Stadt). Questions submitted were limited to eight major points of interest:

1. To which expert, in your Canton or Town, does the examining magistrate, or chief of the criminal police have recourse for medico-legal examinations or pathological examinations?

2. To which expert, does the examining magistrate, or chief of the criminal police, have recourse for the examination of blood, semen, or saliva (for group determination or alcotest)?
3. To whom do you submit samples for forensic toxicological examination?
4. To whom are materials for criminalistic examination submitted? Such examinations include the identification of traces from biological and non-biological origins, of fingerprints, palmprints, footprints, shoeprints, tyre-prints identification, identification of hairs, textile fibres, of paint fragments, glass particles and soils. In addition this area also covers toolmarks, firearms identification and ballistics problems, for criminalistic studies associated with fires, arson, explosions, traffic and other kinds of accidents.
5. Does your Canton or town maintain a "Service d'identification judiciaire"? perhaps best translated by "Legal Identification Department" which is responsible for providing a fingerprinting and photographic service, especially for scene of crime officers. If the answer to this question is yes, then what numbers of staff are involved and to what technical equipment do they have access?
6. Does your Canton or town maintain a Forensic Science Laboratory, or Criminalistics Laboratory? If yes, how many staff do you employ and to what technical equipment do they have access?
7. What is the background training of the personnel and their subordinates for their role in the "Service d'identité judiciaire" (Identification Department)?
8. What is the background training of personnel and their technical support for the Forensic Science Laboratory?

Out of 29 questionnaires distributed, 27 responses were received which give an interesting insight into Forensic Science Services. Firstly, there is a clear distinction between the answers to questions 1, 2 and 3 relating to forensic medicine, toxicology, serology and alcohol measurements and, in answer to the question concerned with criminalistics, almost all the police forces of the Cantons and Towns send their cases of forensic medicine and toxicology to the Forensic Medicine and Toxicological Department of the nearest University. There are five Universities with Faculties of Medicine in Switzerland, namely Basle, Bern, Zürich, Genève and Lausanne. The one exception, Saint Gallen, used the sevices of the nearest important hospital. The same was generally done for blood grouping and the alcotest, although some Cantons made use of private analytical laboratories. A similar result was found for toxicology, only two Cantons making use of private laboratories.

In the area of criminalistics involving trace evidence obeying Locard's Exchange Principle, there is, with the exception of Zürich (see below), only one place with a real Forensic Science Laboratory. All the Cantons and towns provide their own identification departments ("Services d'identité judiciaire" in French or, in German, "Erkennungsdienst" or "Kriminaltechnische Abteilung"). Normally, such departments are with, or are part of, a scene of crime group collecting all kinds of micro-traces and taking finger and palm-prints, shoe and tyre-prints and tool-marks, etc. The staff of such departments vary from as many as fifty people for the Canton of Bern, to two people in the half-Canton of Obwald. Such staff are mainly recruited from amongst police officers and are trained for varying periods of time depending on the Canton and the police department. Some Cantons make use of training facilities in Cantons where they may have an opportunity to attend lectures on special subjects. Fifteen diplomates of the Institut de police scientifique et de criminologie belong to staffs of ten of these criminalistics departments in the ten Cantons. These diplomates are able to present evidence in more serious and difficult cases. Generally, most of these Identification Departments or "simple criminalistics departments" send cases they consider too difficult for their knowledge or too important, to the main forensic science laboratories in Zürich. One exception is in the Canton of Bern, where serious cases are sent mainly to various departments in the University of Bern, although some may be sent to Zürich. The technical equipment available in these departments, in general, varies considerably. Most of them possess what may be classified as classical, or common equipment such as photographic equipment, stereomicroscopes, comparison microscopes, ultraviolet lamps (short and long waves), infra-red image converters, electrostatic detection apparatus, etc. as well as wet chemistry laboratory equipment. They will also include facilities for the detection and revelation of fingerprints, as for example a Visu-print apparatus for the detection of fingerprints using super-glue.

There are, in Zürich, two forensic science laboratories associated with the Cantons of Zürich and with the City. Both laboratories are located in the same building and work in close and good cooperation. All the cases associated with forensic medicine, forensic toxicology, to blood, semen and saliva grouping and alcohol testing are sent to the Forensic Medicine Laboratories with its chemical-toxicological department. The head of the medico-legal (Forensic medicine) department of the University of Zürich is Professor Dr Hartmann and the Head of the chemical-toxicological department of the same University is Professor Dr Brandenberger, two specialists of international repute. Preliminary examination of blood, semen and saliva in the Canton of Zürich may be made by the Scientific Department of the City Police of Zürich ("Wissenschaftlicher Dienst" or WD in German). The "Kriminaltechnische Abteilung" is divided into four departments: Identification Department or Erkennungsdienst, the photographic department in Winterthur (about 26 km from Zürich), the Document urkundenlabor laboratory and the Criminal Photographic department or Kriminal-Photodienst. The Identification Department has two functions, one to assist at scenes of crime in collaboration with one of the "criminal photographic units, and the other one as a forensic laboratory, specialising in the identification of traces such as finger and palm-prints, shoe-prints, tool-marks and so on, in the same way as other similar departments in any other Canton. The "Wissenschaftlicher Dienst" (Scientific Department of the City Police of Zürich, founded in 1952 by the late Dr Max Frey-Sulzer) is conversant with all the other forensic science problems such as fire-arm identification and ballistics, hairs and textile fibre identification, the examination of paint flakes and varnishes, glass particles, soils, fire investigation, explosions. This department, "Wissenschaftlicher Forschungsdienst" (Scientific Research Department), works especially for the General Attorney of the Swiss Confederation. In addition the "Unfall-photodienst", attached to the Traffic Police (Photographic Accident Department) is called out to the scenes of accidents, including traffic accidents;

however, the forensic study of each particular case is conducted, and the report written, by the Scientific Department. The "Urkundenlabor" (Document Laboratory) is involved with the examination of handwritings and signatures, typewritten and printed documents, as well as papers, inks, glues and adhesives, etc. which make up the materials of such documents.

The scientific equipment of all these departments is very comprehensive and up to date, going from simple magnifying glasses to the Scanning Electron Microscope, through spectrophotometers, infra-red spectrophotometers, gas-chromatographs, etc. These two Zürich laboratories are amongst the best equipped, in material and men, in Western Europe. They also maintain collections of reference materials of all kinds such as firearms, typewriter specimens, inks, rubber shoe-soles, cigarettes and tobaccos, etc. The Scientific Service of the City Police of Zürich is under the direction of Dr Jacob Meier who is supported by sixty-seven people, six of whom have a university degree, five of these being at the PhD level in inorganic, organic, analytical chemistry and in biology.

The Criminal Technical Department of the Canton of Zürich is under the direction of Dr P. X. Iten, a chemist who has the support of more than eighty colleagues, among them a former assistant at the University of Lausanne, Dr P. Pfefferli.

On the other side of Switzerland, in the French speaking part, is Geneva which also has an interesting organisation but on a much more modest scale than the one in Zürich. In the Identification Department, there are three diplomates of the Institut de Police scientifique et de criminologie, one a technical chief, one an assistant to the chief and one police officer. They are integrated into a team of about thirty people, sixteen of whom belong to the scene of crime group. In addition, the Canton of Geneva established, some years ago, a Criminalistics Laboratory with a very limited staff. But under the dynamism of its new director, another diplomate of our Institute and former assistant, this laboratory is growing and will increase its staff to five who will be provided with more sophisticated scientific equipment. This laboratory maintains a close collaboration with the Identification Department but, at present, is only active in the Canton of Geneva.

In the opinion of the author, this organisation for Forensic Sciences in Switzerland is not the best. Even if this organisation is sufficient for problems of legal medicine, blood examination and toxicology, the use of recent developments in the field of forensic criminalistics are not being used to maximum benefit. Geographically, both laboratories in Zürich are not in the best position and the requirement for most of the Identification Departments to send their cases to Zürich is not the best solution. Such a system is time-consuming, resulting in delays to obtain the necessary answers. There is also the language problem which necessitates the translation into French, or Italian, of reports written in German in Zürich. These problems are not the fault of the hardworking personnel in Zürich. Such a system leads one to pose a number of questions. Are we sure that all the Identification Departments in each Canton are really making the best use of forensic science? Are we sure that all police officers and their chiefs are aware of the role forensic science can play in their investigations? Are we sure that all cases are studied thoroughly? It is with regret that the answer to these three questions is either "maybe" or, unfortunately, "no".

A paper recently delivered by Dr W. J. Rodger at the Seventh James Brierley Firth Memorial Lecture, on November 1st, 1985, and published in the *Journal of the Forensic Science Society* (1) is apposite to the situation in Switzerland. Three very relevant passages are as follows:

> "I state without hesitation that the United Kingdom currently has arguably the finest forensic science service in the world."
>
> "Universities must be supported and encouraged to ensure that lawyers know more about science and scientists know more about law." (The author agrees totally with this statement.)
>
> "The United Kingdom has one university with a nominated forensic science department providing a course leading to a qualification in forensic science. That University is Strathclyde."

Switzerland also has one university with a nominated forensic science department providing a course leading to a qualification in forensic science. That University is Lausanne.

Other countries have a different perception of forensic science. Last September (1985), the author was invited by Professor Kegel, Head of the Criminalistics Department of the University of Wrocław in Poland, to attend a handwriting identification symposium. In March 1986 Professor Kolecki of the Criminalistics Department of the University of Poznań in Poland, visited the University of Lausanne. Through these colleagues, the opportunity was taken to learn that, in Poland, there are ten universities, seven of which have Departments of Criminalistics attached to the Penal Law Institute of the Faculty of Law and Administration. The lectures in criminalistics take place during the third and the fourth years of the course of studies leading to a Masters degree in Penal Law.

The "Institut de police scientifique et de criminologie" (Institute of Forensic Science and Criminology) of the University of Lausanne, was officially founded in 1909 as the result of the efforts of the late Professor R. A. Reiss, a pioneer of the Forensic Sciences. Reiss wrote in an article published in the *Pall Mall Magazine*, in April 1907 (2), "We have to meet the criminal on equal terms, and to surpass him, if possible in finesse. This is feasible only by giving our Police forces a professional training, based upon scientific methods, i.e. by requisitioning the researches of scientific men for the science of criminal enquiry."

Briefly, some important dates on the history of the "Institut de police scientifique et de criminologie" are as follows:

1909—Foundation of the "Institut de police scientifique". The Institute is attached to the Law, Science and Medicine faculties of the University of Lausanne.

1919—Retirement of Professor Reiss. Professor Marc A. Bischoff appointed as his successor.

1929—Death of Professor Reiss in Belgrade.

1954—Extension in the area of studies. The Institute became the "Institut de police scientifique et de criminologie".

1963 — Retirement of Professor Bischoff and appointment of the author Jacques Mathyer as Professor of scientific photography and criminalistics and as director of the Institute.
1971 — Death of Professor Bischoff in Lausanne.
1986 — September 30th — Retirement of Professor Mathyer.

The Constitution of the University of Lausanne in 1977 identifies the Institute as a "school" attached to the Law Faculty but geographically located in the building of the school of chemistry of the Faculty of Science.

Today, the University of Lausanne offers three degrees in the field of Forensic Science and Criminology: a "Diplôme en police scientifique et criminologie"; a "Diplôme en criminologie"; a Doctor's degree in Police scientifique et criminologie. To obtain the "Diplôme en police scientifique et criminologie", the students have to attend the University for four academic years, or eight university terms. The first begins in October and ends in February (the Winter term) and the Summer term runs from mid April to the end of June. Students normally enter the University at the age of 18–19 years, the entrance qualification being a "Baccalaureat" or "Swiss Federal Matriculation".

During the first year of their studies each student attends lectures in the Science Faculty which covers general, inorganic, organic and analytical chemistry, experimental physics, mathematics and photography. They also have to undertake practical work in chemistry and physics as well as photography. The second year is devoted to further lectures in Forensic Chemistry and Instrumental Analysis applied to Criminalistics, accompanied by appropriate practical work. Special lectures (six hours each week, for the two terms) in criminalistic aspects of Forensic Science are given, all lectures being emphasised by demonstrations and practical work in the laboratories of the Institute. At the same time the students must also attend lectures in the Law Faculty covering such topics as an Introduction to Law, Criminal Law and Criminal Procedure. The third year contains practical work in the forensic science laboratories, lectures given by professors of the Social Sciences Faculty in General Sociology and Psychology and an introduction to Forensic Medicine, Pathology and Psychiatry by the Medicine Faculty. Professor M. Killias of the Institute also lectures on Criminology and Penology. Finally, the fourth year, which is divided into two parts, sees the students spending many hours in laboratories and attending lectures or seminars during which actual cases are presented and studied.

During the practical training in the forensic science laboratory, students have the opportunity to study traces materials associated with documents and which have been found in actual criminal enquiries. They have to prepare reports on their findings illustrated by photographs, etc. During the second year (third and fourth university terms) they have an average of fourteen hours a week in the laboratory and an average of eighteen hours during the fifth and sixth terms and finish with thirty-two hours a week during the seventh term.

For the complete course there are three sets of examinations: one at the end of both the first and second years and the final one during the eighth semester. These examinations take the form of oral interviews, written composition and practical assessment. During their University vacations, students have the possibility of receiving a practical training in an official Police Laboratory. For the "Diplôme en criminologie", the accent is given only on lectures and seminars without any scientific laboratory work. It would be tedious to present the full course of studies, but, very briefly, the students have to attend lectures normally given in the Faculties of Law and Social Sciences. For example, General Sociology and Psychology, Social Psychology, Psychosociology of Social Integration and Deviance, Methodology, Mathematics for the Social Sciences, Statistics and Psychiatry. They also have to attend lectures in Criminalistics. Only those students who already have a Law or Social Sciences degree from any University are allowed to attend this course because this is a postgraduate diploma. For the doctor's degree, candidates have to conduct personal research and to present an original thesis either in Forensic Science or in Criminology or Penology. It must be realised that the "Institut de Police scientifique et de criminologie" is not a Police Forensic Science Laboratory, but belongs solely to the University. Its activities are divided into three main areas:

(a) research and university teaching;
(b) the provision of expertise for Judges and the Courts, usually confined to Switzerland but exceptionally for other countries;
(c) collaboration with the criminal Police forces.

Many of the diplomates have developed their careers in Switzerland but also abroad, often joining Police forces in the country of their choice. For example, Germany, Rumania, Poland, Yugoslavia, Argentina and Brazil were all countries which employed diplomates of the Institute before World War I and between World War I and II. More recently, former students have joined Police Forces in Tunisia, Israel and Canada.

Today, the Institute's staff is composed of two professors, Professor Killias who teaches Criminology and Penology and the author whose speciality is Photography and Criminalistics. Professor Killias is supported by one assistant in Criminology and the Institute itself employs a master-assistant, Dr Tappolet and three assistants, as well as a photographer, a laboratory attendant and, of course, a secretary.

With such a small team, it is difficult to conduct research on a large scale, but we do our best. Professor Killias has just completed a research project on victimisation in the French speaking part of Switzerland while, in the field of criminalistics, we are conducting researches, mainly into the analysis of paints and of liquid writing inks and on the security of valuable documents. Our teaching staff is, needless to say, completed by professors from the various faculties of the university from whom we "borrow" teaching in chemistry, physics, mathematics, law, psychology, sociology, and so on.

Police forces as well as Police Forensic Science Laboratories need generalists, as well as some specialists. Some of our diplomates, who graduate as generalists, may decide to extend their knowledge in a specialised area such as analytical chemistry or toxicology. This view of the roles of the generalist and specialist were confirmed by what my colleague and good friend Professor Stuart S. Kind wrote in a letter he sent to me just after the visit he paid to the Institute of Lausanne and the lecture given to our students in November 1982; he wrote: "I think you have retained in Switzerland some of the generalist attitudes to the involvement of science in crime investigation that perhaps we, in the larger countries, have regrettably lost."

While preparing this article, a question arose in the mind of the author. Was Professor Reiss right to fight for the creation of a course of studies in forensic science and were professors Bischoff and Mathyer right to develop the Institute founded by Reiss? Today, without any doubt, the answer must be "Yes". The creation of the Forensic Science Unit in the University of Strathclyde and the enquiry conducted recently by the General Secretariat of the International Organisation of Criminal Police — INTERPOL (3) (which came to no positive conclusion) are proof that there exists a need for courses of studies in Forensic Science. The ideas proposed by Reiss more than eighty years ago are still relevant and, after having read Dr Rodger's James Brierley Firth Memorial Lecture of November 1985, it can only be concluded that Forensic Science must be taught, not only to scientists, but also to lawyers.

References

1. Rodger, W. J. Forensic Science — Policy Option. The Seventh J. B. Firth Memorial Lecture. *Journal of the Forensic Science Society*, 1986; 26: 69–78.

2. Reiss, R. A. The Training of a Modern Detective. *Pall Mall Magazine*, 1907; 168.

3. International Organisation of Criminal Police Report.

KILROY WAS HERE!

W. J. Rodger

During World War II, the phrase "Kilroy was here" was often found written up wherever the Americans, and in particular Air Transport Command, had been. Its origin is a matter of conjecture. One suggestion is that a certain shipyard inspector in Quincy, Massachusetts, wrote the words on equipment he had inspected.

Unfortunately, when a criminal commits a crime, he does not often write up on the wall at the locus "Naughty Nick was here", but what he surely does on every occasion is leave behind and take away some evidence of his visit.

That evidence may be large or minute, permanent or transient, obvious or invisible — and whether or not it provides a means of identifying Naughty Nick will depend first of all on its being found and then identified. Only at that point will it be known if it has a degree of individuality which may contribute towards the solution of the crime.

Since the subject of this Conference is "The Uses of the Forensic Sciences", it might be appropriate to highlight the potential of forensic science including identifying Kilroy and then relate that to its use.

There is, of course, no limit to what might constitute valuable forensic scientific evidence. [Slides were shown to demonstrate a wide range of positive forensic scientific evidence and in particular relating to physical fits of fabrics and dentures, tachograph route retracing, vehicle identification by paint undercoat systems using a computerised data bank, and bloodstains, semen stains and hairs.]

Clearly, it would seem, the potential requirement for scientific examination of evidence materials should be very great. Indeed, it is difficult to envisage any kind of crime where there could never be a possible scientific involvement. At the locus, for instance, that involvement might be important to establish that a crime had actually been committed. It might be important to establish that a potential suspect was in fact innocent, a somewhat hidden contribution not much appreciated but nonetheless significant.

It would surely be difficult to argue that the scientific evidence, such as we have seen on the slides, is not an infinitely better option than the evidence, for instance, of eye-witnesses, especially in the area of personal identification. In one recent case no less than four eye-witnesses identified three suspects as being those involved in a robbery. There was no other police evidence and the suspects were eventually released. A second robbery occurred for which three different men were apprehended. Other witnesses then correctly identified them as being "the men" involved in the first incident.

The author will certainly never forget a personal experience in which he was "volunteered" to take part in an identity parade in a sexual assault. He was picked out three times! The panic which engulfed him was more than enough to quench any misconceived notions he might have had arising from having been considered capable of the deeds under investigation. This occurred not a few years ago, and he decided there and then that, like the members of the jury on the very long trials who are subsequently excused from jury duty for life, he had just made the one significant and final contribution to identity parades. Clearly, in all eye-witness situations, investigative procedures must always seek additional corroborative evidence, and that should surely include scientific evidence!

What about the potential of forensic science in supporting the demands of the law and society for action in dealing with the major problems of today? That we have a serious drugs situation is beyond debate. How many convictions would be achieved without scientific identification of drugs and, where appropriate, quantification? Last year there was a 29 per cent increase in reported rapes in England and Wales, with London itself showing a 56 per cent increase in sexual attacks on women. If that does not involve a similarly greater input from forensic scientists, someone should wish to know why. In addition, it should be said that DNA fingerprinting of seminal stains in such cases has a future potential which is, to say the least, exciting. Quite apart from the 29 per cent increase in rapes, what is more disturbing is the much-held belief that only about 10 per cent of such cases are ever reported. These unreported cases are a prime example of the "dark figure of crime" referred to no less than 22 years ago by Alistair Brownlie (1) who called it "the greatest single factor weakening such deterrent effects as punishment possesses". We would no doubt all agree that one of the greatest deterrents is the certainty of detection. That being so, and if it is accepted that Forensic Science has much to offer in the way of detection and conviction, then statistics should reveal that it is being used to maximum advantage. Let us look at the statistics for Scotland.

In 1984 there were 334,537 reported offences, such as breach of the peace, reckless driving, vehicle defect offences and so on — areas which understandably would not usually require a forensic scientific input. In these offences there was a commendable 95·7 per cent clear-up.

In the same year, there were 474,913 reported crimes, i.e. crimes of violence, crimes of indecency, housebreaking, fraud, fire raising, drugs and so on, in all of which areas a scientific input must be at least a possibility. In these crimes, the clear-up rate was 30·8 per cent.

In that year, 7,676 cases were submitted for forensic scientific examination, which is 1·6 per cent of the total — in other words, of every 1,000 crime cases, 16 were submitted to the forensic science laboratory. Further analysis of the 1984 figures reveal that crime cases sent to the laboratory averaged out at 0·57 cases per police officer — in other words, from ten police officers each working for a full year, the laboratory could expect to receive less than six cases.

If we look at the police gross expenditure in 1984, for every £100 spent, the amount allocated to forensic science would have bought two postage stamps — mind you, that's 1st class stamps!

There are lies, damned lies, and statistics — and the use of statistics, especially in relation to crime trends, is notoriously dangerous and misleading. It is difficult to understand, for instance, the hysteria which overtakes the media around Christmas and the New Year on the subject of the numbers of drinking drivers apprehended. It gives them a fair amount of copy, but what does it actually mean? A fortnight ago, the Scottish crime figures for the first half of 1985 were published, indicating a reduction of just under 1 per cent overall, compared with the corresponding period in 1984. A spokesman was quoted as saying that this slight fall in recorded crime was encouraging — but was there a real reduction in crime or were the figures reflecting the fact that financial restrictions enforced on Chief Constables reduced their ability to deal effectively with the caseload?

Is dealing effectively with crime the same as dealing cost-effectively with crime? Is it possible to deal effectively with crime on a cost-effective basis? At what stage is it no longer cost-effective to pursue a housebreaker, or a rapist or even a murderer? It would certainly seem that cost-effectiveness is more and more a determining criterion in crime investigation, but how important is cost-effectiveness in a legal system which can apparently spend £5,000,000 on one trial alone, more than was spent on Forensic Science in Scotland in the last five years? What is cost-effective about a legal system which insists on police officers sitting around court rooms to the tune of several million pounds a year in Strathclyde alone, especially when one survey showed that in almost three-quarters of the cases, the officers were never called to give evidence? Official reaction on this particular subject seems to be that there is a need for improvement, provided it does not involve any change in the law. Let me respectfully suggest that even the law isn't perfect, and if it can be improved, why should it not be improved, especially if it makes it more efficient. In this country over the last few years, reasons of economy have been used to justify highly significant social and environmental changes affecting the lives of millions of people to varying degrees. It is certainly not an overstatement to say that some economies introduced have meant life or death to a number of people, not least of course, in the health services. Wasn't it Bill Shankly, the football manager, who said "Football is not a matter of life and death. It's more important than that." Is that how the law is to be considered? If economies can justify a limited police resource to investigate crime, if economies can justify a cut-back in health services to the stage of denying some people their very lives, they can surely justify a look at the laws of evidence to weed out those archaic, inefficient procedural requirements which have long outlived their relevance in contemporary society. Wasn't it only last year in Scotland that two prisoners claimed their apparently competent right to trial by combat, where each of them would do battle with no less than the Lord Advocate himself each armed with wooden staves in a man-to-man fight which would continue until either combatant cried "craven" — or the stars came out? The motion was in fact withdrawn, much to the relief presumably of the Lord Advocate, for several reasons.

Let me quote Sir Edward Coke (2) "How longsoever it hath continued, if it be against reason it is of no force in law." Unfortunately, that was over 350 years ago and it would seem to be a sentiment which has enjoyed very little favour ever since.

The law's purpose is to serve and protect society. The law should be shaped to suit the just requirements of that society, NOT vice versa. It should be seen as a horse, rather than a sacred cow. It should be fed by sensible modification — and adaptation to today's needs, not worshipped like some stone-carved edict brought down from the mountains.

It is fundamental that the law should have the respect of society, but it should be prepared to earn that respect rather than take it for granted. In the first instance, respect for the law must be demonstrated by all of us involved in the process of law — police officers, forensic scientists, police surgeons and, dare I say it, even lawyers.

How much respect was shown for the process of law by the lawyer who agreed a minute of admission that a forensic scientist's report identified a piece of cannabis as a controlled drug? The prosecution, therefore, did not call the forensic scientist. At the summing up, the defence then claimed that the report as it stood did not in fact legally identify cannabis. How much respect was shown for the process of law in a case where the Crown forensic scientist had stated a degree of common origin on the basis of his examination of control and suspect fibres? Defence lawyers took the samples to a defence analyst who carried out his own examination using the same techniques and additionally using microspectrophotometry. Using all these techniques, including microspectrophotometry, he came to the same conclusion as the Crown scientist. At the trial, however, the defence did not call their analyst but attacked the Crown scientist on the basis that he had not used microspectrophotometry to come to his conclusions, and they then contended that had he used a microspectrophotometer he might have found that the samples were different. If we can't get a moral approach to and a demonstration of respect for the courts by professionals how can we expect it from anyone else?

Since we are here to discuss the Uses of the Forensic Sciences, it is worth addressing ourselves also to the misuse and abuse of the Forensic Sciences such as these examples demonstrate.

The forensic scientist need not be concerned as to whether or not his evidence is or is not considered valuable in any particular case, provided that any limited value assigned to it relates to its relevance to the circumstances in that case rather than to some implied deficiency in its own quality.

However, every forensic scientist, whether for the prosecution or the defence, should be concerned to ensure that his evidence is not misused or abused by counsel. The forensic scientist has a responsibility to the court of law at all times. He also has a responsibility to his profession and to his fellow professionals.

He must ensure that he attends to these responsibilities primarily and is not induced to neglect them as a result of manipulation by the kind of advocate who clearly does not accept that such responsibilities exist and who, it would seem, is apparently prepared, for instance, robustly to deny any primary duty existing between the scientist and the court. That is a recipe for professional disaster. All of us, scientific, medical or whatever, must strive to demonstrate neutrality in the witness box and that can only be done by placing our respect for the law and our own profession at the highest level.

Forensic science has much to offer the court of law in many, many areas, including identifying Kilroy. Advances in our technology require a rethink by all responsible for structuring our legal system so that we move away from the kind of philosophy which produces staffing formulae specifically designed to avoid increasing numbers of staff in proportion to the numbers of cases received, the kind of philosophy which seems to generate a trial procedure with an existence and purpose independent of such general considerations as the truth, the kind of philosophy which seems more and more prepared to accept that justice may not be done but that can be tolerated so long as justice is not seen not to be done.

References

1. Editorial. *Journal of the Forensic Science Society*, 1964; 4: 110.

2. *Penguin Dictionary of Quotations*, Cohen, J. M. and Cohen, M. J., Eds. 1973; 114; ref. 2. Institute commentary upon Littleton; 1: 80.

FIRE BUGS — THE ROLE OF BACTERIA AND FUNGI IN SPONTANEOUS HEAT GENERATION

R. E. H. Skelton

The term "fire bug" is commonly associated with pyromaniacs who start fires for pleasure, or arsonists who do so for profit, but in the world of microbiology there are many organisms including bacteria, actinomyces and fungi which in the normal course of their development, may raise the temperature of their host substrates to the point where chemical oxidation leading to so-called spontaneous combustion begins.

None of these organisms are capable of photosynthesis owing to the absence of chlorophyll in their make-up; consequently they can develop only on substrates providing a ready-made carbohydrate food supply. Depending on the type of organism, the substrates are either degraded or fermented to produce the materials needed for microbial growth.

Chains of enzymes produced by the organisms catalyse and control these degrading or fermenting reactions, but since only the hydrolytic ones such as cellulases can spread from their parent bacterium into substrate fibres it is unlikely that the enzymes themselves are directly involved in heat generation. The enzyme complement varies considerably between genera, also between species and sub-species, so the relationship between these variations and the ability of associated organisms to raise substrate temperatures merits further study. Many factors combine to determine the nature and extent of microbial colonisation possible in a particular substrate. Initial temperature, aeration, water content, water activity, i.e. the ratio of water pressure over the substrate to that of pure water at the same temperature and pressure, pH, the mass, density and food value of the substrate, each contributes in some way to determining the identity and numbers of organisms that it can support, and consequently the extent to which its temperature can be raised by microbial activity.

Given the number of variables that may affect the ability of any particular substrate to self-ignite, it is not surprising that many fire investigators treat with suspicion claims that certain fires have ignited spontaneously.

But such fires do occur and many substances including agricultural and forest products, various types of waste materials, composts and manures (1), Table 1, are prone to spontaneous heating if sufficiently infected by thermotolerant/thermophylic organisms. Heating up to 40–42°C may be due to cellular and/or microbial activity, the former being due to respiration of the still living "parenchymal cells" of cellulosics such as wool wastes, hay and straw, etc., during the first 7–8 days after stacking and the latter by microbial colonies with growth temperatures ranging from 12°C for *Aspergillus fumigatus* as minima, to maxima of 75–80°C for *Bacillus calfactor* (3), Table 2.

Since the growth temperatures and other related factors affecting microbial colonisation overlap in some cases, various genera and species may co-exist on the same substrate. As many as forty-five different categories per sample including bacteria, actinomyces and fungi have been reported (3) in

TABLE 1

Substrates Supporting Spontaneous Heating (1)

Agricultural produce	Hay and straw Cereal grains and other seeds Fermenting foods Cocoa, coffee and tea Tobacco Cotton Wool
Forest products	Wood chip piles
Waste materials	Sugar cane bagasse Vegetable composts and hot beds Manure of herbivorous animals Municipal wastes
Mushroom compost	
Retting guayule	
Nests of Mallee fowl	

TABLE 2

Spontaneous Heating by Pure Cultures (2)

Species	*Min. Growth Temp.* (°C)	*Max. Growth Temp.* (°C)	*Heated Substrate To* (°C)
Fungi			
Rhizopus nigricans	1	35–40	38
Aspergillus glaucus group (?)	?	41	39
A. niger	7–10	50–55	53·5
A. fumigatus	12–15	55–60	57 Amb 40°C 54 Amb 20°C
Absidia corymbifera	20	60	56·6
Malbranchea pulchella var *sulfurea*	29	55–60	58
Humicola languinosa	30	60–65	62·5
Bacteria			
Bacillus calfactor	30	75–80	51 Amb 40°C 68 Amb 60°C
Thermoactinomyces vulgaris (?) (as *Actinomyces thermophilus*)	30	60–65	63

studies of moulding hay. There is also evidence that different organisms may interact to increase or decrease the spontaneous heating potential of a particular substrate. Samples of hay with 50 per cent moisture content inoculated with *Bacillus stearothermophilus* and *Thermoactinomyces vulgaris* showed a temperature increase from 30°C to 55–57°C. Other samples inoculated with the Bacillus only, continued heating into the chemical oxidation stage up to 260°C (4).

In the Morrum Sulphate Mill Fire of 1971, involving an out-door storage pile of 250,000 m^3 of wood chips, fire seat temperatures of 100°C maximum were recorded (5). Unburned samples removed from the stack burst into flames at 90°C, immediately on exposure to air. This phenomenon has been attributed (6) to the presence of *Cronartium flaccidum* infection in the wood.

A review of several fire incidents involving spontaneous combustion of wood wastes (7), describes one fire which started in an accumulation of sawdust and cutterdust around a wooden ventilation duct. The temperature of air passing through the duct had been at maximum, 65°C, the lowest recorded ambient temperature for a fire involving forest products. One possible explanation for this event is that piles of moist sawdust can develop high concentrations of carbon dioxide in the early stages of self-heating due to cellular or microbial activity.

The enzyme for interconversion of carbon dioxide, water and carbonic acid is carbonic anhydrase:

$$CO_2 + H_2O \xrightleftharpoons[]{\text{Carbonic anhydrase}} H_2CO_3$$

This enzyme is capable of converting 600,000 molecules of carbon dioxide per second into carbonic acid, the fastest known reaction rate for an enzyme and ten million times faster than the same reaction un-catalysed.

In wood wastes containing "tramp" steel objects such as cutterdust or nails, etc., these conditions can lead to the dissemination of iron salts throughout the contiguous volume of the pile, which at a mean temperature of 65°C may oxidise, for example, green aspen at about 1·6 Wkg^{-1}, or Douglas fir at 0·41 Wkg^{-1} (8).

While most fungi and actinomycetes are obligate aerobes, bacteria are usually anaerobic especially the methanogens of which, up to a few years ago, only two or three species had been identified. The list however is steadily growing. This identification problem stems from the fact that these organisms never grow alone in nature and are always found as part of a mixed microbial system. This situation occurs because the only substrates on which methanogens can develop, hydrogen plus carbon dioxide or the equivalent formate and the acetate, are found only as products of metabolism by other microbes. Methanogens such as for example *Methanosarcina, Methanospirillum, Methanobacterium*, etc., do not generate heat but produce instead methane gas which in appropriate stoichiometric ratios with air can be ignited by a secondary heat source such as a spark.

Explosions involving farm slurry tankers, some fatal, have been investigated and reported many times by different authors. In each of these cases methane had been generated and the build-up in the tanker was due to a variety of causes such as standing in sunlight. Owing to defective (or tied down) safety valves, tanks have been over-pressurised to the point of rupturing and sparks generated by tearing metal or of similar origin, have explosively ignited the contents (9). With a lower explosive limit of only 5 per cent in air, naturally occurring methane is hazardous at all times.

Mud and soil bacteria mainly species of *Clostridium*, with others such as *Sporolactobacillus, Sporosarcina, Sarcina*, etc., nearly all produce hydrogen and acetate; they also produce alcohols. When methanogens or sulphate reducing bacteria (SRB's) such as *Desulfovibrio* and *Desulfotomaculum* grow with these fermentative species the hydrogen produced is removed by the SRB's stimulating further production of hydrogen and acetate which may be released as flammable vapours. SRB's also convert sulphate to sulphides including H_2S, another flammable gas.

In the early 1970s following a series of unexplained fires and explosions which occurred over a two-day period at the Townsville Sugar Terminal in Queensland, South Australia, investigators discovered a colony of *Clostridium butyricum*, an anaerobic species of bacteria. The organisms in metabolising waste sugar washed into the drainage system had produced a mixture of hydrogen and carbon dioxide. The former, being lighter than air, had risen from the drains to be ignited in random locations on coming into contact with various indigenous heat sources. Since hydrogen burns without incandescing the actual number of free burning sites caused by the bacteria could not be determined.

Not all microbial heating is problematical. Food fermentation involving spontaneous heating, a feature of some oriental and South American dishes, utilises pure cultures of certain fungi (10). One example is "miso", a preparation involving rice fermented by *Aspergillus oryzae*. The flavouring of cocoa, coffee and black teas also requires microbial fermentation (11). In nature the Mallee fowl utilises microbial colonisation by arranging for some composting material to surround and incubate its eggs, the bird using its beak as a probe for controlling the temperature (12). The successful composting of municipal wastes using thermophylic actinomycetes has also been reported (13, 14).

Finally, there is the contentious issue of spontaneous human combustion (SHC) dating back to 1692. In that year in Copenhagen, "a woman of the lower class who for three years had used spirituous liquors to such an extent that she took no other nourishment, having sat down one evening on a chair to sleep, was consumed in the night time so that next morning no part of her was found but the skull and extreme joints of her fingers. All the rest of her body was reduced to ashes."

By 1824 no less than eighteen cases of SHC had been recorded and reported (15). Cases were reported from Italy in 1736 and 1771, France in 1725, England in 1744, 1888 and 1902, Germany in 1811 and sporadically in the U.S.A. up to 1888. Letters to the *Lancet* in 1902 provide graphic descriptions of two cases of non-fatal SHC involving elderly males, one suffering from severe atonic dyspepsia, the other an alcoholic, from chronic gastritis. In both cases the patients reported explosive flashes causing beard and facial burns when they eructated (belched) while lighting in one case a pipe and in the other a short piece of cigar.

In 1977 in the Irish Republic, a 54-year-old female taken into custody while drunk and incapable, later burned to death in a police cell. The coroner's verdict in this case was that the unfortunate victim had probably ignited her clothing while trying to light a cigarette. Spent matches in an unburned box were found by the police after the incident, located under the bunk on which the woman had been placed, but no cigarettes or matches were listed among the woman's possessions at the time she was brought into the station. The possibility of the matches having been brought in by an earlier occupant of the cell, does not appear to have been considered.

In all of the reported cases of SHC the victims were mostly female and almost all given to immoderate use of alcohol. They were also elderly and therefore perhaps more prone to fermentive decomposition of the stomach contents than younger persons. It is beyond dispute that bacterial activity in the human stomach is capable of producing gases which, if exposed to air and a suitable heat source simultaneously, can burn fiercely and even explosively. Peritonial and gastric fluids for example frequently include alcohols, the products of bacterial fermentation of foodstuffs.

Lactose rejection among infants is today detected by measuring the hydrogen content of a baby's breath. Hydrogen is a highly combustible gas and its derivative hydrogen phosphide is one of many gases which will spontaneously burst into flames on contact with air.

Because SHC is no longer medically recognised it is consequently not considered as a possible cause of death in fire fatalities. There are, however, many investigators who have been confronted with corpses in post-fire searches, exhibiting burn patterns not consistent with the type of fire being investigated. Unfortunately the professional gulf that exists between the fire-fighters and investigators on the one hand and medical practitioners on the other, means that such anomalies are rarely if ever given the consideration they perhaps deserve.

Given the extensive knowledge now available on the ignition and burning characteristics of clothing and improvements, etc., in medical and physiological practices since the nineteenth-century rejection of SHC, it is possible that some form of joint study between the two disciplines might now indicate that this rejection was premature?

Acknowledgements

The author wishes to record his sincere appreciation of the generous assistance and guidance received from Dr John Lacey of the Rothamstead Experimental Station, Professor Thomas Thornqvist of the Royal Swedish College of Forestry, Dr Peter N. Hobson of the Rowett Research Institute and Professor J. N. P. Davies of Medico-Legal Consultants P.C., Albany, N.Y.

References

1. Lacey, J. Colonisation of damp organic substrates and spontaneous heating. *Microbial growth and survival in extremes of environment*. Society for Applied Bacteriology Technical Series, 15, 53–70. London, Academic Press (1980).

2. Miehe, H. Uber die Selbsterhitzung des Heues. 2 Auflage, *Arbeiten der Deutschen Landwirtschafts-Gesellschaft*, 196, 1930; 1–47.

3. Gregory, P. H., Lacey, M. E., Festenstein, G. N. and Skinner, F. A. Microbial and biochemical changes during the moulding of hay. *Journal of General Microbiology*, 1963; 33: 147–174.

4. Hussain, H. M. Okologische Untersuchungen uber die Bedeutung thermophiler Mikroorganismen fur die Selbsterhitzung von Heu. *Zeitschrift fur Allgemeine Mikrobiologie*, 1973; 13: 323–334.

5. Bergman, O. Thermal degradation and spontaneous ignition in outdoor chip storage. Department of Forest Products. Sweden 1974; Report No. 291, 2–5.

6. Thornqvist, T. Royal College of Forestry, Uppsala, Sweden. Private Communication (1986).

7. Virtala, V., Oksanen, S. and Frilund, F. Methods for the determination of the tendency to spontaneous ignition. State Dept. for Technical Research Publication No. 14 (1949).

8. Springer, E. L., Hajny, G. L. and Feist, W. C. TAPPI 53: 85–86 (1970).

9. Hobson, P. H. The Rowett Research Institute, Aberdeen, Scotland. Private Communication (1986).

10. Tansey, M. R. and Brock, T. D. *Microbial Life in Extreme Environments*, ed. Kushner, D. J., London: Academic Press (1978).

11. Broadbent, J. A. and Oyenizan, J. O. *Biodeterioration of Materials*, eds. Walter, A. H. and Elphick, J. J. London: Elsevier Publishing Co. Ltd. (1968).

12. Frith, H. L. *The Mallee Fowl. The Bird that builds an incubator.* Sydney: Angus Roberts Ltd. (1962).

13. Stutzenberger, F. J., Kaufman, A. J. and Lassin, R. D. Cellulolytic activity in municipal solid waste composting. *Canadian Journal of Microbiology*, 1970; 16: 553–560.

14. Kane, B. E. and Mullins, J. T. Thermophyllic Fungi in municipal waste compost systems. *Mycologia*, 1973; 65: 1087–1100.

15. Beck, S. *Elements of Jurisprudence* (1824).

BLOOD, SWEAT AND TEARS

P. H. Whitehead

Many concerned with the investigation of crimes against the person, be it a pub brawl, rape or murder, will be familiar with the following type of phrase found on the forensic scientist's statement of witness: "Bloodstains found on the blade of the knife (exhibit 1) were tested and found to be human of blood-groups A, PGM2-1, Hp 1-1. One person in fifty in the United Kingdom has blood-groups of this combination including that of the deceased SMITH. The blood could not have come from BROWN."

It is the intention of this article to first explain the meaning of these hieroglyphics — the magic symbols of the new priests of crime investigation that allow them to differentiate one person from another by examining their blood.

Blood grouping in Forensic Science is concerned with discriminating between individuals on the basis of differences found in their blood. In reviewing the subject a period of time of really a very few years will be covered from which we have moved from an inability to distinguish at all on this basis to the new-found ability to distinguish everybody. A major jump in technology achieved in less than 100 years!

In this review will be discussed what blood groups are and the history of their use in Forensic Science from the start of the twentieth century to the present day. This latter will be expanded to detail our present abilities and achievements and the problems faced in interpretation of bloodstain evidence. The related difficulties associated with the grouping of secretions such as semen and saliva will also be covered. Recent developments and what they hold for the future will be commented upon.

Blood Groups

Before describing what blood groups are, it is necessary to describe the composition of a drop of blood. Blood consists of a very large number of red cells together with a relatively small number of white cells floating in a yellow fluid — the plasma. The main function of the blood is to act as a transport medium for all manner of things from vitamins to traces of copper but principally, of course, to carry oxygen through haemoglobin in the red blood cells. An important feature of the red cells is that they do not have a nucleus and have no chromosomes (the bodies which carry the genetic material known as DNA). This is in contrast to the white cells.

Blood groups are of three types:

1. Those which represent the chemical architecture of the walls, or membrane, of the red cell such as the ABO groups. They are usually made of protein and carbohydrate, and may be envisaged as "floating" islands in the lipid (or fat) membrane of the cell. The most important component is the carbohydrate structure which determines the blood-

group activity. When blood dries in the form of a stain, the cell-wall is ruptured but it retains its carbohydrate structure and hence group activity.

2. Those which represent different forms of proteins *inside* the red cell, e.g. PGM, EAP and others. These proteins are catalysts (enzymes) which aid the conversion of one chemical to another within the cell.
3. Different forms of proteins within the plasma, e.g. Hp. These proteins are often "transport proteins".

A witness statement involving blood grouping may have all three types describing a stain. For example:

A	*PGM 2-1, EAP BA, AK, 1*	*Hp 2-2*
membrane	intracellular	extracellular

Genetics

Blood groups are inherited characteristics: that is they are inherited from one's parents and are associated with an individual for life. These two features are most important in forensic science and have important consequences in both disputed paternity investigations and the field of crime investigation.

Each living organism is composed of microscopic cells of many different types representing different functions. Each cell in the human, excluding red blood cells, has a nucleus wherein lies the genetic material which determines the number and variety of our inherited characteristics.

General Theory of Inheritance

The nucleus of each cell of the body contains thread-like structures called chromosomes which can be observed down the microscope. These chromosomes are divided along their length into more or less discrete regions each of which has distinct genetic properties. These regions are called "genes" and a large number of them are present on each chromosome. It is the gene which contains the "computer programme" which determines our inherited characteristics, including blood groups. They are arranged in a characteristic order along its length so that each gene always occupies its own special position (or locus) on a particular chromosome. In man, it is known that there are 46 chromosomes in 23 pairs. Each member of a pair contains the same number of genes and the gene loci are arranged in the same order. (The sex chromosomes are the only known exceptions to this rule.) The significance of the *paired* chromosomes can be seen in consideration of the sex cells, i.e. the male sperm and female ovum.

In the sperm and ova there are only 23 chromosomes in each nucleus. This position is reached by special cell divisions in which the homologous paired chromosomes part, one going into each of the two sex cells. Thus the sex cells contain exactly half of the chromosome material of the body cells. When fusion of the male and female sex cells occurs, the chromosome material doubles up again, each chromosome finding its homologue among chromosomes derived from the opposite sex, subsequent divisions giving rise to body cells containing 46 chromosomes in 23 pairs. Thus every body cell (as opposed to sex cell) contains the same genes in its nucleus as every other body cell. Moreover, half of them have been derived from the male parent and half from the female.

A single gene is responsible for a particular characteristic, e.g. eye colour. However, to account for the great variety of different forms of that characteristic, e.g. blue, brown, green, grey eyes, etc. it is clear there must exist genes with the same objective but a slightly different programme. These are called alleles or allelomorphic genes and they occur on the same position on the chromosome. An individual possesses two and only two alleles for that characteristic, one from each parent. If the *same* allele is derived from each parent, the individual is said to be homozygous for the particular gene and if different, heterozygous. It follows, therefore, that if two alleles which can be designated L and l exist at a particular position, three genetically different types of individual can occur, L-L, L-l, and l-l. Sometimes it is possible to distinguish clearly each of these from the other but often only two classes can be recognised, one which may be called "L" comprising LL and Ll and the other "l". In such circumstances L is said to be dominant to l and l recessive to L.

The ABO System

We can now apply this genetic theory to a consideration of the best known of the blood group systems — the ABO system. This system, discovered by Landsteiner at the start of the century (1), is of importance because of its significance in blood transfusions; however, not all groups are important in this respect. The ABO groups may be thought of as chemical structures made of carbohydrate which "stick out" from the red cell membrane, being anchored to the membrane by a protein core. People who are group A have the "A" chemical; B have the "B" chemical and group O have neither "A" nor "B".

The characters A, B and O are inherited by means of three allelomorphic genes, which are also called A, B and O. Every individual has two chromosomes each carrying either A, B or O — one from each parent. Thus a person may have AA, AO, BB, BO, AB or OO. As A and B are dominant over O, so one is either group A, B, AB or O.

The various ABO matings and the children derived from them are now easily explained. The same reasoning may be applied to other systems, e.g. haptoglobin or Hp. There are two types, or alleles, Hp 1 and Hp 2. There are thus only three kinds of blood group Hp 1-1 (abbreviated to Hp 1), Hp 2-1 and Hp 2-2 (or Hp 2).

Hence the importance of blood groups in disputed paternity cases. There are many other blood group systems in use now and the effect of adding other grouping systems to the problem of disputed paternity is to progressively reduce the number of people who could be the parents of any given child. Similarly with bloodstains. It is the combination of blood group systems that makes them such a powerful tool in discriminating the blood of one person from another. Whereas approximately 42 per cent of the population are group "A", 50 per cent are PGM 2-1 and 10 per cent approximately are Hp 1-1. Hence a combination of the systems A, PGM 2-1, Hp 1-1 is only found in approximately 2 per cent of the population of 1 in 50.

Bloodstains

The origins of our ability to discriminate the blood, and bloodstains, of one individual from another began with Landsteiner's discovery of the human ABO blood groups at the start of the century. Once the basic genetics of the ABO system had been understood and a terminology agreed, we began to see early publications on the application of this exciting discovery to the problem of dried bloodstains.

The next system to be applied to dried blood was the MN system, rather similar to the ABO system in being on the red cell membrane, which Landsteiner and Levine (2) showed to be detectable in dried blood shortly after they had discovered them in 1927. Over the next 20 years we see the ABO system being consolidated and successfully used in many crime cases and — with perhaps rather less success — the MN system. The next most interesting phase in the detection of genetic markers came in the 1950s and 1960s with new micro-techniques for the ABO system allowing reliable grouping of minute fragments of dried blood.

Biochemical

While progress in the discrimination of bloodstains by studying groups associated with the cell membrane has been one of steady progress since 1900, punctuated by bursts of activity, the discrimination of stains by studying proteins *in* the red cell and *in* the plasma has been an explosive one over the past 20 years. Nearly twenty "polymorphic" enzyme and protein systems have been shown to be potential discriminating markers of bloodstains. These include the widely used systems such as PGM and Hp already mentioned. However, other systems in use include EAP, AK, ADA, GLO, GC and others, the initials in each case representing an abbreviated name of a protein.

Problems

The most obvious problem which our technological success had brought us is one of choice — which system or systems are to be used in any given case? In practice, of course, this is not a choice without limit as we are constrained by both physical conditions relating to the bloodstain, e.g. size, age and also inevitably by financial and resource considerations. Very few laboratories indeed, even given a large fresh stain, will have staff and time to use every discriminating system available even if they so wished. One is obliged after considering the number of staff and types of skills available, to choose those systems which are most likely to discriminate between the blood of different individuals.

Secretions: Semen and Saliva

The grouping of bloodstains has then obvious significance in cases of assault and murder. However, the grouping of secretions such as semen or saliva is also possible but to a much lesser degree. The detection of blood groups in these secretions — and the chemicals responsible for the blood groups which may be present in these secretions even in the absence of blood — is more difficult. Two main systems are used: the ABO and PGM systems.

However, even further complications arise as very often in cases of a sexual nature we are dealing with a mixture of secretions from both the man and the woman. For example, following a case of rape, the police surgeon will take a sample of the fluids from the vagina — usually on a cotton swab. If intercourse has indeed taken place then the vaginal swab may contain components of both semen and secretions from the woman herself. As both secretions may contain blood groups it is important in the interpretation of such grouping results to take full account of the contribution from both individuals. Often, of course, in cases of rape the question is not did intercourse take place and with whom, but rather was it with consent. In such circumstances the most useful evidence is likely to be evidence of violence such as bruising and torn clothes; the grouping evidence may then be of little significance.

Significance of Grouping Results

Four specific features occur in nearly all reports relating to bloodstains — distribution, species, grouping results, and frequency of occurrence of the recorded group(s) in a *relevant* population.

Depending on the circumstances of the case each or all of these features will be of greater or lesser significance. It is important that we weigh carefully the significance of each feature and not exaggerate one feature over the others. For example the presence of a large human bloodstain stretching from the elbow to the cuff of a man's jacket, which is indisputably *not* his own blood group (e.g. group A), may in itself be of greater significance (in terms of discrimination) than the fact that it is blood group O and 50 per cent of the population have such a group. In such circumstances we are more interested in the number of people who have large amounts of human blood on their sleeves than the fact that in theory it could have originated from 50 per cent of the population.

In brief the significance of blood grouping evidence is proportional to the ratio of:

$$\frac{\text{PROBABILITY this defendant would have blood on him if the incident was as alleged}}{\text{PROBABILITY anyone else would have comparable blood evidence on his clothes as the defendant}}$$

It is this ratio which determines the value of the blood evidence in any given case. Obviously this ratio is very dependent on the environment in which the offence is committed. We must, therefore, be very wary of trying to calculate from blood grouping frequency figures alone the probability that a given suspect was involved in crime simply because he has on his clothes blood which is not his own and which is of a group(s) which "only" belongs to a small percentage of the population.

Characterisation of the Individual

DNA-profiling

Given a human bloodstain only a few days old and about the size of a new penny it may be possible to group it in a number of systems — as already mentioned. The combination of such groups may on calculation mean that only one person in several thousand has such a series of blood groups. In a "closed" situation this may prove decisive. However, in the "open" crime situation it still means that in theory, at least, large numbers of people may be involved. For a number of reasons already mentioned, given a seminal stain it is likely that only one or two grouping systems are applicable and in such circumstances, again in theory, very large numbers of men could be the donor of the semen — perhaps nearly half the population in the U.K.

In other words our present systems are of great value in eliminating individuals but are of no value in positively identifying individuals.

All of this will change with the introduction in the future of "DNA-profiling". This system, which is based on studying the genetic material present in blood and other body fluids, will provide an identification system unique to the individual. At present trials to test the system are still going on at the Home Office Central Research Establishment under Drs Gill and Werett (3) but it is expected that the system will be in use in criminal trials in one to two years.

It is not the intention of this article to go into great detail concerning the technique other than to say that the basis of the method lies in studying the genetic material which is responsible for determining all of our individual characteristics from our sex to the colours of our eyes, from intelligence to blood groups. The genetic material which is responsible for storing all of the information which leads to the production of the individual is DNA — or "de-oxyribo-nucleic acid".

DNA may be visualised as a long ribbon coiled in a complex manner inside the chromosome. The ribbon made up of a series of chemicals may be considered as the blue-print which directs the production in each cell (with a nucleus) of proteins which in turn finally "build" the individual with all of his/her unique characteristics. It is the ability of our scientists to read and interpret the molecular code which makes up the DNA-ribbon which allows us to finally associate a bloodstain with a specific individual. And not only bloodstains but also semen stains.

The future looks very exciting, but it is a time-consuming technique and requires skilled operators. Many problems, some technical, others organisational still have to be overcome, but there is no doubt that the final goal of the forensic expert in blood grouping has now been achieved — the association of a given blood with its donor.

References

1. Landsteiner, K. Uber Agglutinationserscheinungen Normale Menschicher Blutes. *Wiener Klinische Wochenschrift*, 1901; 14: 1132.

2. Landsteiner, K. and Levine, P. A new agglutinable factor differentiating individual human bloods. *Proceedings of the Society of Experimental Biology and Medicine* (NY), 1927; 24: 600–602.

3. Gill, P., Jeffreys, A. J. and Werett, D. J. Forensic Application of DNA fingerprints. *Nature*, 1985; 318: 577–579.

LEGAL

THE SOLICITOR AND FORENSIC SCIENCE

A. R. Brownlie

Since the Forensic Science Society and the British Academy of Forensic Sciences came into being in 1959 they have achieved much for the forensic sciences. They have by their meetings and by their Journals stimulated consideration of the uses of forensic science, and have spread around the world knowledge and awareness of the developments which are going on in the field, and have helped scientists and to a lesser extent lawyers to be more aware of what is being achieved and what may yet be achieved. Strathclyde University has played a unique and notable part not only in training scientists to fit them for a career in clinical and laboratory work at home and abroad, but by exposing them in some degree to the kind of situation in which they will meet with lawyers in the court-going phase of their duties. The British Academy has always had a strong legal component and the Forensic Science Society has enrolled a respectable number of lawyers in its membership but has rarely been able to engage them in confrontation or dialogue with scientists save to a limited degree. The fact that in a participants list of over 170 persons attending this Conference — probably the most sophisticated of its kind ever to be held in Scotland — there are but a handful of lawyers present — suggests that all is not well with the science/law relationship in this country; and English experience has been no better. This is the more remarkable because in a real sense lawyers are the consumers of forensic science. The product of the scientists' enquiries, examinations, conclusions and reports is the input of expert evidence, oral or written, which the forensic scientists provide in Court for the lawyers — the judge and jury and the opposing Counsel on either side. Where have all the lawyers gone?

Now I must not succumb to the ecclesiastical temptation of denouncing from the pulpit the non-churchgoers: I should then be addressing the wrong audience. But I am not sure how to reach the consumers of forensic science who have not realised the benefits to be gained for themselves and their clients from contacts with the scientific community.

It is, of course, well known that there is a cultural barrier to be crossed between science and law. Superficially it may seem that since each is involved in playing a part in the administration of justice, co-operation should be easy. But law and science are deceptively similar and radically different. Both disciplines seek for reliable fact on which to build. All fact having rational probative value is admissible, unless there exists some specific rule or reason excluding it. Science and law can both equally accept these guidelines. Truthful, reliable data must be the basis for true judgment. And both law and science are now accepted as part of our culture. But the difference between law and science can be highlighted and simplified by saying that law is prescriptive (concerned with guiding conduct) while science is descriptive or explicative (concerned with providing data and principles to follow observed phenomena). Law presupposes at least a degree of permanence: the very word carries the suggestion of rigidity and persistence. Science proceeds from hypothesis to hypothesis and is immediately ready to discard one hypothesis as soon as an awkward fact emerges requiring that the hypothesis be reformulated. The hypothesis is the scientist's principal intellectual instrument in research. Yet in practice this disadvantage of seeming fluidity is more apparent than real. Law reaches out towards stability: science seems perpetually tentative. Each rule and datum is open to challenge and to testing. Law proceeds by deductive processes; science by inductive. Hopefully neither jumps to conclusions on insufficient evidence.

Yet these incompatibilities should not mean that scientist and lawyer cannot co-operate; and thankfully they do not often prevent practical co-operation. What is needed is that the scientist should better understand the stance of the lawyer, and the lawyer the stance of the scientist. The differences between them are at least in part, a function of the differing tasks performed by science and law in our society.

Law — at least in the circumstances in which the forensic scientists meet it — proceeds on a case-by-case basis. Each case has to be looked at within its own framework, and what is learned by way of evidence in one is not carried through into another; it must be repeated. Moreover each case has to be dealt with against a time-table. Legal fact-finding cannot wait for elaborate experiment or endless testing of theories or ideas. In the real world there have to be bounds set to any enquiry; the judge and jury have to get home for their tea. And lawyers make no pretensions to be revealing ultimate truth. They are simply doing the best they can with the materials at hand. That is why there have to be so many opportunities for appeal. Lawyers are always conscious of their capacity for error, and thankful if opportunity exists to have error corrected. Scientists seem more concerned that what they espouse as evidence shall be seen as true for all time and in all places, or at least to all others in the scientific community.

Perhaps a greater difficulty for scientists — and it is one that lawyers have to take seriously — is that scientists distrust the legal method of enquiry, based as it is almost entirely on the testing of the recollection of observers of fact — the testimony of witnesses; and the method of eliciting this evidence which is by question and answer, is a subjective approach. By contrast the scientific method is founded upon an examination of what is objective and demonstrable and generally replicable; a highly persuasive procedure. Most lawyers do not realise that scientists have reservations about the validity of legal methods of fact-finding. There is a substantial body of scientific data undermining the reliability of testimonial evidence and the powers of retention and recall by witnesses of past events (often long past events), or the effectiveness of examination and cross-examination as a means of checking and testing these recollections, especially when they are concerned with questions of visual identification. It is well known that even two honest observers of the same scene rarely give identical accounts. All of us are prone to see what we want or expect to see. The point at which the fibres and blood vessels pass through the retina of our eyes to reach the brain produces in each of us a genuine blind spot. But the real blind spot is not physical in origin.

For centuries lawyers have believed, and still believe, that the best way to resolve a conflict of fact or opinion is to argue the issues openly within the rules of advocacy, and that the best way to reach the truth of a witness statement is to expose its maker to examination and cross-examination by skilled advocates. To the scientist that truth is far from self evident, and there is much aversion to the adversary process. My own personal answer to these misgivings is to look to that comment of Aristotle (Metaphysics) when he said that "A man shall more easily and discreetly judge of things if he have heard the reasons on both sides contending like adversaries". Put that way, my intuition and my experience is that the comment is true.

Given then that there are these differences of approach and of method, what can be done to encourage the scientist and the lawyer to come closer to co-operation in the matter of the forensic sciences? How can the use of the forensic sciences be widened and the intelligent understanding of the forensic sciences deepened?

Obviously there has to be a greater interchange of information and ideas between the scientist and the lawyer. The one must learn more about the other and must try to respect the other's integrity. It used to be said that one reason for the law's slow acceptance of science was that judges were mostly brought up in a literary training, innocent of scientific knowledge. There may have been some truth in this in the past but in Scotland, at least, all judges now regularly encounter scientific witnesses, and it is arguable that the Senator sitting as a judge in the High Court of Justiciary has *more* exposure to scientific evidence than any other kind of lawyer. Yet lawyers do need education in the field of science and no doubt scientists in the field of law. Neither can substitute for the other and neither should presume to poach on the preserves of the other. Lawyers are proud of their traditions, but it is salutary to remember that sorcery and witchcraft were tolerated by the law as lately as the sixteenth and seventeenth centuries. And in pursuit of a point in one of my own cases recently I found it necessary to establish the legal authority for the proposition that torture is no longer permitted as a means of eliciting evidence in the Law of Scotland. I can confirm to any anxious forensic scientists that this is indeed truly the case. Those who give expert evidence in Court may feel that they have a view on this matter; but if they do it is a feature of the scientist's aversion to adversary proceedings for which one must have considerable sympathy.

Much has been written about the problems of giving evidence by question and answer on a technical matter. Obviously the question of language becomes of the greatest importance, and the witness must strive to give evidence clearly, simply, economically and without straying (or being led) beyond the bounds of his or her expertise. "It is a rare privilege", wrote Sir William Willcox in 1924 in a pamphlet (1) on the giving of expert evidence, "not to be lightly undertaken." "The real strength of any evidence", said Sir Keith Simpson in his popular book (2), *Forty Years of Murder*, "is its reasonableness: it has to be both sound and defensible, and to look so to the jury." These things are easy to say but difficult to perform.

It is true that the questioner in these adversary proceedings is dominant, but sometimes an unexpected answer stops him in his tracks. The plight of the expert who is being led unwillingly step by step into territory or in a direction he does not wish to take, so that his evidence is being given a slant that it should not have, is a difficult one. However all questioning comes to an end, and the expert witness who feels ill-used must remonstrate, and if he remains dissatisfied, should stand his ground until the judge enquires why he lingers in the witness box. This is the expert's opportunity to say that having taken an oath to tell the whole truth he feels there is more to be said: and nine times out of ten he will be invited by the judge further to explain the reasons for his discomfiture.

I suppose that the lawyer's ready facility with words and the weapon of cross-examination are the two things which cause most concern to forensic scientists. You know the kind of thing exemplified by Rufus Isaacs' question, "Do you drink?" Answer, "That's my business". Question (as quick as lightning) "Have you any other business?" Cross-examination is certainly what lawyers find most difficult, in dealing with a technical expert. It is the duty of the Court to prevent cheap-jack cross-examination which aims only to unsettle or demean or distress the witness. My own view is that judges should deal more strictly with cross-examiners who put suggestions to expert witnesses which turn out never to have had the slightest foundation in fact, but perhaps this is a grey area of the law. It is certainly the case that effective cross-examination requires in the questioner a considerable knowledge of the subject professed by the expert witness, and much of the dissatisfaction caused by cross-examination stems from questions asked by persons who do not understand what they are enquiring about. It is said that Sir Edward Clarke who defended Adelaide Bartlett on a charge of murdering her husband by poisoning him with liquid chloroform in 1886 shut himself up for a week with medical textbooks before the trial to make himself master of the medical aspects of the subject, which he assuredly did to good effect.

Certainly when Geoffrey Lawrence, in the Dr John Bodkin Adams trial in 1957 (3) for murdering an old lady, rose to cross-examine the Crown doctor he seemed to know as much about the action of morphia, heroin and paraldehyde in the management of acute terminal illness as did the witness. And so he was able to detect the expert's desperate last minute formulation of the theory that the accused had withdrawn morphia for four days in order that it might be fatally reintroduced following the reduction of the patient's acquired tolerance.

"That theory", persisted Lawrence, having led the witness on to found upon it, "is *nonsense*"; for, he argued, the chemical similarity of the drugs involved meant that despite withdrawal of morphia there remained a fair degree of cross-tolerance. And in face of this knowledge of his subject the Crown expert could only fall silent.

I hope I have said enough to show that while a lawyer should never aspire to become a chemist or a pathologist or a doctor, there is much benefit to be derived by solicitors and counsel who may be involved in civil or criminal litigation with a technical aspect having some prior familiarity with the kind of specialised evidence likely to be given by the expert and with the ways of thinking of such experts. This observation in itself is in my submission a sufficient reason for supporting the proposition that lawyers should have some elementary knowledge of and contact with the forensic sciences. When in 1967 the Law Society of Scotland submitted their Memorandum of Evidence to the Monopolies Commission (4) describing the then state of the profession they listed as one of the areas of study which litigation lawyers ought to be familiar with, the forensic sciences. I know, because I wrote that paragraph myself. In the intervening years, however, the profession has failed to take very much heed of the opportunities for becoming familiar with the detailed work of scientists in the numerous branches of science which can contribute to the process of the administration of justice. They are the losers, and the treatment of scientific evidence in Court is meantime less effective than it might otherwise be. It is to be hoped that the presence of so many internationally distinguished forensic scientists in Glasgow this weekend, giving so enthusiastically of their skills to the service of the law, will draw attention to the opportunities which still exist for Scottish lawyers to participate in this developing field not least in connection with Strathclyde University and that a growing interest in both directions will begin to manifest itself.

I would add only one or two other points.

Solicitors and forensic scientists should make it their business to meet one another more often, and not in the context of the adversary process. There should be a greater effort to communicate. They should share their experiences. In the field of publishing there should be greater exchange of information; more publishing in one another's journals. More efforts should be made at joint-author publishing. More effort should be made to capitalise on the work being done by groups such as the Forensic Science Unit of this University. The rewards both for participants and for society would be considerable.

There is a story of the Glasgow wean who had been to a children's party and was being accompanied home on the Auchenshuggle tram by his mother. She enquired if he had enjoyed the party and he replied despondently "I wished I hadny goed". "No, no," said his mother, "that's no proper English. You mean 'I wish to Goad I hadny went'."

I may have mildly criticised my professional colleagues the legal absentees today, but I am absolutely confident that none of us present will so colourfully regret our attendance at this remarkable Conference on the Uses of the Forensic Sciences.

References

1. Willcox, W. M. *The Influence of Chemical Research on Medicine and Forensic Medicine*. Institute of Chemistry of Great Britain and Ireland, 1924; 16.

2. Simpson, K. *Forty Years of Murder: An Autobiography*. London: Harrap, 1978; 217.

3. Hoskins, P. *Two Men were Acquitted; The Trial and Acquittal of Dr John Bodkin Adams*, London: Secker and Warburg, 1984; 152.

4. Memorandum of Evidence by the Council of the Law Society of Scotland to the Monopolies Commission; 1967, para 3(a), 5.

THE PLACE OF THE EXPERT IN CRIMINAL COURT PROCEEDINGS, WITH SPECIAL REFERENCE TO RECENT PROPOSALS FOR CHANGE

C. Goodwin Jones

Over the past few years, against a background of growing concern about falling recruitment, low morale, absence of career structure, attacks on impartiality and allegations of partisanship, a debate has grown up concerning the appropriate role and organisation of forensic expertise in the criminal justice system. It is not the purpose of this article to go into these proposals for change which have been mooted as solutions to the perceived problems. It should be stated at the outset some of these proposals may be considered to be rather misguided attempts at problem-solving not because they are in themselves deficient in thought or understanding, but because they fail to address fundamental issues. The most fundamental issue of all is the notion that it is possible, through some sort of fine tuning of our forensic sciences and a honing down of organisation and skills, to meet the requirements of the criminal justice system, thereby to purge injustice, partiality and error from our system. To aim for some ideal stratagem whereby our scientific and legal procedures may be so designed to meet the joint goals of efficiency and accuracy is in itself not a bad thing; what we must temper this ideal with, it must be argued, is a good dose of realism which makes us regard every failure to meet the ideal not as a travesty of justice nor a perversion of the scientific method, but as an expected consequence of an imperfect and imperfectible system. It has been said that forensic scientists must aim for the highest standards. There is no doubt that more money, better facilities, incentives and a rewarding career structure all assist the achievement of such standards. By the same argument, it is said that poor funding, bad organisation, falling standards and pressure of work may lead to the "odd one or two" crimes and criminals slipping through the net cast by the forensic scientist. This too is true. What must be argued here is that changes in the organisation and funding of forensic science designed to improve the mesh of that net — to fashion, if you like, a dragnet (an image which would have recommended itself to the founders of the FBI) — these measures cannot of themselves put things to rights, nor can they in any way guarantee that injustices, bias, error and partisanship will be "designed out" of the system.

It is proposed to give a brief synopsis of the main options which have figured in recent discussions. In the limited space available it is not possible to do justice to each but it is hoped, in passing, to establish that few of the so-called "new" proposals for change are in fact not new at all — most have been, if not already tried and rejected, hanging up in the law's lumber room awaiting revival for some hundreds of years.

At the risk of provoking controversy, it is suggested that one way forward for forensic science might be to knock fairly and squarely on the head for all time the notion that thoroughgoing scientific impartiality is what the criminal justice system requires of its agencies. Our system is not alone in its faults:

other systems fail to permit and encourage scientific neutrality just as much as our own. Leaving aside for the moment the issue of whether such neutrality is theoretically possible, it is nevertheless clear to those closely involved with the legal system that legal procedures, both formal and informal, operate to make scientific neutrality practically difficult to achieve. It is not at all obvious that this neutrality is, in any event, what the law wants. Forensic science is applied science — courts like it when it is useful and blame it when it is not. Applying science to crime may assist different parties in different ways. For example for the judiciary, scientific expertise may assist the accuracy of judicial decision making (and if it does not, well at least there is someone else to blame) while for the prosecution and defence, scientific expertise is an aid to advocacy, that is it can help win cases or assist in the defeat of the other side's case. Decisions seen to be based upon a scientific foundation gain an added legitimacy and public credit. Lawyers and law have successfully co-opted sciences of all kinds in much the same way as once upon a time they would have sought support from religious and moral orders. Given the limits of the state of the art, forensic scientists make their contribution to the pursuit of "the truth, the whole truth, and nothing but the truth" whilst the public expect this assistance to aid the aims of justice. What both suffer from is the idea that the whole truth and justice are of paramount importance to the law and lawyers. Aiming for such ideals might be a noble pursuit, and we can assume that they are fair enough ideals to aim for, but the Realpolitik of the legal system guarantees that such ideals are but rarely attainable and not always desirable. Cynicism does not mean, however, that we need to abandon the ideals altogether in favour of thoroughgoing pragmatism. What we do need to do is recognise the limits of our scientific and legal procedures. We have made the mistake of beginning to believe in our own myths of perfectibility. If this is correct, we are mistaken to pursue some ideal alliance between law and science and should settle instead for some kind of "best possible fit" wherein we recognise that faults and even abuses may occur, and that when they do so, we adopt a "no fault liability" approach to their occurrence.

Turning now to the specific proposals for change which it is felt would better meet our ideals of justice, equality and impartiality, we have in the main two kinds of suggestions:

(a) Improvements within the existing system. For example, access for the defence to its own or to Home Office forensic science facilities so as to counteract what is seen as the present inequality of access to expertise. Reorganisation of forensic pathology so as to bring pathologists into closer alignment with their so-called "clients", the police and the coroners.
(b) Radical changes, or so-called radical changes, in the organisation of forensic expertise.

For example, the establishment of a system of court experts to replace that system whereby each side is free to call its own expert witness in support of its case. The reorganisation of forensic science into one central and/or several Regional Institutes, along the lines of the Continental model much admired from a distance.

Lastly, the proposal which manages to somehow straddle this dichotomy between radical and piecemeal solution to perceived problems, namely the privatisation of forensic work, the so-called "putting out to tender" option much discussed in 1985.

Taking the *ad hoc* or piecemeal approaches first, these seem to recommend themselves firstly on the basis of not interfering too much with the way things are and, some would have us believe, the way things always have been. Tradition has long been a prized feature of both the English and the Scottish criminal justice systems, the feeling being that the systems we have, while open to improvement, suit our history, our culture, and answers best those needs we have developed over time and with substantial experience. Within this doctrine, we allow for change in so far as it is compelled by the interests of justice. Equality before the law, it has been argued, is an empty piece of rhetoric unless it be backed up by the facilities and support needed to make it real. Thus we have permitted a number of changes to take place which better gear our system up to this aim of achieving access to justice for all. Despite this, there has been a certain dogged opposition, born perhaps of blindness, to the calls for better defence access to forensic services. Until very recently there has been a dearth of suitably qualified experts available on a free-lance basis to defendants in criminal cases. Indeed, this position persists very much so in England and is not improved by problems particular to the provision of legal aid for experts in that country. In Scotland the position is slightly better. In the absence of similar Home Office forensic science centres, it is possible in Scotland for the accused to secure the services of one or other of the admittedly small, and diminishing, pool of experts available, and the provision for fees on legal aid is slightly better. In England it has long been recognised, not least by those within the Law Society, that an undesirable inequality exists between the defence and prosecution *vis-à-vis* forensic expertise, facilities and funding. Home Office and free-lance experts work under very different regimes, conditions of employment and within very different environments. By this we are simply referring here to the much-vaunted view of the Home Office experts as "police experts", a view which fails to take account of the integrity of Home Office scientists working under conditions which do not always encourage a high commitment to work and the best possible results. If state-funded forensic science has its problems in times where economic and bureaucratic efficiency have become the marker, how much more difficult then is the position of the free-lance defence expert whose continuity of employment is not guaranteed, whose income fluctuates and is, very often, restricted by the level of legal aid fees permitted and whose impartiality frequently faces the challenge of being a "hired expert"? In the absence of steady work — and defence work is inherently dispersed and intermittent — free-lance experts face problems of capital investment, being unable to purchase equipment which might aid their work. Furthermore, unless one becomes an expert to whom defence lawyers frequently turn, purchase of expensive items of laboratory equipment (which may be rarely but importantly used) cannot be justified. Again, the high-sounding critique of the defence expert as a partisan "hired gun" fails to do justice to the integrity of such experts as men of science doing their job under difficult conditions. It must also be added that under our present system this "partisan expert" is a product of our own fashioning since defence experts in our existing system *must* be privately hired experts. We make no other provision for the supply of scientific expertise to the accused.

The English Law Society, in an effort to improve access to experts working on a free-lance basis, provides a list of names of those experts in the pool. In reply to the author's own research on the usefulness of such a list, she was informed by English lawyers that many of its listed experts were either retired, out of the country or dead, and that they preferred to keep their own lists of tried and trusted experts, chosen as much for their willingness to accept instructions without argument as for their scientific reputations. In order to get on the list of one of these legal firms it was necessary to be recommended, a system of access which perhaps suits a peculiarly English way of doing things. It is not, one may think, a system designed to obtain the best expert. This suspicion is confirmed by the numerous instances whereby an expert was put on the list and used only after numerous others had been approached and had refused to do what the lawyers wanted. As long ago as 1876 Lord Jessel (1) made comment upon a state of affairs which remains with us today. In his words:

> "Now in the present instance I have as usual the evidence of experts on the one side and on the other and, as usual, the experts do not agree in their opinion. There is no reason why they should. As I have often explained since I have had the honour of a seat on this Bench the opinion of an expert may be honestly obtained and it may be quite different from the opinion of another expert also honestly obtained. But the mode in which expert evidence is obtained is such as not to give the fair result of scientific opinion to the court. A man may go, and does sometimes, to half a dozen experts. I have known it in cases of valuation within my own experience at the Bar. He takes their honest opinions, he finds three in his favour and three against him; he says to the three in his favour, will you be kind enough to give evidence? and he pays the three against him their fees and leaves them alone; the other side does the same. It may not be three out of six, it may be three out of fifty. I was told in one case where a person wanted a certain thing done, that they went to sixty eight people before they found one."

It is unlikely that modern lawyers would go to quite such lengths to find a suitable expert, unless perhaps the case was "big enough" to justify such an expenditure of time, energy and money. It is more likely to be the case today that legal firms requiring expert evidence on a regular basis will have built up their network of information more efficiently than in Jessel's day, and will be able to access their chosen expert with the minimum of fuss. Though there are quite distinct differences between law firms as regards their skills in this field (differences related to the nature of their clientele and economic factors), it is clear that "justice" and "equality" are not going to be attained simply by improving access *to* experts. There must also be the necessary back-up to ensure that experts thereby made available can, and will, be used by litigants. In the current climate of cutbacks to the provisions of legal aid, it is unlikely that this funding will be forthcoming.

In any event, increased financial funding for the accused can only be part of the answer. One further suggestion has been the provision of a state forensic service for the defence, to match exactly the facilities of the Home Office laboratories. Quite apart from this crucial question of where the necessary funding would come from, such a proposal lacks understanding of the nature of much forensic work. It would be difficult, for example, to see how two separate laboratories could carry out tests on materials which tend to be destroyed or altered by the first set of tests. Victims of crime as much as its purveyors tend not to leave excess evidence sufficient for the detection purposes of one forensic examination, let alone two. Problems also arise from the fact that since it is the police who arrive at and organise scene of crime investigations, it tends to be the Crown which gets "first shot" at any collection and examination of forensic evidence. Whilst it is possible to foresee a system whereby two sets of scene of crime teams could be notified and despatched, it strains credulity to expect such duplication to be workable, efficient, or necessary, and again, there is the question of expense.

One alternative proposal has concerned itself with access to Crown facilities and examinations by defence experts, and indeed, this works well in certain areas though is much dependent upon relationships of trust and co-operation being established on an informal basis, perhaps through former working relationships. This suggestion was mooted as long ago as the nineteenth century in the murder trial of Lamson (2), a poisoning trial. Though the defendant had requested that his expert be present during the experiments of the Crown's expert, permission was refused by the court as being "contrary to all practice" in reply to which Lamson's counsel objected that: "If this is contrary to all practice, the sooner the practice is remedied the better. To try a man on speculative theories on the one hand, and upon the other on an analysis taken behind his back is trifling with life." Perhaps it has been the abolition of the death penalty which has led to the demise of such impassioned cries. Certainly very little notice was taken of Lamson's lawyer in any event, the impact of his rhetoric being, as with a great deal of legal rhetoric, more imagined than real.

The tenor of more recent cries has indeed been less "defence-minded" than "prosecution-minded", in so far as they aim to further the imbalance between Crown and accused by drawing the forensic scientist more closely into contact with the police. Thus, for instance, in his report following the Confait case, Fisher (3) listed amongst his recommendation ways in which the pathologist (in the employ of the coroner in England) might more closely liaise with the police in order that he/she might better appreciate police lines of investigation and incorporate such understanding into his or her own approach to forensic examination. As has been expressed elsewhere, this sort of move could well be thought to compromise the position of the pathologist as a "man/woman of science" and lead to their being well and truly labelled "police pathologists", subject to the orders and wishes of the police with, as Professor Alan Usher has pointed out (4), "all that could mean for the quality of evidence".

Given that historically there has been much made of the imbalance between state and accused *vis-à-vis* provision of expert forensic services, and given that the experts have themselves, over time, expressed a wish to work outwith this narrow conception of forensic science, it is all the more surprising to find that proposals to privatise the forensic services recommend closer "consumer/expert" relations. By the same token, it is hard to see that this approach is what the Home Office termed "a fresh look" at the organisation of the forensic sciences. What its glance does demonstrate is a more blatant statement of what it sees as the role of forensic science, revealed in that chilling phrase "consumer interests".

There are, undoubtedly, problems with privatising the forensic science services. Putting work out to tender entails the notion of giving work to the department (university, health service and otherwise) which can deliver the goods within an acceptable price range, with the possibility of work going to the lowest bidder. Even given that departments might receive contracts for five or ten year periods, which on first sight might seem a fair prospect, experience of scientific workers employed elsewhere on short-term contracts subject to uncertain renewal has demonstrated the knock-on effects of such terms of employment on recruitment. In the universities, where this type of contract is already used, research staff find problems shifting from one place to another as and when their contracts expire, a problem which persists to fairly high levels in the career structure. Universities would find it problematic to fund chairs in those subjects which have a forensic use, already a problem with forensic medicine. Career prospects too would be curtailed when departments lost their contracts as future bids undercut their own. The prospect of getting forensic work done for the lowest possible price must seem attractive to the present government, though the inherent danger of cutting corners in the quality of forensic services resulting from such a scheme hardly augments the rhetoric of its "law and order" platform. Catching the criminals is one thing, conducting fair and high quality forensic investigations to enable conviction or acquittal is another. The net result of privatisation could mean more "miscarriages of justice" than at present. In short, though the forensic scientists working within the present civil service pay guidelines must relish the prospect of higher rewards for their good works promised by privatisation, in the long run, privatisation might well turn out to be bad both for forensic scientists and, perhaps more importantly, for forensic science. Improved salaries for forensic scientists could as easily be achieved by the creation of a flourishing private sector working for the defence, properly funded and offering reasonable career prospects. In effect, this is the sort of system we presently offer to the accused *vis-à-vis* legal services, and it is possible for lawyers to change between the private and state sectors in mid-career should they so wish. For forensic scientists, such a system might offer opportunities to see life from both sides of the fence, hence avoiding the danger of becoming "prosecution" or "defence" minded. It would also provide insight into the problems faced by either side and possibly lead to a fairer appraisal of each other's work. It could even give rise to working relationships between forensic scientists on either side whereby knowledge, methods and facilities were, to some degree, shared. Though there are problems with this scheme, and they mainly relate to proper funding of the private forensic scientist working for legally-aided accused, the creation of a flourishing private sector in the provision of forensic services may well offer us a solution to some of the problems identified as iniquitous by critics of the present system.

Against the kind of piecemeal reforms outlined thus far stand the so-called radical proposals for change which, on the whole, argue that the grass is very much greener on the other side of the hill — or Channel as the case may be. Many Continental jurisdictions operate on what is termed the Inquisitorial system. In such systems there is a single investigating magistrate who conducts all enquiries, interviews witnesses, and hears the evidence in court. To assist him in this task he may call upon the services of a court-appointed expert. General opinion has it that such experts, being appointed independently of either side in a case, are thereby more neutral in their opinions about the evidence. Get rid of the expert on either side, so the argument goes, and that's an end to improper and partisan scientific evidence. This model has attracted much admiration both here and in America. Learned papers (5) have been written urging us to adopt this "Continental Court Expert System" (especially popular in America in the 1940s). Twentieth century English responses to such proposals have been typically phrased in anti-European terms — "it's all right for them, but we have a different legal tradition and it suits our national character". Every time the idea has been mooted, Royal Commissions and the like have tended to come up with the same negative response, viz.: The adoption of such a system would interfere with our legal tradition in too radical a fashion. It would entail the setting up of national scientific institutes to provide the requisite experts for court duties. Only those qualifying through the tests set by such institutes would be eligible. The system would, then, also cost money and be subject to a level of regulation by the scientists themselves which is outwith the experience of the prevailing system. Moreover, one scientific expert will tend towards one viewpoint. A fair cross-section of opinion is not heard and so on. But there are other drawbacks too and they are by no means new to the British. History belies those who advocate the court expert as a new and radical departure which will solve all our problems. It may come as a bit of a surprise to some to learn that we have already tried this system, didn't like it, and stopped using it in all but some jurisdictions (Admiralty & Patent court still regularly use court appointed experts or "assessors" as they are termed; provision for use of court experts in other courts remains on the books but is seldom used). For the most part, the English stopped using court experts in criminal trials towards the middle of the eighteenth century. Their place was taken by experts in the witness box as English law developed the use of trial by jury. Before this date, court experts were used at least by 1345. Texts speak of their use as a well established practice within the criminal justice system by that date. Records note their use in trials in 1353, 1429, 1554, 1597, 1673, 1753, 1755, 1782, 1791 and in numerous trials throughout the eighteenth century. It is not thus convincing to argue, as many American and English authors have argued, that the court expert is a "Radically Different creature which Foreigners use and we might Adopt!" Like many other things, the British had already tried court experts and rejected them. One attempted revival of the court expert by Lord Denning in the 1960s faltered when it was thought that use of a court expert appointed by the judge might in fact lead to a situation whereby each party sought to call their own evidence to rebut that of the court expert, thus bringing three rather than one expert opinion before the judge. Other efforts at revival of the court expert have faced problems endemic to the system. Instead of the opposing defence and Crown expert being accused of partisanship, critics of the Continental systems point to disquiet within those systems concerning the monolithic nature of the court expert's evidence and his lack of accountability. Justice may be being done, but is it being seen to be done? Further opposition arose within British legal circles, and notably from the judiciary itself, when it was thought that appeals from courts using court experts were going not from judge to judge but from expert to expert, all the way to the House of Lords. This perhaps might be no bad thing but, quite apart from any vested interest the judiciary might have in keeping decision-making within its own province, scientific adjudication of legal problems and factual questions of guilt is, and was seen, as alien to the principles and ethos of the criminal justice system. We see something of this in present-day controversies concerning the replacement of juries by expert assessors in fraud trials where we again see rhetoric about the layman's role in law fully rehearsed whilst other issues are overshadowed.

What then are we left with? The so-called radical ways of reorganising forensic evidence better to meet the ends of justice turn out to be old and trusted friends while piecemeal adjustments to the existing system seem inadequate. Neither approach seems to have had much success in the past, whether it be on this or some other Continent. Is the search for some perfect system which will marry the power of science to the needs of law a fruitless search? Is it impossible to devise some system which will better approach our ideals of justice, answer the needs of the courts, provide adequate working environments and incentives to forensic scientists without compromising their impartiality?

In one sense the search for answers in other criminal justice systems is both futile and misguided. An examination of the history and practice of such systems demonstrates that whatever the means of organising forensic evidence in that jurisdiction, problems equal to our own arise. But it may be that some forms of organisation do not cause as many problems as they solve. It may also be the case that rather than searching for a once-and-for-all solution (which by the by also fits in with our expenditure limits) we should employ a plural approach, using whatever facilities are available as and when appropriate. There may be a case, for example, for employing one kind of organised forensic service to tackle some sorts of problems, whilst another form of organisation might better suit another. It has, in the past, been possible to marry the use of court experts with freelance experts, private laboratories with public service laboratories, defence experts with Crown experts and so on. It has to be said, however, that in matters of this kind, it is very often funding levels which dictate the success of each domain, a problem which we already face. Indeed, it may well seem here that, having criticised the various proposals for change, we are left with the system very much as it now exists, and this is in part true, with the one difference that insists upon proper funding for a plurality of institutions so that our presently suffering system might be given the chance to perform properly. There are certain advantages in retaining a plural system wherein experts may be drawn from universities, hospitals, specialised laboratories and the like, not the least of these advantages being the maintenance of some plurality of viewpoint, something approaching the "open scientific community" which Karl Popper advocated (6). Against this it may be said that retaining the fabric of the existing system is to retain its problems, not all of which can be remedied by the injection of more cash. Not least of these problems is the accusation of partisanship or lack of impartiality on the part of the forensic expert him or herself. On this subject there are two things to be said. The first is to emphasise what to some must seem an anathema, namely that we cease to regard forensic science as a perfect science which will, if used properly by scientists whose vision is unblurred by partisan considerations, enable our law courts to always reach the right conclusions. Against a background of financial and bureaucratic constraints, such expectations are unattainable even by those who wholeheartedly believe in their possibility. Secondly, and more importantly, it should be possible to educate both lawyers and the public at large about the limits of forensic science and its practitioners, thereby removing this general expectation of perfection which so often increases the chances that any blame for error, "miscarriages of justice" and the like is laid at the door of the forensic scientist. Blameworthiness is encouraged by an expectation of perfection. One consequence of this is an atmosphere of secrecy, a witch-hunt mentality of shock, horror probe character. In turn, exposure of imperfection may engender low morale and the possibility of greater secrecy as a profession closes ranks. All this is unnecessary luggage for the forensic scientists to carry about with them in their already difficult work. Appended to any reorganisation of the forensic science services should be some form of "no fault liability" clause which will encourage greater openness in the admitting of mistakes, less hysteria on the part of the public and greater willingness on the part of the courts in remedying "miscarriages of justice" if, and only if, a conviction has wrongly and unjustly resulted from any scientific error of method, judgement or opinion. We should, in other words, drop the rhetoric and grow up and in so doing realise that even competent practitioners make mistakes. Only where they can be shown to have been deliberately negligent should some form of blame attach itself to their conduct and even here we should be prepared to examine our own consciences to ask whether there but for the grace of God go I. Reproval, should it follow, should be debated publicly rather than privately. Otherwise we deny the wrongdoer that very justice we so properly seek to see done to the wrongly convicted.

We must also recognise that, serious though wrongful conviction is, it is going to happen within our criminal justice system whether we like it or not, that it is bound to happen even on the law of averages, and that it is, unfortunately, the case that all legal systems are equally imperfect. This is so whatever system we adopt to improve our forensic services. One of the most important things we rely upon is the personal integrity of those administering the legal system, an integrity which is hardly rewarded by low pay levels, poor facilities and an unpromising career structure, not to mention the awful prospect of one day being hoisted with one's own petard. If we can get away from the notion of having someone's head roll every time a forensic scientist is shown to be in error and if we can properly reward work done by defence and prosecution experts in the pursuit of justice, law and order, then we must be on the way to a system which recognises and encourages integrity and fair-mindedness.

References

1. Jessel, M. R. 1876. Thorn v. Worthing Skating Rink Co.
2. See Rowland, J., *Murder Revisited.* John Long: London, 1981.
3. Fisher, Hon. Sir Henry. Report of an Inquiry into the circumstances leading to the trial of three persons on charges arising out of the death of Maxwell Confait and the fire at 27 Dogget Road, London SE6, 1977. H.C. 90, para. 2.4–2.4g.

4. Usher, A., *The Guardian*, July 31, 1985.

5. Hand, L. Historical and Practical Considerations Regarding Expert Testimony. 15 H.L.R. 40, 1901. See also Hammelman. Expert Evidence. 10 M.L.R. 1947.

6. Popper, Sir Karl. *Conjectures and Refutations*. Hutchison, 1963.

THE EXPERT IN THE ADVERSARIAL PROCESS

M. Hill, Q.C.

Introduction

My instructions from the conference organiser were to be provocative. Like all good barristers I obey my instructions. However, I have had some qualms. As Mr Brownlie has commented, there are far more of you here than there are of us and I have to acknowledge, regretfully, on behalf of my profession that the cross-discipline learning drive is not as obvious within the practising legal profession as it ought to be.

That said, if I have anything to offer a conference such as this, it is to puncture a few balloons of self esteem from which any profession inevitably suffers.

I am an English criminal advocate, prosecutor, defender — and cynic. When I started, starry-eyed, determined to emulate the greats, I believed everybody who gave evidence, eye-witnesses, policemen, experts, defendants and alibi witnesses. As a result, I went through agonies as I began to realise that people lied on oath and, more disturbingly, that even the honest witnesses were unable to tell the whole truth, however hard they tried. By the time that I became one of the Treasury Counsel (prosecuting counsel to the Crown) at the Old Bailey, I believed no-one. My attitude now is, I hope, more sophisticated but those years as Treasury Counsel and my years in silk have taught me to accept nothing, to test everything and to base my arguments only on those assertions of fact that the testing has shown to be sustainable.

That attitude applies to all witnesses and, perhaps especially, to experts. Not that I question their honesty. I question the reality of the detachment and independence with which they seek to clothe their opinions and which they brandish resentfully when those opinions are questioned in court. The expert is retained by one of the parties. The objective may be professional independence but experience of barristers suggests that, too often, objective and attainment do not coincide, although the clothing is ostentatiously worn. This is the first main theme of what I have to say.

My second main theme is the imbalance in forensic scientific resources available under the English and Welsh criminal justice system to prosecution and defence. At the end, I shall seek to draw the two themes together by suggesting that balancing resources may have a beneficial effect on the quality of expert evidence.

I was minded to start with a passage to be entitled "experts I have known" but I see that as invidious. I have, however, promised myself not to make a comment which is not based on personally observed events — although I will deliberately camouflage all but one of the particular cases to which I refer by changing the factual details without diminishing the lessons which I suggest should be drawn from them.

Professional Detachment of Expert Witnesses

I think I ought to say something at the outset about the nature of criminal litigation in England and Wales. Many of the experts with whom I have argued function have appeared not to understand the purpose of our criminal trials. We all know the basic principles — the prosecution must prove its case to a very high standard, the defendant is not required to prove his innocence, contentious witnesses for prosecution and defence must give evidence in the presence of the defendant and must submit themselves to cross-examination, the defendant is not required to incriminate himself so that, during the investigation, he can refuse to answer any questions and, during the trial, he is not obliged to give evidence. These principles, each of which has a strong jurisprudential basis, have been evolved over the centuries as society has strained for a criminal justice system which maintains a balance of fairness between "the state" and the individual. Some people hanker after a different system, almost always demonstrating the truth of the saying that the grass is greener on the other side of the hill and frequently the danger of a little knowledge. Contacts with lawyers and others from different systems throw up the same kind of hankering, this time after our system: they have doubts about the inquisitorial system as a route to criminal justice, just as some in England and Wales are doubtful about the adversarial system as a route. Such debates tend to obscure what *our* criminal trial process is about. The search for truth, in theory, occurs during the investigation: the function of the trial is to examine whether the prosecution can prove that the results of the investigation are the truth. The criminal court — magistrates, judge and jury — is not itself engaged in a search for the truth although many trials in fact turn into such a search. The criminal court is charged with the duty of acquitting a defendant because the prosecution has failed to prove his guilt, not because the defendant has proved his innocence. Even when he has proved his innocence, so that although a crime was committed, it was not committed by the defendant, the criminal court is not charged with the duty of identifying, nor is it equipped with the resources to identify, the true criminal.

The first time I came across an expert in court was not, in fact, in a criminal case. I was just starting my common law pupillage. I walked into a case before the Official Referee about an allegedly defective machine. The purchasers complained that the machine did not do its job properly and that, when their experts had examined it, they had found that the cause was that an important part of it was out of true. My pupil master was acting for the manufacturers and, in so far as I understood a word of the case, their defence was that (a) the part was out of true only to an extent which was within the acceptable margin of tolerance and (b) the reason for the failure of the machine to function properly was that it was not being used properly. The case lasted six weeks; each side called two experts, one each on manufacture and one each on user. Altogether, their evidence lasted nearly five weeks. All the experts were leaders in their fields, there had been a full exchange of reports and there were irreconcilable disputes between them. I could understand how there could be disputes about the proper use of the machine: what I was unable to understand was how there could be a fundamental dispute about the extent to which the machine was out of true which, after all, was a matter of measurement. At the end, I asked my pupil master why the experts could not have got together to see if they could resolve their differences before the case came to court — thereby avoiding the very intense acrimony that developed between them as the case proceeded. Experts in the audience will recognise that as a question which many of them have asked, based upon their own experiences.

He said two things: first, that the court was charged with the responsibility of publicly resolving the dispute, so that private and untested agreements between experts elevated them to the status of judges, which they were not; that I could understand even if it did not seem to me to be a complete explanation in a *civil* case. It was his second statement that caused the alarm and served to open my eyes: he said that at least one of the "manufacturing" experts was either incompetent or worse and that neither party should be led into a situation in which that expert was able to dominate the other into changing his mind for the sake of professional harmony. "Incompetent experts" was a contradiction in terms: the "worse" was inconceivable to my naive mind.

Later, in a homicide case, the Prison Medical officer (P.M.O.) had found nothing mentally wrong with the defendant but, since the killing was so bizarre, he had called in a consultant psychiatrist who had confirmed the P.M.O.'s opinion. The defence had done their homework very carefully and had gone to a consultant psychiatrist who had a particular expertise which seemed to the defence lawyers to be pertinent to the defendant and to the killing. He reported that the defendant was suffering from an abnormality of mind such as substantially impaired his mental responsibility. There was no obligation on the defence to disclose their consultant's report but they chose to do so in the hope that prosecution and defence would be able to agree on diminished responsibility, thereby probably avoiding a trial. The prosecution response was to seek a further expert report from someone else specialising in this field. He disagreed with the defence expert but the defence persisted in trying to reach agreement before trial. The consultants were put together: when they came out, they had agreed that the defence expert was right. The prosecution reluctantly agreed to accept the plea of guilty to manslaughter if the judge approved but, faced with the reports, the judge would not. There was a trial, at the end of which the jury acquitted of murder and convicted of manslaughter on the grounds of diminished responsibility. What came out very clearly in the trial, to me at any rate, was that the pursuit of intra-professional harmony had far too much to do with the eventual agreement between the consultants and this, of course, bore out my master's argument that this kind of expert conflict should be resolved only by the proper tribunal.

I suppose those two cases, involving different kinds of experts and conducted in different jurisdictions, had more effect on my attitude to experts than any other cases. To adapt a phrase, they were my seminal cases.

Not that the picture was always the same — far from it. There was a series of very efficiently planned shop burglaries in the mid-1960s. Careful police investigation, lasting over several months, led to their identifying the team responsible and to their acquiring information about the crimes then being planned. The information did not allow the team of detectives to be sure about the actual premises next to be attacked but they were fairly sure of when that attack was to take place. As soon as the anticipated crime was reported they swung into action, taking with them not just the equivalent of a scenes of crimes officer but a forensic scientist from the laboratory which serviced the particular police force. In the end, the conviction of the burglary team turned on the forensic scientific evidence. The prosecution knew that the defence had retained their own expert and, although it was not usable in court as part of their evidence, gained some moral support for what they were doing from the fact that the defence did not call any expert evidence. Moreover, the prosecution expert had reported strongly against any scientifically demonstrable connection between the man suspected as being the leader of the burglars and the scenes of the crimes. The case against that suspected leader was dropped in the absence of any other evidence. Neither the experts team nor the prosecution team was popular with the police but each had managed to do its job properly.

This case stands out in my mind because of the ways in which it demonstrated the experts truly doing their jobs. I do not say that it was the only case in which I have experienced that — far from it — but it is inevitable, I suppose, that one remembers most clearly the cases which went wrong. After all, it is remembering one's own and others' mistakes — and learning from them — which is the most significant way in which the professional improves himself.

Counsel has to learn his way into the expert's field. The learning is, of course, incomplete, it has to work on certain untested basic assumptions, it is bound to be narrow and, very often, I regret, will be superficial. What counsel is trying to achieve is a degree of understanding so that he can translate the professional jargon into language and concepts more easily understood by the lay tribunal (including the judge) and so that he can test the expert's conclusions by pertinent questions. The easiest way of doing this case-by-case learning is by conferring with the expert retained for the party whom counsel is representing. I deplore the fact, whatever its cause, that such conferences do not occur as a matter of course. What counsel needs to be able to do as well, of course, is to test the accuracy of the facts upon which the conclusions are based: which means treating the expert as an investigator. My own view is that it is the almost inevitable and entirely desirable involvement of the expert in investigation, in discovering facts, which most often leads to his becoming partisan and to the quite considerable dissension which can develop between counsel and the expert whom he is cross-examining.

There was a dramatic example of this some years ago. In escaping from a crime, the villains made off in a motor car, described by some eye-witnesses by make and colour. The escape route led over open ground and passed through some bushes. The track of the escaping vehicle was clearly shown by the tyre marks which were left on the soft open ground. The expert came to the scene and claimed to be able to identify which marks had been left by which wheel of the vehicle and to be able to find such clear tread patterns of each tyre as to make it worthwhile taking moulds of those patterns. About 24 hours later, police enquiries led them to a particular house, in the garage of which they found a car of the right make and colour. They reported that, caught up in the bumper assembly was a twig showing all the signs of having been recently broken from a bush similar to those through which the escaping car had travelled. The car was taken for examination by the expert. He returned to the open ground and searched successfully for the bush from which the twig on the car had been broken: he said that he found an exact mechanical fit, an assertion clearly supported by the photographs that were taken. He produced tread patterns from each of the tyres (and from the spare) of the car and then compared the tread moulds with the patterns, finding what he described as a remarkable similarity between three of the moulds and three of the patterns, those from the two front wheels and one of the rear. "In my opinion," he said, "this car was the escape vehicle." He did not deal explicitly in his statement with the fourth tread mould. In evidence, he said that he could find no similarity between that mould and any of the tyres on the vehicle when he examined it. It was put to him that that absence of similarity raised very serious questions about the rest of his evidence. The riposte was obvious — you can never be quite certain how a tyre will conform to the ground and, anyhow, the ("original") fourth tyre might have been changed and disposed of between escape and discovery. Moreover, he strongly relied on the mechanical fit of the twig and the broken bush. The defence had retained their own expert. He pointed out that the unconnected tyre mould was from a tyre of a different make from the tyres producing the other three moulds and from those on the car and said that, if the prosecution forensic scientist had been doing his job properly, he would have spotted that. He said, moreover, that tyre patterns were not like fingerprints and that the prosecution expert was far too positive about the significance of the similarities between the three moulds and three patterns. He was the person who discovered that the prosecution's scientist had identified the mechanical bush/twig fit before he had compared moulds and patterns. In light of what the defence expert had said, the defence had gathered together a good deal of evidence to show that the car in question had not gone through any wheel or tyre changes between the "escape" time and the discovery and examination of the car. When the defence cross-examined the prosecution expert, he was disconcerted by the information, which he eventually confirmed, that the "missing" tyre was of a different make from the others, embarrassed by the questions demonstrating the order in which he had done his work and irritated by the criticism that his conclusions (on the three tread moulds) went too far. When he was asked whether he had considered the possibility that the broken twig had been put there for him to find, he would have none of it. In the event, the defendant (the owner of the car) was acquitted. I have no idea whether the defendant's car had been the "escape" car: what I was and remain quite sure is that the prosecution's expert had been convinced by the mechanical fit which he had discovered that it *was* the "escape" car and that this had coloured his professional judgment and the way in which he presented his evidence. In truth, he had become "involved" in the prosecution's case and, in the witness box, was defending that case rather than giving independent evidence.

That experience was not unique. Not so long ago, there was a case in which a forensic scientist was giving evidence about blood at the scene of a crime. He had examined the scene and had been responsible for deciding what samples the scene of crime officer (S.O.C.O.) should take. He had been shown a summary of what the police had themselves discovered, necessarily because he had to have some idea of where to look and what to be looking for. The prosecution were able to establish, through his evidence, something as to the order of events at the time of the crime and something indicating the way in which the injuries had been inflicted. The use to which the groupings of the blood could be put as part of the evidence identifying the offender was limited: the defendant could not be excluded but, since his blood groupings were identical in most instances to those of the victim, traces of blood (on his clothes) had minimal significance. The defence were interested in the "negative" indications and since there had been a very thorough and painstaking examination of the scene by the S.O.C.O. and a very detailed report produced by him accompanied by photographs and drawings, they had a fair amount of material to examine. What they discovered was that there was other blood at the scene which, from its position, was unlikely to have come from the victim and, since there was some evidence that the victim had inflicted injury on his assailant, might well have come from the assailant. That blood had not been sampled. Moreover, there were fibres on and about the victim which could have come from the assailant, had been examined in the laboratory with care and could not be connected with the defendant. The only way in which the prosecution scientist could properly have dealt with those matters when they were put to him was to accept them for what they were but he did not. He expended a great deal of effort in arguing in the witness box that they were insignificant matters. What he was doing was defending the prosecution's case. Jurors react against that kind of thing and they did so very obviously in that case. I am not saying that it was the expert's performance in the witness box that was the sole cause of the eventual acquittal but I think that all the barristers involved in the case regarded the way in which the expert gave his evidence as being the turning point.

I could multiply these examples, showing, for example, how a defence expert called to undermine the validity of the tests carried out by the prosecution expert had fudged his results thereby avoiding, he hoped, giving evidence of inconvenient experimental results, how a doctor examining an alleged victim of a violent rape had not included in her statement that the "victim" had said that there was no violence, doing so on the ground that the "victim" was so distressed that what she said should not be treated as reliable. But I do not because my purpose is not to paint all experts as incompetent (or worse), which would be a grossly inaccurate picture, but to point out that experts are fallible and that our process is designed to identify that fallibility.

Fallibility was most clearly shown in the sorry story of the Confait (1) case, upon which I trespass with some trepidation. Barristers have had to learn many lessons from the course of that case about their own job but one of the most chilling lessons ought to have been learnt by experts — that if they do not look at the real problem and the real evidence but make or accept assumptions and become enmeshed in arguments which, to the outsider, appear to have been affected by other considerations, the value of what they have to say is totally diminished and harm can be done. The great expert argument was about time of death. The criticism of the prosecution's pathologist was that he had managed to make the facts, discovered by him on post-mortem examination, wrongly produce a time of death which deprived the accused of the benefits of their genuine alibi for the time when, it was said, Confait was really killed. When the case was referred to the Court of Appeal by the Home Office, it was doubt about the evidence which led to the quashing of the convictions. The subsequent Fisher Enquiry (2) went over the whole of the case and a good deal of time was spent on the pathology evidence. In the trial, in the Home Office reference and in the Enquiry, everybody approached the issue on the basis that death had occurred within eight hours (based upon some non-expert evidence) of the discovery of the body and the question was "when in that eight hour period?" For reasons that I really cannot talk about, it became clear some years later that death had probably occurred two days previously, somcthing which was confirmed as a real possibility by an examination of the histological slides which had been produced at and immediately after the post-mortem examination. The significance of those slides was that they demonstrated that death had occurred at least eighteen hours prior to the discovery of the body. If you examine the Fisher Enquiry Report, particularly paragraphs 7.26–27, you will see that harsh words were being said about the prosecution's pathologist's report of his observation of the presence of post-mortem changes. It was said that, since such changes would not be apparent within the time span which everyone was considering, the pathologist could not tell the difference between a bruise and a post-mortem change. If anybody had actually bothered to go back to the original post-mortem reports and to have read them with an enquiring mind, they would have seen that there had always been a basis for checking whether post-mortem changes had, indeed, occurred. No-one did. I do not *know* why, but I have the uncomfortable feeling that it was because those involved were too much concerned with advancing cases and protecting positions than doing an expert's true job.

Forensic Facilities for the Defence

I turn now to my second main theme — balance in the criminal justice system. Balance is crucial. Much current argument seems to equate the discovery of balance as a desirable feature of the system with the Report of the Royal Commission on Criminal Procedure (3): "balance" has become a magic word. In fact, as I said at the outset, our system has evolved through a search for balance.

The balance with which I am concerned is a balance of resources. At least 90 per cent of all criminal litigation in which the defendant is represented is wholly funded from the public purse. The prosecution have access to laboratories for their forensic scientific investigations and evidence — the Home Office laboratories, their own establishment laboratories. With all their problems of funding, they attract and retain qualified scientists of different disciplines, to whom are available physical and group intellectual resources which the forensic scientist in private practice can hardly hope to match and, in my experience, does not match. The legally-aided defendant is at an obvious disadvantage. Save in very exceptional cases, he will not be able to go abroad for expert evidence and the restrictions on legal aid expenditure make it very difficult for him to mount a root-and-branch re-examination of the prosecution's scientific evidence. Even a privately-funding defendant has problems, although he can go abroad for experts.

There is one route available to the defence which would give them access to the same resources as are available to the police and that is by submitting their enquiries through the police to one of the Home Office laboratories. That has obvious disadvantages, since not only the request but the response has to be channelled through the police and that is something which any properly advised defendant would be reluctant to do, not just because of the desire to retain the advantage of surprise which may not matter much, but because, under such circumstances, the confidentiality essential to the proper preparation of a case for trial would be lost.

Nobody regards this as a satisfactory situation. If a forensic scientific or medical expert is to be retained by one party to criminal litigation, then that party must be entitled and enabled to conduct the scientific or medical investigation in confidence and to decide whether to use the results without having the other side knowing what is going on and what those results are. Even the privately-funding defendant who is able to go abroad for his expert may be faced with the same problem if the expert is a member of a laboratory equivalent to our Home Office laboratories, in that the request and response would probably have to be channelled through Interpol and, therefore, initially through the national police.

Something needs to be done about this — and quickly. After all it is not a new problem recently discovered. I am told by the Home Office that they are looking for a solution. I do not see the difficulty. I do not see why a defence request to a Home Office laboratory arising out of a criminal case needs to be channelled through the police and why it cannot be sent to a different laboratory from that which has been used by the police investigating the particular case.

The advantages to the defence and to the administration of justice are obvious. What may not be so obvious are the advantages to the forensic scientists. It is very significant that we do not have the same problem with obtaining the services of pathologists and psychiatrists. They are retained for their expertise directly by the party seeking their opinion. They undoubtedly talk about their "discoveries" to the experts on the other side but the specific enquiries made of them and their reports are confidential to the party retaining them until the system requires (if it does) disclosure of their reports. My experience is that, as a consequence, there is a greater willingness and opportunity to use such experts, there is less partisanship in the evidence given by them and, perhaps more importantly, because they are retained by the competing parties, it is far more difficult for them to hide any partisanship under the appearance of disinterested professional independence. The quality of the evidence that is given by such witnesses, I believe as a result, tends to be much higher. As a side product — but a very important one — I believe that we may be sowing the seeds of revival in the general quality of forensic pathology in England and Wales arising from this greater use of forensic medical experts on both sides in criminal trials. I firmly believe that we would see the same all-round improvement if the defence had similar facilities available in the field of forensic science.

There is no doubting the importance of forensic science in the detection of crime and in the trial of alleged criminals. I believe that the public knows it as well. The experts themselves must realise that they have to work within the criminal justice system which is an adversarial system, that they have no special privilege to be believed or to be sheltered from cross-examination, that they are not judges and juries but witnesses, the testing of whose evidence is a fundamental element in our imperfect human attempt to find a method of trial which convicts the guilty and acquits the innocent but is prepared to accept the acquittal of the guilty as the price to be paid for protecting the innocent. If experts want their professionalism and opinions to be respected then they must accept the system for what it is and not try to pretend that, when they operate, it changes in some way. Experts can be wrong and the other party is entitled to demonstrate the error. Knowledge that the other party has commensurate resources available to it will make those experts who are prone to slipshod work or inclined to descend into partial investigations and partisan opinions less inclined to do so and more careful in what they do and say.

References

1. R. v Lattimore, Salih and Leighton; Central Criminal Court, November, 1972; Chapman, J. and jury: Court of Appeal (Criminal Division), 26th July, 1973: Court of Appeal (Criminal Division), 18th June, 1975.

2. The Report of the Enquiry into the death of Maxwell Confait and the fire at 27 Doggett Road, London, SE6; by Sir Henry A. P. Fisher; House of Commons Paper, 90, 77/78,

3. Report of the Royal Commission on Criminal Procedure, Chairman Sir Cyril Philips; January, 1981; Cmnd. 8092.

FORENSIC MEDICINE — AN INDEPENDENT SCIENCE?

Lord Morton, QC

Forensic Science is an expertise which assists a Court to come to a correct decision. If the Forensic Scientist as an expert witness is to be of any use to the Court he must be seen to be impartial, fair and objective and above all, accurate.

The standard expected of the expert scientific witness has been expressed in various ways: one was "There should be a rigorous obligation on all experts to give the Court, as clearly as they can, the limits of accuracy of this evidence, whether it is experimental or theoretical, and to disclose, if it be the fact, that other views exist in their profession. It should also be their duty to the Court to indicate what inferences cannot properly be drawn from their evidence" (1).

The Court in the case of Preece (2) expressed the same idea in a negative way when it said "No reasonable jury would have convicted once it became clear on a consideration of the serological chapter of his evidence that Dr Clift was discredited not only as a scientist but as a witness upon the accuracy, fairness and objectivity of where evidence reliance could be placed."

The unfortunate history of the cases in which Dr Clift was concerned has done damage to the standing of forensic scientists as witnesses and it is essential that they are restored to the position, which they deserve, of being witnesses on whose accuracy, fairness and objectivity reliance can be placed.

In Scotland compared with almost everywhere else the forensic scientist is the poor relation of his more fortunate colleagues elsewhere. In Scotland they are grossly overloaded, have inadequate space, without adequate modern equipment and without a proper career structure.

It is almost impossible for someone who is overworked to keep up with new ideas, with reports on research and so on. This makes it difficult to produce evidence of other views which may exist. If you haven't had time to read them how do you know they are there?

In Scotland the forensic scientists are, in the main, divided among Police laboratories of three of the Police forces. This is not the equivalent of the Home Office Laboratory.

My theme, therefore, is a plea that the forensic science facilities in Scotland should be removed from the Police laboratories and greatly expanded in a Central Laboratory — run, presumably, under the Home and Health Department.

It is not the purpose of this paper to deal with the facilities provided by the Departments of Forensic Medicine in the Universities. Nor is it intended to say anything much about the Forensic Science Department at Strathclyde University except to point out that it is the only available resource for the Defence in cases when advice is desired and it is abundantly clear that this Department is the appropriate place for research which is required and is absolutely necessary and that some arrangement somehow must be found to finance research.

The idea of a large Central Laboratory has been raised many times over the last thirty years. I am merely adding my voice to many much more well informed than I.

It is natural and inevitable that the main use of forensic science is by the police and on the prosecution side forensic science is used to determine if a crime has been committed and if so by whom. But, far more frequently it is used by the police *after* arrest of the accused, to add to the available evidence or to produce sufficient evidence to get conviction.

If the forensic scientist tells the jury that he is employed by Strathclyde Police and works at Police Headquarters, it is much more likely that a juror will say "well he's bound to be on the police side". If he says "I am employed at the Government Laboratory" he is one stage removed from the police and so more likely to be regarded as independent.

Arguments in favour of an expansion of forensic science in Scotland and the establishment of a Central Laboratory are to my mind overwhelming.

In one case in England 41 scientists were involved. That is more than the total employed in Police Laboratories in Scotland. If we had such a case, as we may have had, we could not provide the resources.

Some years ago police estimates were that if the facilities were available they would refer 30 per cent more cases to forensic scientists but could not do so at present because the scientists were so overworked.

It is quite clear that the actual physical space used for laboratories in Scotland is minute compared with England. One can't work properly if productions are propped up along corridors.

Scottish laboratories do not have all the more sophisticated equipment which can only be justified in a large laboratory. If they had this facility a lot of the work could be done more quickly.

Some years ago, it was recommended that to give a similar standard of provision as exists in England, it would be necessary to have about sixty forensic scientists in Scotland in such a Central Laboratory and that these figures now probably require upward revision.

It would be possible, if there was such a laboratory, for it to be used, on occasions and on payment, by the defence or in civil litigations in the same way as the pathologists of the Forensic Medicine Departments of the Universities are regularly used by the defence. This helps the public impression of impartial objectivity of the scientist if his expertise can be seen to be available to both sides.

All the arguments exist in favour of such a provision; the argument against it is lost.

I have never understood the way governments approach costs, with each area of expenditure left in its separate compartment and its financial year. It is frequently the case that because money has not been spent towards the end of March people rush around trying to spend it. On one occasion the Procurator Fiscal in Stornoway suddenly found himself allocated six copies of the standard text book on the Factories Act as if Stornoway was an industrial centre and March is certainly the time for sudden purity in the Courts. It is as absurd to consider forensic science by itself as it is to force all spending into twelve-month periods.

If expenditure on forensic science was considered as part of the whole crime and court expenditure it could well be that increases in expenditure on forensic science would in fact reduce the total court expenditure and produce a net saving.

It seems impossible to get a government to look at the whole picture. The Government, at this time, are putting through a Legal Aid Bill partly, at least, because of the increasing cost of Legal Aid Bill and partly, at least, because of the increasing cost of Legal Aid which in Scotland is running at around £35 million a year. No one seems to be prepared to consider whether alterations in procedure might save costs. For example, in the ordinary case in which forensic scientists examine articles, in addition to the two scientists who perform and report, the Crown has to cite the police officer who took possession of the articles, and the other officer who delivered them. All the defence gets is a list of names of witnesses. Each has to be seen and interviewed at a considerable cost to Legal Aid. If at an early stage the police statements and the scientist's report were served on the defence, it would be quite easy to alter the law so that the statements themselves would be admitted as evidence unless the defence intimated that they requested the witnesses to be present, in order that they could test the evidence by cross-examination.

This sort of procedure would save considerable legal aid costs, it would save time for the forensic scientist and the police because in 90 per cent of cases the scientist's evidence is unchallenged and the police carrier of production is rarely, if ever, challenged. But this sort of approach is *not* considered and I would urge that it should be. Both the police and the forensic scientist have regularly complained about time wasted attending courts. It is avoidable and should be avoided.

I have not much hope that it will because I made similar suggestions in the debate on the Legal Aid Bill and the Government seem determined that the Legal Aid authority should not look at ways of changing procedures to save money.

There are other ways in which use of scientific resources saves rather than costs money. If I am defending an accused and explain to him that the crucial evidence against him is his alleged spontaneous confession to a police officer who was asking him his name, age and occupation, I am likely to be told that the police officer had made it up and it's all lies. If I can tell him that the evidence against him is fibres or hairs left at the scene of the crime, or his fingerprints on the weapon, he is almost certain to accept advice.

Recently in Stirling two out of a group of boys who had escaped from an approved school were picked up by the police. The Police Officer said they confessed to breaking into a garage and stealing a van and a lot of welding equipment, including gas cylinders which they carried to an upstairs flat in a block of houses. The police went to the flat and the property was there. Predictably no examination of thc articles for fingerprints or anything else took place and the prosecution relied on the confession. Equally predictably, the boys denied stealing it and because neighbours had found the articles at about the same time as the police found the boys, there was a suspicion that the police might have made it up. After a long investigation and the eventual trial of the police the officers were acquitted. I am reasonably sure that boys of 15 on the run from an approved school must have left some fingerprints on the cylinder or got oil from the equipment on their clothes. A scientific examination would have decided that issue. Instead there was a two-day trial of the boys and a four-day trial of the police. The cost of that episode must have been well over £10,000.

I find the arguments that a proper Forensic Science facility under adequate staff cannot be provided because of cost totally unconvincing. It is also, apart from the cost, quite unjustifiable that one part of the U.K. should be required to exist on a provision that is so wildly out of step with the rest of Britain, especially on an issue as serious as Law and Order.

It is essential that in Scotland, which has a considerable crime rate, there should be an adequate forensic science service. If it is to be adequate there must be a proper career structure and a possibility of promotion for those who wish to seek it. If the position remains as it is, anyone who wishes to advance his career, or to do research, or just not to be grossly overworked, has to go elsewhere.

Research is vital to the health of any scientific institution. Without some research it tends to stultify. In my view the obvious place for research is the Department at Strathclyde University. It is difficult to see under present arrangements how this could be funded. Legal Aid is arranged on a case by case basis and so does not have the provision to make a grant for general research. The Law Society representing solicitors and the Faculty of Advocates representing the Bar seem most unlikely sources of funding of research, though it would be logical as the legal profession would be one of the ultimate beneficiaries. In the end, I can only see the Government, in one form or another, as the source of funds. I hope they will be made available because it would be tragic if the Department could not continue.

References

1. Ormrod, J. Scientific Evidence in Court. *Criminal Law Review*, 1968; 240.

2. Preece *v.* H.M.A. *Criminal Law Review*, 1981; 783.

PROOF OF FACT IN CRIMINAL TRIALS

M. Stone

Introduction

The Forensic Sciences contribute to criminal justice by their probative effect, not their technical virtuosity. The term "forensic" rather than the term "science" needs emphasis. Forensic scientists testify in a crossfire of lay evidence about contested facts, which are decided by non-scientific criteria. This paper, based on my book of the same title (1), outlines the overall fact-finding process, as background for Forensic Scientists. By its very nature this paper has to be selective.

Fact-finding is the essential task in criminal trials. The real issue is nearly always one of fact. Few verdicts turn on disputed points of law. Facts are not decided by even the most relevant rules of law. Legal thinkers have ignored fact-finding. Legal texts expound the law on the basis of neat and tidy statements of facts, disregarding how they were proved.

For conviction, the Crown must prove firstly that the crime was committed, and secondly that the accused was the offender. But almost every factual defence will contest only one of these assertions, so that the other will be proved formally. Experts may testify about disputed or undisputed issues.

Witnesses are the eyes and ears of the court. They were there; the court was not. Facts are decided by assessing the reliability and credibility of what they say. Reliability refers to absence of error, and credibility to truthfulness. Accepted evidence must be both reliable and credible.

Reliability of Evidence

Observation and memory are fallible. No one can compete with a video camera. But Courts could not exist without a basic view that, generally, honest and positive evidence is likely to be accurate enough for a proper verdict, although details may be mistaken. Common sense would support this. But some psychologists attack the general validity of testimony. For example, "... the testimony of legal witnesses is shown to be deplorably unreliable. Courts should not rely on such testimony except when it is absolutely necessary, which it usually is ..." (2). Such unreasonable contentions are based on 100 years of experimental research on artificial tasks in laboratories, remote from the realities of the courtroom. It has made no significant discoveries about perception and memory. Many psychologists do accept the general reliability of testimony.

Errors of Observation

Features in the event may cause error, e.g. brevity, number of persons, movement, violence, ambiguity, obscurity, facts commanding attention, subjectivity of perception of abstract qualities such as time, sequence, distance, place, layout, sounds, touch, taste, and smell. The conditions of observation may reduce accuracy, e.g. distance from the incident, lighting, weather, obstructions.

Apart from permanent traits, temporary physical or mental states may impair observation, e.g. drink, injury or illness. A witness's perceptual activities, i.e. thoughts, feelings and actions, may reduce the degree of attention given to various facts, or expectations may colour what he perceives, especially in ambiguous or obscure situations.

This is a one-sided picture of observation, like a text on pathology which ignores health. Favourable factors also exist. Unless there is objective evidence of some real obstacle to good observation, a positive report may be acceptable. The basis for believing evidence is often the court's trust in the self-assessment of an honest and confident witness, rather than incidental facts. Would you accept the report of someone you trust?

Errors of Memory

Memory is the basis of all honest oral evidence. Although the event was seen clearly, forgetting or suggestion may make evidence incomplete, unsure or mistaken.

Forgetting: The delay between crime and trial, needed for investigation, tracing and apprehending the accused, and preparation of the case, may cause some fading of memory, loss of detail, unsureness or inaccuracy. But statements taken soon after the event which prompt recall, may offset this.

Suggestion: A faded memory is vulnerable to new information which, by suggestion, can increase or reduce doubts, exclude facts or insinuate imagined elements. One compromise memory is formed which the witness takes for genuine. Discussion of evidence, the main problem, is inevitable and is not unlawful unless it is done in order to falsify evidence. Memory may also be changed by auto-suggestion arising from the witness's thoughts, feelings and wishes, guessing to fill gaps, working things out, or rehearsing the evidence to make it more coherent, consistent and complete.

Assessment of Memory: Again, the self-assessment of an honest witness is the usual basis for accepting that his memory is accurate. Common sense and psychology would agree that we are less likely to forget, or to be misled by suggestion about, the essential facts and meaning of an event than about secondary details. Memory for a complex event takes the form of reconstruction of its general sense, as the witness responded to it. So whatever defence counsel may suggest, a lady's memory of rape will not mellow in the fullness of time into last summer's romance, nor a burglary into a charitable donation.

There can be no rules about what will be remembered or forgotten in any given period. Most psychologists agree that forgetting is rapid at first and slower thereafter, but some doubt if this applies to memory for faces.

Subtle suggestive influences are hard to detect or assess in Court. It is usually impossible to know the extent and effect of discussion of evidence. Even otherwise honest witnesses seem reluctant to admit discussion or that it may have swayed them.

Identification Evidence

In trials, identification of the offender is the most common question of fact. Evidence of visual recognition needs special care. As visual patterns, many faces are similar. Undetected misidentification can lead to wrongful conviction or acquittal. Courts know the risks of even sincere and positive evidence of recognition of a stranger from a fleeting glimpse, or under poor conditions, or after a long delay, or where any form of suggestion, such as discussion, may have played a part. But many reassuring facts indicate that verdicts based on misidentification are exceptional.

Presumably, identification is correct if the accused pleads guilty, as occurs in about 90 per cent of cases. Frequently the crime, not identity, is the issue. Often witnesses know the accused personally. In many trials, the accused cannot deny that he was at the locus, e.g. if he was arrested there. If he still denies any part in the crime, observation of his actions, not recognition, is the question. Visual identification of the accused may be supported or replaced by circumstantial evidence from which his implication can be inferred. Forensic science may show physical traces of the accused at the locus or on the victim, or physical traces of the crime on the accused. Many accused admit guilt to the police. To deny this in Court involves credibility, not identity. Awareness of the risks of identification evidence is reflected in vigorous advocacy, warnings to juries, the need for corroboration, and the onus of proving guilt beyond reasonable doubt.

Credibility of Evidence

In trials, there are far more lies about crucial facts than errors. Psychology offers no insight into lying or techniques for exposing it. It has ignored the subject, e.g. Scheibe: "... because the artificial limitations of laboratory research make it extremely difficult to replicate the conditions of actual lie detection. ... This work seemed to fall outside the territory of traditional psychological theory" (3). Behaviourist-type research into lying is futile. Psychiatry and depth psychology deal with motivation only in clinical settings. Their conflicting theories and techniques offer no help in judging testimony. Their concepts would only confuse clear-cut issues of credibility with irrelevant complexities.

Court's Approach to Credibility: To expose lying effectively requires the holistic approach of a criminal court. To judge one person without supporting facts is unsafe. Psychology's neglect of lying supports this view. Experience is private. If not communicated openly, it can only be inferred. There is no magic key, no sure way of knowing intuitively if someone is lying, or what is hidden. In private interview, a plausible, planned, uncontradicted but false story, may be impenetrable. Study of what a speaker says, as well as his manner, is essential. The test then is not his private inner world, but the world of fact, the common reality shared with others. Here, the court scores. Statements about the same points, from various angles, by many witnesses, liable to penalties for perjury, are tested for consistency, contradiction, possibility and probability while the witnesses' character, motives and demeanour, are also studied. This total and comprehensive approach, interlinking everything, is the unique form of enquiry into credibility undertaken by a criminal court.

Content of Evidence

The credibility of evidence depends greatly on its consistency, probability, and realistic qualities.

Consistency and Inconsistency: Consistent evidence from unconnected witnesses, which fits together to the same effect, may be persuasive. But absence of normal discrepancies between several associated witnesses may suggest lying.

Verbal inconsistency means that, regardless of the facts, two statements cannot both be true, e.g. that a car is black and white. Either statement, or both, could be wrong.

Factual inconsistency occurs when the connections between facts show that two statements cannot both be true, e.g. that a car had not been driven, and that the engine was warm. Factual inconsistency, ranging from total conflict to improbability, may depend on a chain of related facts.

Inconsistency about major facts may affect the verdict directly. Under cross-examination, minor discrepancies may be exploited so as to discredit the evidence more widely. Self-contradiction, even if corrected, may be fatal. If a witness changes his evidence when confronted with his associates' different evidence, he may contradict himself. Inconsistency of witnesses on one side, especially about essential facts, may damage their credibility. If found in Crown evidence, because of the onus of proof, acquittal may be inevitable. The essential conflict between Crown and defence evidence is a ground for decision. An uncontradicted witness may lie plausibly and resist cross-examination. But although nothing appears to be wrong with a witness or his evidence, falsity is often exposed by contrary evidence.

Possibility and Probability: Courts may find evidence impossible or improbable, in the light of their practical experience of life and knowledge of facts requiring no proof, including human nature and affairs. Usually, impossibility is shown by other evidence, e.g. that a wall prevented observation. More often, probability is a test of credibility. Improbability may be found in single statements, combinations of facts, or the whole story. Mathematical probability has little application, but qualitative probability — mainly how people normally behave — is often crucial, e.g. was a youth on a roof for the view?

As part of a court's total approach, probability is only one test of credibility, albeit an important one. But one must maintain on open mind. Courts hear many strange, but true, tales. Emphatically, probability is not the test for conviction. For proof of guilt, everything must converge to reach the standard of proof beyond reasonable doubt.

Unrealistic Qualities in Lying Evidence: False stories are often unrealistic in form and lack the ring of truth. Typically, they may be brief, bare, one-sided, anxious versions of the main points, lacking detail and the richness and colouring of real life. True stories often mention, spontaneously, facts which precede, accompany and follow the main event, making the report more vivid. Truthful witnesses often fail to separate their observations from their feelings and thoughts, and they mention their personal involvement in or reactions to, the event, unlike lying witnesses. Even a single genuine remark may be illuminating and convincing. Of course some evidence must be matter-of-fact.

Stories may cover essentials by one-way evidence pointing wholly to one version of disputed facts. The situation shows whether such positive evidence is likely to be truthful or not. True stories often state that something happened, simply because it did, and not because it tends to prove anything. They may include unnecessary complications, irrelevant, unexpected, obscure, inexplicable facts, items which deviate from the main theme, or suggest opposing conclusions. An honest witness may omit or decline to state facts supporting the general tendency of his testimony, or he may admit to uncertainties or doubts. It would be surprising to find such elements in a false story.

In judging credibility, a court studies what is said while it also forms a view of the witness. This integrated process is separable, only for the purpose of analysis.

Assessing the Witness

Judging credibility from an impression of the witness, apart from his words, is mainly intuitive. We can all respond to others in this way, but with variations in insight.

Character: Usually, only a surface view of a witness's moral character is possible. Alone, this is a limited guide to credibility. It is safer to assume that witnesses have no fixed quantum of veracity, which decides if they will be truthful, regardless of their situation. Many persons, of impeccable repute, have denied, and been convicted of, embezzlement, sexual crimes, shoplifting, road traffic or other offences, or have lied to save friends or relatives from conviction.

Motives: Witnesses with no motive for lying, are often trusted. Fear of penalties for perjury motivates all witnesses, but this has little value in assessing credibility. Perjury is rife, but is rarely prosecuted. Some forms of false evidence would not be perjury. It is realistic to treat the oath as a neutral formality and to decide credibility on other grounds.

A witness's motives in connection with his situation are usually obvious and specific. Veracity may be related to, but does not depend wholly on such motives.

Official police motivation to enforce the law forbids lying and is, therefore, no guide to police credibility in a given trial. Only some unlawful motive, or mistaken conception of duty, would lead to perjury by police witnesses.

Motivation for acquittal cannot, alone, settle the truth of defence evidence. Either innocence or guilt could explain it. The same tests of credibility apply to all evidence. Defence evidence must be assessed on its merits with an open mind, fairly, though motivation not reality may dictate it.

Sometimes a witness, unconcerned with the verdict, may lie for a personal reason, e.g. fear of publicity, embarrassment or vanity. Lies due to such motives are unlikely to distort essential facts seriously. The intimidated witness, who could be harmful, is usually obvious and is discredited.

Demeanour: Many people believe that a witness's demeanour shows if he is telling the truth or not. I wish to stress the limitations of this approach. Demeanour includes everything perceived in a witness, except the meaning of his words.

Unless one is swayed by stereotypes, fixed traits like sex, age, build, or hair say nothing about credibility. Visible signs during the evidence may be changes in facial expression, gaze or posture; gestures, tremors, movements or perspiration. Audible qualities or changes in speech may include volume, articulation, tone, pitch, rate, hesitation, or emphasis. Complex behaviour patterns may occur like anger, tears, distress, illness, hysteria, fainting, needing to go to the toilet, or having to drink water. This list is not exhaustive. Are such signs a good guide to credibility? Psychology, court experience, and common sense answer this question.

Psychological research into non-verbal communication reveals no typical signs of veracity. Lying is a cognitive process not necessarily associated with any specific emotional state or distinctive form of physical expression. Fixed signs of veracity are precluded by the complexity, flexibility, and individual variation of our responses.

Each Court decides what weight, if any, demeanour merits. The author's judicial experience accords with the caution of Lord Devlin, who relied on it as little as he could. "The great virtue of the English trial is usually said to be the opportunity it gives to the judge to tell from the demeanour of the witness whether or not he is telling the truth. I think that this is overrated ..." (4). Common sense supports this caution. Certainly, speech means more than words. A witness's manner may seem to confirm or contradict what he says. He may show feelings by involuntary signs. But some expressions of feelings may be deliberately controlled, suppressed or simulated. Everyone can act to some extent, and what is expressed may be uncertain. Also, although intuitive insight into others is a universal ability, it varies in individuals and is usually limited. In view of the uncertainty both about what demeanour may actually express, and about the capacity to decipher it, the risk of deciding credibility by this alone becomes clear.

Anxiety may be related to lying. But in my court I have seen countless lying witnesses who seemed quite relaxed, and truthful ones who appeared anxious. A witness may simply be an anxious kind of person. One cannot compare his everyday demeanour. As is common, he may be anxious about giving evidence, or about the outcome of the trial. One cannot assume that an anxious witness must be lying. Anxiety can mean many things depending on circumstances. By itself, then, the demeanour of witnesses, and especially of a single witness, is not a safe guide to credibility.

Conclusion

It has been stressed that, by itself, each way of assessing evidence has limited value. This was not done to cast doubt on the accuracy of decisions, but rather to emphasise that the heart of the matter is the holistic judgment which integrates the multiple approaches. Essentially, this is how Courts decide facts.

For Forensic Scientists, an apt analogy is that the constituent elements of a human body are only a few unimpressive chemicals. But when they are all properly assembled, the marvel of the organism emerges. Holistic judgment in court, or in daily life, is similar. It transcends reductive analysis, but we all have experience of it.

References

1. Stone, M. *Proof of Fact in Criminal Trials.* Edinburgh: W. Green & Son (1984).

2. Neissen, U. *Memory Observed — Remembering in Natural Contexts.* San Francisco: W. H. Freeman (1982), p. 93.

3. Scheibe, K. *Mirrors, Masks, Lies and Secrets — The Limits of Human Predictability* (1979), p. 87.

4. The Rt. Hon. Lord Patrick Devlin. *The Judge*, p. 63.

FORENSIC MEDICINE

POST-MORTEM INTERVAL BY MICROWAVE THERMOGRAPHY

L. M. Al-Alousi and R. A. Anderson

Introduction

The estimation of the time of death is one of the most important and fundamental problems which are regularly encountered by forensic pathologists, especially in cases of suspicious death (1–4). The answer to this problem frequently becomes of decisive value in the outcome of the case (5). Accordingly, the subject has been repeatedly and often extensively studied. However, an accurate, reliable and easily applicable method of estimating the time since death has not yet been found (5–7) and therefore it is usually accepted amongst forensic pathologists that estimations of the post-mortem interval have an investigational rather than evidential value (9).

There is therefore a continuing need for more accurate and reliable (albeit more complicated) methods for the estimation of the post-mortem interval or, at least, to achieve a better understanding of the problems. This goal has become more possible and practicable in recent years by the application to forensic medicine of sophisticated modern equipment and techniques for the analysis of biological materials and the acquisition and processing of data. Of particular value are recent advances in computing science.

Apart from entomological estimation of the post-mortem interval, all methods depend on the chemical, biochemical and physical changes that occur in the body after death. Several reviews of existing methods have been published (1, 4, 7, 10, 11). Considerable effort has been directed towards the analysis of body tissues and fluids such as blood, urine, cerebrospinal fluid, intraocular fluid and pericardial fluid to find regularly and constantly occurring post-mortem changes to be used as a "post-mortem clock" (3, 12–15). These methods, in general, have been found both cumbersome and inaccurate (1, 3). Methods which depend on general physical post-mortem changes such as *rigor mortis, livor mortis* and others lack objectivity and are, moreover, not suitable for quantitative calculations (1, 16).

The Post-Mortem Rate of Cooling

Methods of estimation of the time of death based on post-mortem cooling are regarded as the most reliable in practice, the easiest to implement and the most likely to be of value, especially during the first 18–24 hours post mortem (1, 4–7, 17, 18). Reviews have been written by many authors (1, 7, 19, 21). Published methods may be classified according to the mathematical expression used to describe the post-mortem cooling curve:

1. *Studies using a single exponential model (Newtonian Model)*
   Newton's Law states that "the rate of loss of heat from the surface of a solid body to the surrounding fluid is directly proportional to the difference in temperature between the surface and the fluid". It is worth noting that this law was originally applied to homogeneous and

thermally-thin bodies. Studies using this model include all the early work in the nineteenth and first half of the twentieth centuries (20, 22, 23). Molnar and Brown and Marshall have given excellent discussions on the application of Newton's Law to the human body (20, 22, 24, 25).

2. *Studies using a linear cooling model*
The linear cooling model is the traditional "rule of thumb" procedure used in the field. This model and the single exponential model are mathematically different; it is correctly stated by Green & Wright (26) that "the 'rule of thumb' method implies a linear drop in temperature, though it was generally assumed that it obeyed Newton's Law of Cooling which is exponential".

3. *Extended exponential and linear models*
Although these still follow the principle of linear or exponential models, many modifications have been introduced to compensate for factors such as body size, clothes and environmental conditions and some extended "rules of thumb", reference charts and formulae have been proposed (8, 19, 27, 28). Most workers in this area are aware of the initial temperature lag or plateau which has been observed for some time (20, 22) but only seriously considered in the last 30 years (29, 30).

4. *Studies that follow the "Heat Transmission Theory"*
According to the heat transmission theory, the cooling curve of any body of non-uniform temperature distribution (i.e. not thermally-thin) varies with its shape. In practice this theory has been applied to the human body either directly as the "Infinite Cylinder Model", which derived from work by Carslaw and Jager (31), or in a slightly modified form as an infinite sum of exponential terms (32). Williamson & Adams have also used the cooling curves and formulae for a solid sphere according to the "Infinite Sphere Model" (33). The Infinite Cylinder means that all or most of the heat of the cylinder flows radially and not axially. The cylinder and sphere models and their formulae simply mean that the temperature gradient along a radius from the centre to the surface at any moment of cooling can be described by the sum of an infinite number of exponential terms. The validity of this formula for the human body has been shown by many authors (16, 20, 24, 31, 34, 35). Also, although Marshall in 1969 stated that "the more exponential terms in the series the more accurate is the formula" (9) a more recent conclusion was that only the first few terms of the formula were important for the cooling of the human body (20).

A prominent and well known formula is the double exponential formula of Marshall & Hoare (23). This equation and its revision by Brown & Marshall (20) are actually modified forms of the Infinite Cylinder Model applied to the post-mortem rectal cooling curve. While the double exponential formula is widely accepted, it has the disadvantage that the body has to be monitored until twelve hours after death before its parameters can be determined. This presupposes a knowledge of the approximate time of death, which is obviously unknown in practice (16). Also, the formula requires information on the height, weight and situation of the body at the locus.

To overcome the latter problem, several modifications to this formula have been devised to obtain "non-dimensional" or average equations (3, 26, 36). The formula has also been converted to a computer-applicable form (37). Although these formulae are more accurate than earlier methods in describing the actual rectal cooling curve, recent studies have shown that significant time errors may still occur when these formulae are applied (3, 26).

There is wide agreement that the body core is the most useful site for temperature measurements. Although this may be best represented by the temperatures of the deep organs such as the liver and the brain, these are seldom employed in practice and the rectal temperature is more widely used. This is mainly because these organs are not easily accessed unless an invasive method is adopted, which is ethically less acceptable.

In the present study, the ethical problem has been avoided by using a new technique, microwave thermography, which enables temperature measurements of the deep organs or tissues to be made by a non-invasive method.

Experimental

Cases

The work described in this article was carried out in the Glasgow City Mortuary. Cases were selected according to the following criteria:

1. The exact time of death should be known.
2. The elapsed time between death and the arrival of the body in the mortuary should be as short as possible, preferably less than 1 hour, so that the body should feel quite warm to touch.
3. The circumstances of the death should allow the body to be kept at the mortuary for a period of at least 20–36 hours, preferably up to 60 hours or more, to allow many hours of monitoring. In practice this criterion meant that cases were restricted to those for which the cause of death was either natural or non-suspicious.

On the arrival of a case satisfying the criteria above, the body was accurately weighed using a weighing trolley, its height was measured with an autopsy ruler and the circumference of the head and the width of the hip were then obtained with a tape measure. The body was then laid in a supine position, either naked or covered with two cotton blankets and monitoring was started as described below. Information concerning the name, age, sex, body measurements and the exact times of the beginning and end of monitoring were recorded.

Temperature Measurements

The device used for temperature measurements was the Microwave Thermography System, constructed in the Department of Natural Philosophy, Glasgow University. This consisted of a microwave radio receiver unit fitted with two microwave radio aerials (microwave probes) and two digital pyrometers fitted with thermocouples.

Each microwave probe was cylindrical in shape, 2·8 cm in diameter and 6·5 cm in length, and connected to the receiver unit through a 1·5 m flexible microwave cable assembly. The temperature resolution of the system was 0·1°C and the response time was 2 seconds. The absolute accuracy of temperature measurements by the microwave probe was in the range of + (0·5–1·0)°C. The system was calibrated with solutions of glycerol in water (1:3 v/v) at different temperatures using a mercury thermometer as a control. During monitoring, the microwave probes were placed in contact with the skin of one of the temporal regions and of the right hypochondrium to monitor the temperature of the brain and liver respectively.

The thermocouples were used to monitor the rectum and also the environment as the temperature of the room in which the experiments were carried out was not regulated. The rectal thermocouple was specially made, having a length of 30 cm and a diameter of 0·5 cm, to allow it to be inserted as far as possible into the rectum. The environmental thermocouple was wall-mounted adjacent to the body at a height of 2 m. The accuracy of temperatures measured by the thermocouples was ± 0·1°C.

Temperature measurements were taken sequentially from the probes and thermocouples with a cycle time of 5 minutes.

Data Acquisition and Processing

Analogue to digital conversion of the signals from the microwave receiver and pyrometers was carried out using a BBC Model B microcomputer and the data were recorded on a cassette tape. The computer also provided a logical timing scale which was also recorded on the tape.

Tapes were taken in batches to the Department and the data were transferred to disk. Initial data processing to calculate temperature differences between each body site and the environment, temperature ratios between sites and temperature difference ratios was carried out using a second BBC Model B computer. Temperature difference ratios, calculated according to equation (1) below, were transferred to a mainframe computer (ICL 2988) for regression analysis and statistics.

$$\text{Temperature difference ratio} = \frac{(T_b - T_e)\,t}{(T_{bo} - T_{et})} \qquad \text{Equation (1)}$$

where T_b = Temperature at any body site
T_e = Temperature of the environment

at a time denoted by o (zero time) or t (any subsequent time).

Curve fitting was carried out using programme P_3R of the Biomedical Programme (BMDP) package, a collection of statistical software routines (38). Averaging of curves for each body site in groups of related cases was carried out by curve fitting to average temperature difference ratios calculated from the equation of each curve.

Results

The total number of cases studied was 117, including 74 cases (63%) monitored as naked bodies and 43 cases (37%) monitored as covered bodies.

The age distribution of the cases ranged from 30 to 90 years: most of the cases were between 60–85 years (66%) while a further 30% were in the range 35–55 years. The male to female ratio was 3:1. Body weights ranged from 40–120 kg and heights were between 1·52–2·00 m. Two-thirds of the bodies monitored weighed 60–90 kg, and of these most were between 60–70 kg (28% of all cases). Three-quarters of the cases had heights between 1·65–1·88 m and 27% were in the range 1·70–1·75 m.

The causes of death in all cases studied were natural. In 17 cases (15%) the death certificate was issued without an autopsy. Most of the deaths were due to heart diseases (86 cases, 74%). Few of them were due to respiratory diseases (11 cases, 9·4%) and only three were alcohol-related, due to alcohol intoxication or inhalation of gastric contents. It is also to be noted that there were only eight deaths (6·8%) due to infection; these were either chronic bronchitis (with or without emphysaema) or bronchopneumonia. The last group, in which elevation of body temperature might be expected, consisted of only two cases.

The monitoring periods ranged from 6–60 hours with most cases (56%) being monitored for 20–36 hours. There was only one case in which the body was monitored for less than 10 hours. Also, no bodies were received within 15 minutes after death and only 2 cases were received after a lapse of more than 2 hours. Most of the bodies were received within 15–45 minutes after death (74 cases, 63%).

The microwave thermography system operated reliably during the study and was found to be easy to use. For each case the temperatures of the brain, liver, rectum and environment were monitored: measurements were taken every 5 minutes during the monitoring period and recorded on magnetic tape prior to processing. Initial data reduction was satisfactorily carried out using a microcomputer to produce, for example, plots of temperature versus time, temperature difference (body site minus environment) versus time, temperature ratio (ratio of temperatures at two body sites) versus time and temperature difference ratio (Equation 1) versus time. An important step in the calculation of difference ratios was to establish the body temperature at the time of death (T_{bo}). This was obtained for each body site by curve fitting of a single exponential equation to the data for the first three hours and then extrapolating backwards over the post-mortem interval prior to the start of monitoring, as discussed below. The average temperatures at the moment of death for brain, liver and rectum are given in Table 1.

TABLE 1

Average values for body site temperatures at time of death

Body site	*Average temperature* (°C)	*Standard Deviation*
Brain (naked)	26·5	3·1
Brain (covered)	27·7	3·7
Liver (naked)	27·5	3·1
Liver (covered)	32·7	2·9
Rectum (naked)	36·6	2·0
Rectum (covered)	32·2	4·8

Following initial treatment, the data were analysed on a mainframe computer using a non-linear regression analysis programme for curve-fitting. The programme used (BMDP) was unsuitable for the microcomputer owing to the large number of data points collected for each case. To obtain the optimum fit for each curve, equations involving one, two, three or four exponential functions were compared. The best fit was considered to be the one having the least residual mean square deviation between the actual data and those calculated by the function. Single exponential fits were evaluated for thirty curves, double and triple fits for approximately 200 curves and four exponential fits for fifteen curves. The best fit was found to be given by a triple exponential function of the form given in equation 2 and this was used for all subsequent curve fitting.

$$R = P_1 e^{P_2 t} + P_3 e^{P_4 t} + P_5 e^{P_6 t} \qquad \text{Equation (2)}$$

where R = Temperature difference ratio (equation 1)
P_1–P_6 are parameters
and t is the time after death in hours.

For each curve, therefore, six parameters were obtained which described the curve accurately throughout the whole time course of the monitoring period. Average parameters were calculated for brain, liver and rectum in the naked and covered groups as described earlier (Table 2). The effects of other

TABLE 2

Parameters for average equations

	*Parameters**					
Body site	P_1	P_2	P_3	P_4	P_5	P_6
Brain (naked)	−5·94	−0·198	4·51	−0·210	2·43	−0·162
Brain (covered)	−5·90	−0·102	4·50	−0·120	2·40	−0·084
Liver (naked)	−6·00	−0·102	5·10	−0·090	1·90	−0·132
Liver (covered)	−5·86	−0·144	5·10	−0·150	1·76	−0·054
Rectum (naked)	−6·01	−0·186	5·10	−0·144	1·91	−0·228
Rectum (covered)	−5·99	−0·192	5·10	−0·204	1·89	−0·084

* parameters are those defined in equation 2.

body variables such as size, weight, surface and hip diameter on the rate of cooling were also evaluated but no significant correlations were found. However, significant differences were observed in many cases between rectal cooling curves for fat and thin naked bodies. Average curves for these groups are shown in Figures 1–3.

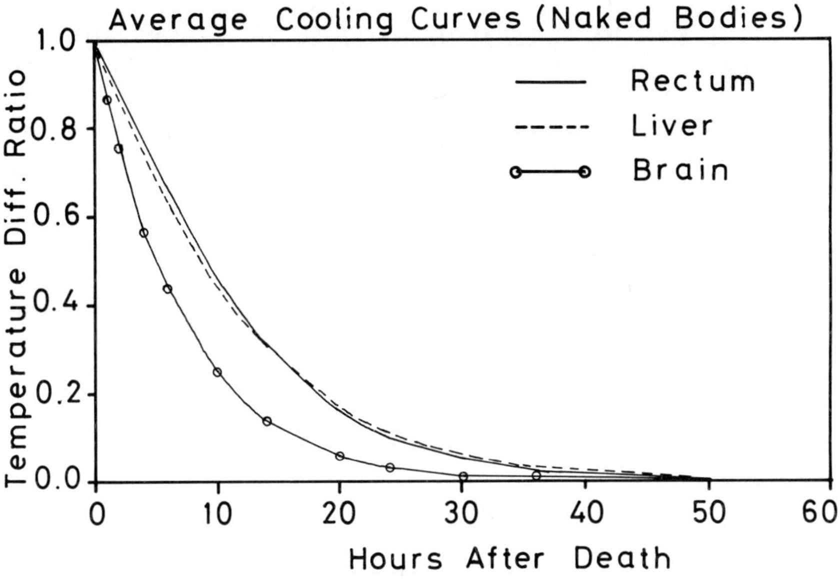

Figure 1. Average cooling curves for naked bodies.

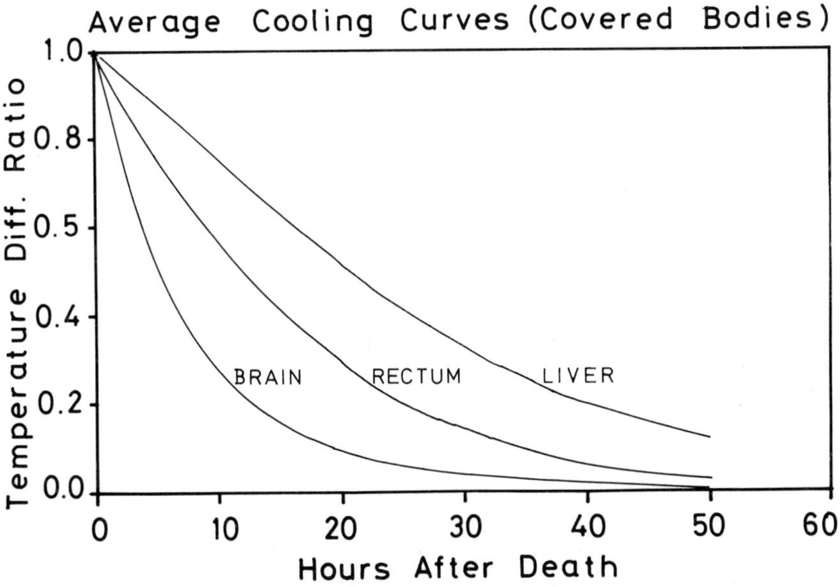

Figure 2. Average cooling curves for covered bodies.

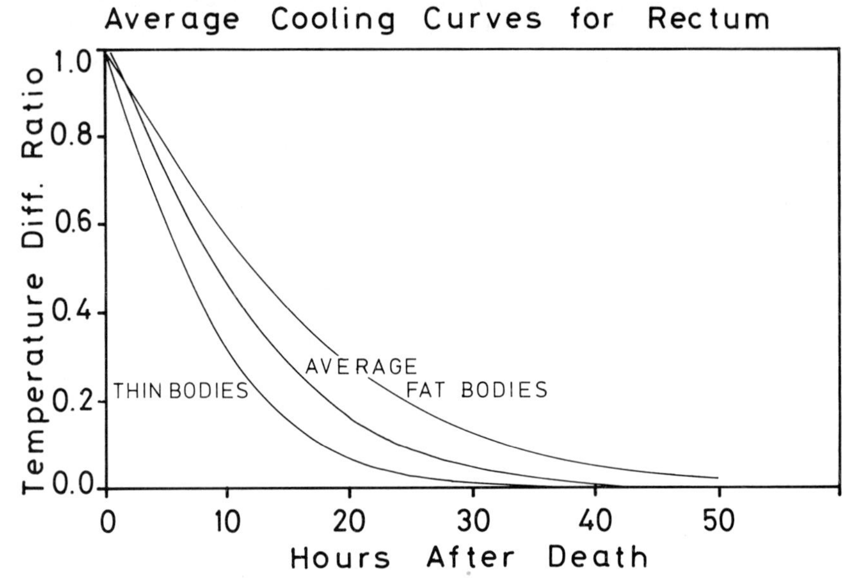

Figure 3. Average Rectal cooling curves for fat and thin bodies.

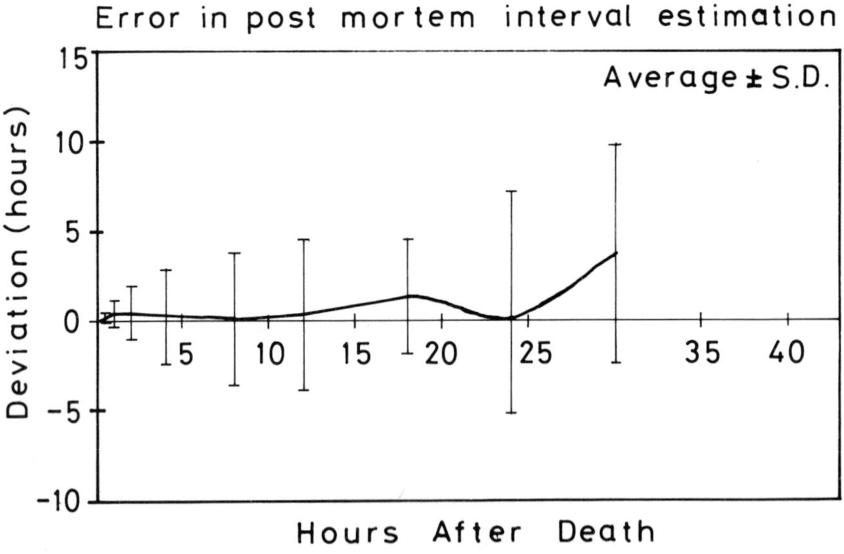

Figure 4. Error in Post-Mortem Interval Estimation versus Time. (Rectal temperature measurements in covered bodies.)

The final step was to return to the raw data and to refit them using, this time, the average formulae. Thus the deviation of the estimated time from the actual time could be assessed throughout the monitoring period for each body site in each case. This was in effect a measure of the accuracy of the average formulae in estimating the post-mortem interval. As an example, the expected errors in estimates of the post-mortem interval versus time after death for rectal temperature measurements in covered bodies are given in Figure 4. This is likely to be the most commonly encountered situation.

Discussion

It is now well accepted and documented that the cooling rate offers, so far, one of the most reliable and easiest methods of estimating the post-mortem interval during the first 24 hours after death (1, 4, 6, 7, 17, 18). Other methods for time of death estimation have, so far, failed to find empirically useful parameters; in other words, they are unable to provide better estimates of the time of death than those given by the temperature method. Nevertheless, this does not mean that the rate of cooling is absolutely reliable and accurate as it has been shown that even the best of the cooling models may give significant errors in the estimation of the time since death (3, 26).

As mentioned earlier, the time of death is often of vital importance in a medico-legal investigation (7). In the literature, many factors affecting the post-mortem drop in body temperature are discussed: as will now be apparent, the overall picture is rather complicated. Accordingly, simple models are intrinsically insufficient and the mathematical complexity of more sophisticated models or formulae should not be a restriction on their use in practice, whenever such a model or formula can offer even a slight improvement. This is particularly true today when almost every discipline has been partially or even totally affected by the computer. Using the computer it is now easy, in practice, to use even the most complicated formulae.

The present study represents a novel approach to the use of cooling models in that it used microwave thermography to measure temperatures of body organs by non-invasive techniques and also extensively used computer-based methods for data acquisition and processing. A useful practical version of the triple exponential formula was developed and evaluated for the first time.

The microwave device used was recently developed in the Department of Natural Philosophy at Glasgow University. Apart from its application to forensic medicine in this research, it has also been used for the diagnosis of disease in rheumatology, clinical oncology and gastro-enterology (39, 40). Its mode of operation depends on the fact that body tissues are relatively transparent to electro-magnetic radiation in the microwave region (39). Thus this technique is able to detect and measure the microwave emission of internal organs using detectors placed on the skin and thereby we can obtain the temperature of tissues several centimetres below the body surface (41).

Few studies have been carried out on the post-mortem temperature drop of the brain and liver, mainly because there is no easy way to access these organs. A thermometer or electrical thermocouple has to be introduced through a puncture wound in the abdomen (6) or one of the eyes (5). This may not only be ethically unacceptable but also may affect the actual cooling process. Using the microwave thermography technique it is now possible to take the temperature of these and other organs by a non-invasive and ethically acceptable method.

Several authors have anticipated that measurement of the brain temperature would yield valuable information. Thus Simonson *et al.* wrote (5) "The philosophy underlying the investigation of the temperature of the brain has yet been that the head and hence the brain are approximately globe-shaped, that its size from individual to individual does not vary very much, that the clothing of the body — apart from head-covering, if any, plays no role and that the amount of hair, of course varies, but seldom very much. The centre of the brain is rather uniformly insulated by brain tissue and CSF."

Lyle and Cleveland found that the temperature fall in the brain showed the least individual variation (2) and Naeve and Apel concluded that the measurement of the brain temperature was the most useful of all temperature measurement (42).

There has been controversy in the literature concerning the conditions under which studies of this type should be conducted. Some authors have suggested that controlled conditions are not relevant to the actual situation in the field. However, our view is that if the problem is to be approached systematically, the post-mortem drop in body temperature should only be studied under controlled conditions. It is impossible to interpret results from studies of randomly selected cases, whereas it is more practicable to study the problem under different sets of controlled conditions which are likely to be met in practice.

The cases used in the present study were chosen to satisfy the criteria given earlier. Firstly, the death should be due to natural causes: this had the twin advantages that the body was not urgently needed for autopsy nor was it involved in medico-legal investigations normally required in suspicious deaths. Most of the cases used died as a result of heart diseases, reflecting their high incidence in the Glasgow area. Also, apart from two cases of broncho-pneumonia, deaths involving hypo- or hyperthermia were excluded to avoid wide variation of the body temperature at the moment of death. There were no children amongst our cases but the age groups studied covered those most likely to be involved in practice. Also, as the effects of age on cooling are primarily related to those of body size, this shortcoming could be overcome by taking into account the effects of size in the analysis of our data.

Monitoring was started as soon after death as possible and was continued for as long as possible, so that both early and late cooling periods were studied. In each case, additional body measurements were collected such as the head circumference and the width of the hip. This was to establish which factors have significant effects on the cooling rate, particularly because some models, for example, the Infinite Cylinder Model, assume a knowledge of the cylinder radius. Where possible, monitoring was continued for at least 30 hours, at which point the temperature difference between the body and the environment was less than a few degrees and a practical limit was imposed by the precision of the device used ($\pm$ 0·1°C). The accuracy of the microwave probes and thermocouples was checked using thermostated media containing glycerol in water to simulate the microwave refraction of body tissues. Apparent temperatures given by the microwave probes were lower than actual as a result of attenuation of the signal by interposed tissues (39).

Body Temperature at the Moment of Death

The need to know the body temperature at the moment of death is a prominent drawback in all methods that depend on the rate of cooling for estimating the post-mortem interval. In life there are both individual and diurnal variations in the body temperature and, moreover, the temperature also varies from one organ or body site to another (6, 7, 43). When life ceases this situation becomes more complicated and obscure. The temperature may then be affected by factors such as the cause and the manner of death and other extrinsic factors such as the temperature and nature of the environment. Some workers have even reported that the body temperature rises by about 0·5°C after death irrespective of the above factors (44).

In this study we estimated the temperatures of the brain, liver and rectum at the moment of death by using the raw data collected during the first 3 hours after death and extrapolating backwards. Problems due to variation between one measuring device and another were also avoided by this approach, particularly with respect to the microwave attenuation by tissues which results in artificially low temperature readings. Nevertheless, the problem still exists in the field where an assumption must be made with respect to the temperature of the chosen body site at the time of death. In this case and if our device is used, the temperatures at death assumed for brain, liver and rectum should be the average values calculated from our results (Table 1).

Evaluation of Cooling Models

Our aim was to find the equation which best described our data regardless of complexity. The linear model (Rule of Thumb) was excluded from the beginning and attention was directed only to exponential functions containing one to four terms. Comparison of the ability of these four functions to fit the data is described earlier. Single exponential functions were generally found to be unable to fit the curves except in a few cases where the fits were poorer than with multi-exponential functions. It was clear that the curve-fitting process was improved by the use of a double exponential function. However, those cooling curves which were only poorly or moderately fitted by single or double exponential formulae were almost exactly fitted by triple exponential formula throughout the whole monitoring period. The four-exponential equation was also tried with some cases but the fit was not improved.

The use of a triple exponential equation may be interpreted in terms of the three cooling stages which have been noted in the literature: the temperature plateau, the fast cooling phase and the slow cooling phase. Each of these stages taken alone can be reasonably well described by a single exponential function.

To apply the model in practice, average curves were required. Two methods of calculating these were tried: by simple numerical averaging of the parameters obtained for each group of related curves and also by repeating the curve-fitting process to average values of temperature difference ratio calculated from the functions obtained from the raw data. The latter method was found to give average curves which were more useful in predicting the time of death (Figures 1–3).

Effects of Body Site, Body Parameters and Clothes

In our study of naked bodies it was found that, on average, the liver and rectum had similar cooling curves whereas the brain temperature dropped more rapidly and therefore the curve was rather steep. The brain temperature in most cases reached that of the environment within 10–15 hours, therefore its applicability is confined to the first few hours after death while the liver and rectum cooled more slowly and could be used for a much longer period. All three body sites had a similar degree of individual variations.

As expected, the brain was found to be unaffected by covering of the torso whereas both the liver and rectum cooled more slowly in covered bodies. This was apparent as a "flattening" of the cooling curves for these organs. The liver was generally more affected than the rectum.

Efforts were made to correlate the cooling factors of each site with body parameters such as weight, height, surface area, hip width, head diameter and cooling size (surface area divided by the weight). No significant correlations were found with the exception that for rectal temperature measurements in naked bodies it was possible to distinguish between fat and thin bodies. However, there were some cases which deviated from this classification, namely thin bodies which behaved as if they were fat and vice versa. The reasons for this are not understood. It was also generally noted that the cooling curves for fat bodies were flatter than those for thin bodies but there was no single parameter which could be used to predict the cooling behaviour.

Assessment of the Method

The usefulness of the method to practising pathologists and police surgeons has been assessed in terms of the error expected in estimates of the post-mortem interval using our average formulae. As the interval after death increases, the error also becomes larger. This is illustrated in Figure 4 for rectal temperature measurements in covered bodies. We have found that the average cooling curves for brain and liver obtained by microwave thermography have given similar accuracy to the rectal curve which was based on temperature measurements made by a thermocouple. Nevertheless the microwave probes were easier and more convenient to use in practice.

It should also be noted that the solution of the average equations developed in this study can be carried out manually using a reference graph or, more accurately, using a pocket computer. It is therefore entirely possible to use our method in the field if the portable version of the microwave system, which has recently become available, is used.

Conclusions

1. The post-mortem rate of cooling of the human body has been studied and found to be a good method for the estimation of the time of death.
2. Microwave thermography has been applied to Forensic Medicine for the first time in this field and found to improve the ease of estimating the time of death. The instrument gives a similar degree of accuracy to other temperature measurement devices.
3. Triple exponential functions were found to be necessary for an adequate description of the cooling curves. Simpler models were unsatisfactory.

4. New average formulae for the brain, liver and rectal cooling curves in naked, covered, fat and thin bodies have been developed. These functions could easily be solved using a pocket computer and would be simple to apply in practice.
5. Estimation of the time of death using this method is of value in forensic investigations but remains insufficiently accurate to be used in evidence.

Acknowledgements

The authors acknowledge the assistance given during this study by Professor Alan A. Watson and other colleagues in the Forensic Medicine Department, Dr David Land and Mrs Diana Worster, Glasgow University and also by Jack Sterling and Fenton Maxwell, the morticians of Glasgow City Mortuary. We also gratefully recall the initial impetus given to the work by the late Professor of Forensic Medicine, W. Arthur Harland.

This study forms part of the work of L. Al-Alousi for the degree of Doctor of Philosophy, University of Glasgow, supported by the Medico-Legal Institute of Baghdad, Iraq.

References

1. Oever, R. Van Den. A review of literature as to the present possibilities and limitations in estimating the time of death. *Medicine, Science and the Law*, 1976; 16: 269–276.

2. Lyle, H. P. and Cleveland, F. P. Determination of the time of death by body heat loss. *Journal of Forensic Sciences*, 1956; 4: 11–23.

3. Brown, A., Hicks, B., Knight, B. and Nokes, L. D. M. Determination of time since death using the double exponential cooling model. *Medicine, Science and the Law*, 1985; 25: 223–227.

4. Marshall, T. K. Changes after death. In: Camps, Lucas, and Robinson, eds., *Gradwohl's Legal Medicine*, 3rd Ed. John Wright and Son Ltd., 1976; Bristol: 78–100.

5. Simonson, J., Voigt, J. and Jeppesen, N. Determination of the time of death by continuous post-mortem temperature measurements. *Medicine, Science and the Law*, 1977; 17: 112–122.

6. Mant, A. K., ed. *Taylor's Principles of Medical Jurisprudence*, 13th Ed., Edinburgh: Churchill Livingstone, 1984.

7. Polson, C. J., Gee, D. J. and Knight, B. In: *The Essentials of Forensic Medicine*, 4th Ed., 1985; Pergamon Press, Oxford.

8. Nokes, L. D. M., Hicks, B. and Knight, B. H. The post-mortem temperature plateau — fact or fiction? *Medicine, Science and the Law*, 1985; 25: 263–64.

9. Marshall, T. K. The use of the body temperature in estimating the time of death and its limitations. *Medicine, Science and the Law*, 1969; 9: 178–82.

10. Coe, J. I. Post-mortem chemistry of blood, CSF and vitreous humor. In: Tedeschi, Eckert and Tedeschi, eds., *Forensic Medicine*, Vol. 2, W. B. Sunders Co., 1977; 1033–1060.

11. Nuorteva, P. Sarcosaprophagous insects as forensic indicators. In: Tedeschi, Eckert and Tedeschi, eds., *Forensic Medicine*, Vol. 2, W. B. Sunders Co., 1977; 1072–1095.

12. Chacon, M. A. and Tildon, J. T. Mode of death and post-mortem time effects on 3,3′,5-triiodothyronine levels. *Life Sciences*, 1984; 35: 2219–2225.

13. Falasoariya, B. A. W., Hill, C. A. and Williams, A. R. The biochemical changes in pericardial fluid after death. *Forensic Science International*, 1984; 26: 93–102.

14. Aoki, T., Yoshiura, M. I., Wamoto, T. and Iriyama, K. Post-mortem changes of uric acid in various fat tissues. Determination of uric acid by reversed-phase HPLC with electrochemical detection. *Analytical Biochemistry*, 1984; 143: 119–124.

15. Sasaki, S., Tsunenari, S. and Kanda, M. The estimation of the time of death by non-protein-nitrogen NPN in cadaveric materials, Report 3: multiple regression analysis of NPN values in human cadaveric materials. *Forensic Science International*, 1983; 84: 11–22.

16. Hiraiwa, K., Ohno, Y., Kuroda, F., Sebetan, I. and Oshida, S. Estimation of post-mortem interval from rectal temperature by use of computer (I). *Medicine Science and the Law*, 1980; 20: 115–125.

17. Mant, A. K. In: Simpson, K., ed., *Modern Trends in Forensic Medicine*, 2nd Ed. London: Butterworths, 1967.

18. Simpson, K. and Knight, B. *Forensic Medicine*, 9th Ed., London: Edward Arnold, 1985.

19. Fiddes, F. S. and Patten, T. D. A percentage method for representing the fall in body temperature after death. *Journal of Forensic Medicine*, 1958; 5: 2–15.

20. Brown, A. and Marshall, T. K. Body temperature as a means of estimating the time of death. *Forensic Science*, 1974; 4: 125–133.

21. Gordon, I. and Shapiro, H. A. *Forensic Medicine. A Guide To Principles*, 2nd Ed., Edinburgh: Churchill Livingstone, 1982.

22. Molnar, G. W., Hurley, H. J. and Ford, R. Application of Newton's law to body cooling. *Pflugers Archives*, 1969; 311: 16–24.

23. Marshall, T. K. and Hoare, F. E. Estimating the time of death. *Journal of Forensic Sciences*, 1962; 7: 56–81.

24. Molnar, G. W. Newton's law of cooling applied to Newton's ingot of iron and to other solids. *Physiologist*, 1969; 12: 137–145.

25. Molnar, G. W. Newton's thermometer: a model for testing Newton's law of cooling. *Physiologist*, 1969; 12: 9–19.

26. Green, M. A. and Wright, J. C. Post-mortem interval estimation from body temperature data only. *Forensic Science International*, 1985; 28: 35–46.

27. James, W. R. L. and Knight, B. H. Errors in estimating time since death. *Medicine, Science and the Law*, 1965; 15: 111–116.

28. de Saram, G. S. W., Webster, G. and Kathigamatamby, N. Post-mortem temperature and time of death. *Journal of Criminal Law Criminology and Police Science*, 1955; 46: 562–577.

29. Shapiro, A. H. Medicolegal mythology. *Journal of Forensic Medicine*, 1953/54; 1: 159.

30. Shapiro, H. A. The post-mortem temperature plateau. *Journal of Forensic Medicine*, 1965; 12: 137–141.

31. Carslaw, H. S. and Jaeger, J. G. In: *Conduction of Heat in Solids*, 2nd Ed., Oxford: Clarendon Press, 1959.

32. Hiraiwa, K., Kudo, T., Kuroda, F., Onno, Y., Sebetan, I. and Oshida, S. Estimation of post-mortem interval from rectal temperature by use of computer. *Medicine, Science and the Law*, 1981; 21: 4–9.

33. Williamson, E. D. and Adams, L. H. Temperature distribution in solids during heating and cooling. *Physical Review*, 2nd Series, 1919; 14: 99–114.

34. Sellier, K. Determination of the time of death by extrapolation of the temperature decrease curve. *Acta*. Medical Legal Society, 1958; 11: 279–302.

35. Joseph, A. E. A. and Schickele, E. A general method for assessing factors controlling post-mortem cooling. *Journal of the Forensic Sciences*, 1970; 15: 364–391.

36. Green, M. A. and Wright, J. C. The theoretical aspects of the time dependent Z equation as a means of post-mortem interval estimation using body temperature data only. *Forensic Science International*, 1985; 28: 53–62.

37. Nokes, L. D. M., Brown, A. and Knight, B. A self-contained method for determining time since death from temperature measurement. *Medicine, Science and the Law*, 1983; 23: 166–169.

38. Dixon, W. J. *BMDP Statistical Software*, Revised printing: University of California Press, 1983.

39. Land, D. V. Microwave Thermography, a new technique for the measurement of inflammation. Private communication.

40. Land, D. V. Clinical microwave thermography, Colloquium on Electromagnetic techniques for the detection and treatment of malignant disease. London: Digest No: 1984; 36.

41. Land, D. V., Fraser, S. M. and Shaw, R. D. A review of clinical experience of microwave thermography. Symposium on the recent development in medical and physiological imaging. London: Royal Photographic Society, 1985.

42. Naeve, W. and Apel, D. Hirntemperatur der Leiche und Todeszeit. *Zeitschrift Rechtsmedizin*, 1973; 23: 159–169.

43. Minard, D. and Copman, L. Elevation of body temperature in health. In: Herzfeld, ed., *Temperature, Its Measurements and Controls in Science and Industry*, Vol. 3 (3), 1963; 527–544.

44. Hutchins, G. M. Body temperature is elevated in the early post-mortem period. *Human Pathology*, 1985; 16: 560–561.

VALUE OF FORENSIC PSYCHIATRY IN A COURT OF LAW

R. N. Antebi

If one looks at forensic science, and compares it with forensic psychiatry, one will soon become aware that forensic science is concerned with the analysis of objects, ranging from dead bodies to other concrete phenomena, and from these facts, tries to establish relationships between the criminal and the offence, and endeavours to reconstruct the past, and in this particular case, the offence, which theoretically, is likely to lead to a proof of fact.

Findings can be challenged. Scientific methods can be superseded by more accurate scientific methods, and finally, the integrity of the expert witness can also be called into question. And now we come to a more difficult area, namely the interpretation of the results. What is initially thought to be logical cause and effect, may not be so at all when challenged by another forensic scientist. Calculations of probability could be used, either to prove or disprove a point, and finally, one must never forget the manner in which evidence is presented in court by the forensic scientist, how articulate and convincing this individual is in the witness box, and a factor which should never be underestimated is the Defence Counsel's skill that may erode a witness, and instil greater and greater doubts in a jury's mind, not only regarding interpretations, but also regarding facts, independently of the personal integrity of the expert witness.

Now, let us relate this whole procedure to forensic psychiatry. What facts have we at hand? We start from an interview with the accused who gives a personal history on request, and may or may not give a history of the circumstances surrounding the alleged offence.

Let us look at the past history in the first place. There are many factors of error regarding the reliability of such history; for example, the anxiety of the accused, what he remembers about the past, what he elects to tell the interviewer, whether he has been advised by his solicitor not to talk, and obviously, there will be a personal bias as to how he presents the material. The past history can be counterchecked by histories from relatives. In some cases, however, one must never forget that relatives have as much interest in giving a biased history to the psychiatrist as the accused himself, even when, as I have experienced, obtaining a history on behalf of his defence. The past history could also be compared with the history available from the Police, which is often rudimentary, or from a social worker, and this indeed, is often biased, and taken sometimes by an inexperienced newcomer to the social work department. The past history may be compared with information which the accused has given to other psychiatrists in the course of his life. This assumes that there was a previous psychiatric contact.

It may well be questionable whether information from other sources, such as National Health medical records where seriously incriminating statements were made several years prior to the accused's arrest, should be accepted by the interviewer, and possibly, in due course, by the court.

Then we have the history of the circumstances surrounding the alleged offence given to us by the accused. Some talk about it, others don't. Some claim amnesia, and some just say that they were not at the locus. This is the most difficult one irrespective of whether one acts for the prosecution or the defence. To what extent should the interviewer make the accused aware of discrepancies in his statements, or indeed, and this is a far more difficult question, discrepancies between statements. Furthermore, should the interviewer make known what has been known or written about him by the Criminal Investigation Branch, information at hand but unknown to the accused? It is not unusual for the psychiatrist to become aware that the accused is telling lies. On the other hand, the psychiatrist should not consider himself/herself to be an interrogator or judge and jury. There is obviously a very difficult balance here to maintain between ethical medical standards, and the standard expected by the courts.

Further psychiatric assessment is made by observed behaviour at the time of the interview, which could be compared with behaviour whilst in custody, or behaviour as described by relatives. Psychological tests such as IQ assessment, or sometimes personality assessments can be of relative value, but medical laboratory investigations should not be forgotten in cases where there is a possibility of a medical condition in the accused which could even be remotely related to the alleged offence. One thinks of an electroencephalogram, or sometimes more elaborate investigation to rule out intracranial pathology or epilepsy. Other medical aspects should not be overlooked, such as generalised or local illnesses; the effect of other drugs known to induce behavioural changes, such as steroids or anti-hypertensive drugs, or even behavioural changes induced through variation of the blood sugar levels in known diabetics, or indeed, in patients where there could be an alcohol induced reactive hypoglycaemia with consequent behavioural changes. Interaction between alcohol and neuroleptic drugs is also known to lead to a lack of inhibition of emotions. Genuine alcohol withdrawal with symptoms of *delirium tremens* should be noted at interview if such states could be at all relevant to the alleged offence. Then one can think of more controversial areas, such as premenstrual tension, and appropriate notes must be made as to the onset of the period of the accused in relation to the alleged offence, as well as a full and detailed account of past behaviour in relation to menstruation.

These are the so-called facts which the psychiatrist uses as a framework to support an opinion. Would you agree that what we have to work on is vague, woolly and possibly unreliable?

Even in psychiatric evidence there will be discrepancies in these so-called facts when given by the various psychiatrists who saw the same accused. This results from the information given by the accused to either the psychiatrist for the prosecution or for the defence. Moreover, there will be a selection by the psychiatrists of the information presented to the court. Such selected information will possibly be based on the ultimate conclusion reached by the psychiatrist, namely whether an accused should or should not be fully responsible for his crime because of various mitigating circumstances. The personal philosophy of the psychiatrist must not be underestimated, whether he or she has liberal ideas, feels sympathy for the underdog, or in fact may have a bee in his bonnet about authority. There is an element of hope in this because the legal profession is very much aware of psychiatrists giving such biased opinions that discreditation of the inadequate expert witness can quickly be demonstrated. This is often sufficient to eliminate such forensic psychiatrists from a court of law or, if they do reappear, their credibility can easily be challenged, and their evidence can be used against the person they are representing to his or her detriment.

Finally, it should not be forgotten that the payment of a fee can bias an expert witness, and defence lawyers have been known to "shop around" before finding the right psychiatrist who will say the right thing for their client.

Let us look now specifically as to what the courts are expecting of psychiatrists. These may be enumerated as follows:

1. An assessment of the mental state at the time of the appearance of the accused in court. This is to say that we are expected to give an opinion to the court as to whether a particular accused is sane and fit to plead.
2. An opinion as to the mental state of an accused at the time of the alleged offence.
3. Once the accused has either pled guilty or has been found guilty, if it appears to the court that the accused will be in need of some psychiatric care, as part of his disposal, then psychiatric opinion is sought prior to sentence.

The request for psychiatric opinion by the Crown is based on several criteria. First of all, it has been the procedure to have two independent psychiatrists to examine anyone accused of murder. This procedure seems to have been put in operation to avoid delays in court procedure when the defence is likely to raise the question of criminal responsibility in relation to mental illness.

Alternatively, psychiatric assessment of the accused may be requested because of information having reached the procurator fiscal from the past history of the accused following preliminary police investigation which indicates that the accused, has been or is, suffering from an abnormal mental condition. Likewise, the behaviour of the accused during his arrest, or in the police cell or even in the prison, could eventually lead to the request for psychiatric assessment. Finally, the cursory assessment of the police surgeon at the time of the arrest could be yet another reason for such an assessment.

There are some areas where forensic psychiatry can be of value in the legal process. These can be summarised as follows: assessment of how dangerous a particular accused may be; the likelihood of repetition of the offence if the offender is allowed back into the community; the motivation of the accused in the perpetration of the crime; the attitude of the accused towards the offence, when he or she is either found or pled guilty. As far as the concept of dangerousness is concerned, work has shown that psychiatrists are no better or worse than others in predicting potential dangerousness of an offender (1). Nevertheless, the court often expects, quite wrongly so with the knowledge presently available, statements about the dangerousness of the accused or criminal. It is a wise psychiatrist who talks about possibilities and probabilities rather than issuing categoric statements.

With regard to the repetition of an offence psychiatrists might perhaps be in a better position than most in giving such opinion, especially if they notice certain criteria such as callousness and a psychopath's typical inability to learn from experience. When talking about the probability of a repetition of a crime which has only been committed once, great caution is called for.

The motivation of the accused in the perpetration of the crime is a very difficult assessment indeed. It really amounts to the interpretation of a person's behaviour. Subjective assessment comes into it, but difficulty may well arise if interpretation is put upon an individual by a psychiatrist which does not coincide, in any way, with that of others, or indeed, with the accused's own interpretation. It is found that, in daily psychiatric work, this area of interpretation is like a minefield, and in individual psychotherapy, such interpretation varies with the therapist's training and philosophy, the patient's accepting or challenging attitude towards the psychiatrist, and the amount of insight both have into each other and in themselves. Humility and modesty must prevail in order to achieve some understanding, but it is difficult to see if this would apply in the relationship between the accused and the examining psychiatrist involved in a trial; the situation being so explosive and so threatening that in general the real motivation rarely surfaces at the time of the trial.

As far as the attitude towards the offence is concerned, we can give some guidance to the court as to how the accused sees the offence, not only in relation to himself, but also in relation to society as a whole, whether he or she understands the implication of the offence, and whether either spontaneous remorse or a desire to compensate has been expressed. These should all be taken into account when sentence is passed.

In rare cases where it has been agreed by all parties in court that the offender has committed an act, such as murder, and where there is some considerable doubt about the mental state at the time of the offence, then psychiatrists for the prosecution and defence have been requested to sit in during the trial, listening to evidence of witnesses before giving their own evidence. This is very unusual, though it has been known to be accepted.

Another use of a forensic psychiatrist is with the Criminal Investigation Department (CID) where exchanges of views could give a further lead in one direction or another to a suspect, or indeed, in guiding the Criminal Investigation Department towards a certain psychological identikit of an offender at large. Bruce Porter (2) discussed at length in a paper entitled "Mind Hunters", the psychological profile team's work of the FBI, and came to the conclusion that the more bizarre and the more abnormal the murder, the easier it was to trace the killer. Understand, however, that in the majority of cases, only a limited amount of help can be given to the CID in terms of a psychological identikit.

Hypnosis has been used in Scotland to elucidate more detailed information from victims or witnesses in difficult situations, and I would refer, for example, to the case of a rape victim who could not remember much about her assailant (3).

Finally, examinations by psychiatrists of witnesses has become more frequent. The information expected from the psychiatrist after such examinations would be to give the court some idea about the possible reliability of the witness. In addition, such assessment may be required to identify the mental state of the victim with particular reference to whether the victim is mentally handicapped or not. An opinion as to the reliability of some witnesses has also been requested in cases of alcohol intoxication, or in severely brain damaged victims. Opinions as to the possible consequences of a victim being asked to give evidence in court, which is likely to endanger her life are also sometimes requested.

Cases of rape victims having retracted statements through threats have been known (4), and cases where victims have threatened to kill themselves should they be subjected to an appearance in court to give evidence have also been known (5). There is room for psychiatric assessment to produce guidance for the court in these cases. To the experienced forensic psychiatrist, simulation of mental illness is not unusual. Symptoms can be produced by malingerers, when detection could be relatively easy, or they could be induced in a person who has either gone through a mental illness in the past, and who therefore knows how to reproduce the symptoms, or could also be reproduced by an individual who has taken psychedelic drugs, and has known madness in his past life.

In conclusion, the question really to be asked at this stage is, if psychiatry is being called upon to give evidence in a court of law, and what psychiatrists have to offer is confined to opinions which could be challenged by other psychiatrists, by advocates, barristers, why does the court still continue to ask for psychiatric opinion if the diagnosis of mental illness is no longer the sole prerogative of the psychiatrist? At the beginning of this article it was mentioned that there was some room, although not a great deal, to manoeuvre in relation to the forensic scientific evidence. By contrast, however, there is much greater latitude in court to allow discussion, sometimes on vague and nebulous statements or findings by psychiatrists. This contentious grey area is absolutely essential in a court of law where prosecution and defence can express their skills in interpretation and demonstrate their techniques in discrediting witnesses; such a system allows the jury time to weigh up certain arguments put forward in relation to a particular case.

Perhaps we are the medical–legal buffer zone which allows not only exposure without commitments or arguments and evidence, but also the projection of ideas which can remain unchallenged by virtue of court procedure. This arises from the skilful abstract generalisation and singularisation processes — the nightmare of the expert witness — who has himself no court of appeal, to dispose of prejudice implanted by those who represent the law.

References

1. Qumsey, V. and Ambthan, R. Variables affecting psychiatrists' and teachers' assessment of mentally ill offenders. *Journal of Consulting and Clinical Psychology*, 1979; 2: 253–262.
2. Porter, B. Mind Hunters. *Psychology Today*, 1983; April: 44–52.
3. Personal experience of unreported cases.
4. Personal experience of 5 unreported cases.
5. Personal experience of 3 unreported cases.

THE AIR INDIA JUMBO JET DISASTER KALISHNA—INJURY ANALYSIS

I. R. Hill

Introduction

The investigation of fatal aircraft accidents is a team procedure, the principles of which have been well established for many years. This approach is necessitated not only because of the complexities of aircraft, but also because air-travel is international and though well-established, its accidents are newsworthy. In this instance the investigation was complicated because the possibility of sabotage had been mooted and on the same day that the Boeing 747 VT–EFO of Air India crashed 120 miles south of Ireland, a bomb exploded in Japan's Narita Airport, shortly after a Canadian CP–Air Boeing 747 had offloaded 374 passengers. The bomb was alleged to have been of Indian origin.

131 bodies of the 329 passengers and crew aboard Flight II–182 (Kalishna) were recovered from the sea. Because of the postulated cause of the accident, each death was treated as being suspicious and it was therefore examined accordingly. Since there were so many bodies and there were varying patterns of injury, mathematical analysis of the injuries was undertaken. This paper describes the investigation and discusses the patterns of observed injuries in relation to the principles of injury causation, in an attempt to establish the crash dynamics of this accident. In doing so, it presents the case for the routine adoption of methods of numerical assessment of injuries in all aircraft accidents, in the interests of flight safety.

Circumstances of the Accident

The aircraft, a Boeing 747 VT–EFO, called Kalishna after an Indian Emperor, took off from Toronto on 22nd June 1985. Its first stop was Montreal which it left at 1710 hours local time en route for London, where it was scheduled to refuel, prior to going on to India. It carried a complement of 307 passengers, 3 flight deck and 19 cabin crew. The passenger load had been reduced by 90, so that a spare engine could be carried from an underwing pod; this is standard practice.

The last radio contact with the aeroplane was at 0807 hours local time, when the crew made a routine positioning report to the Air Traffic Controller at Shannon. At this stage the aircraft was being tracked by secondary surveillance radar. There was no evidence of anything untoward at this stage. At 0813 Kalishna disappeared from the radar screen. Exhaustive attempts were made to contact the aircraft, but to no avail, and at 0902 hours the Shannon air traffic controller notified Irish and British rescue services. An air and sea search was immediately initiated and by 1020 hours the *Laurentian Forest*, the first merchant ship to reach the area, reported that it had sighted wreckage floating on the sea.

All of the 131 bodies recovered were found by 24th June 1985. Of these 130 were found on 23rd June, 92 of whom were landed at Cork by air that day. The remaining bodies were brought in by sea on 24th June 1985. Rescue operations were hampered by the presence of sharks within the area of operation.

The Appearance of the Wreckage

Initially only small fragments of the airframe and baggage were found floating on the surface of the sea. These showed severe destruction and much of the luggage smelt strongly of aviation fuel. Subsequently larger portions of the aeroplane were found scattered on the sea bed at a depth of 6000–7000 feet. The total wreckage spread was said to be over a distance of some 5 miles.

The front and rear of the aeroplane showed considerable damage with Zones A and B lying close to one another, but separate, on the sea bed. Of the remainder, Zone C (page 123) was relatively intact, Zone D (page 124) showed severe damage and Zone E (page 125) was very severely damaged. These were some distance apart from one another.

An examination of some of the seats showed upward buckling, consistent with water impact. Similar signs were seen on the outer skin of Zone E.

Injury Analysis Method

The autopsy findings of each of the pathologists were entered onto proformae. These were examined, and each of the recorded injuries was scored according to the system outlined in Table 1. The results were put onto proformae and analysed on an IBM PC computer.

Injuries occurring on the left and right of the body were entered separately, as were those to the various regions of the body, thus, head, face, neck, upper limbs, chest, abdomen, pelvis and lower limbs. The regional and total body scores were then calculated. These were then compared with the victim's seating position on the aeroplane. They were also compared with a variety of special cases, namely degree of loss of clothing, evidence of decompression, hypoxia and tumbling and signs of vertical impact. The results obtained were examined statistically.

TABLE 1

Injury Scoring System

Severity of Injury	*Score*	*Force Needed*	*Potential Disability*	*Threat-to-life*
None	0	—	—	—
Mild	1	Little	Nil	None
Moderate	2	Moderate	Possible	None
Severe	3	Considerable	Probable	Possible
Fatal	4	Considerable	Not applicable	

Zone C

112 ECONOMY AT 34" PITCH

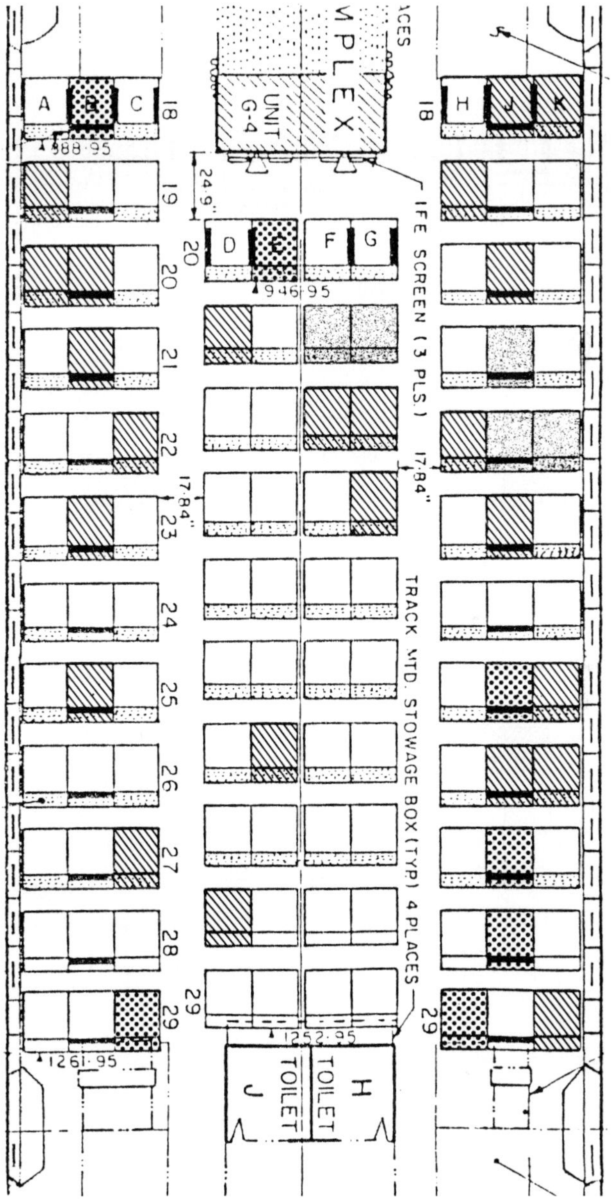

Zone D

86 ECONOMY AT 34" PITCH

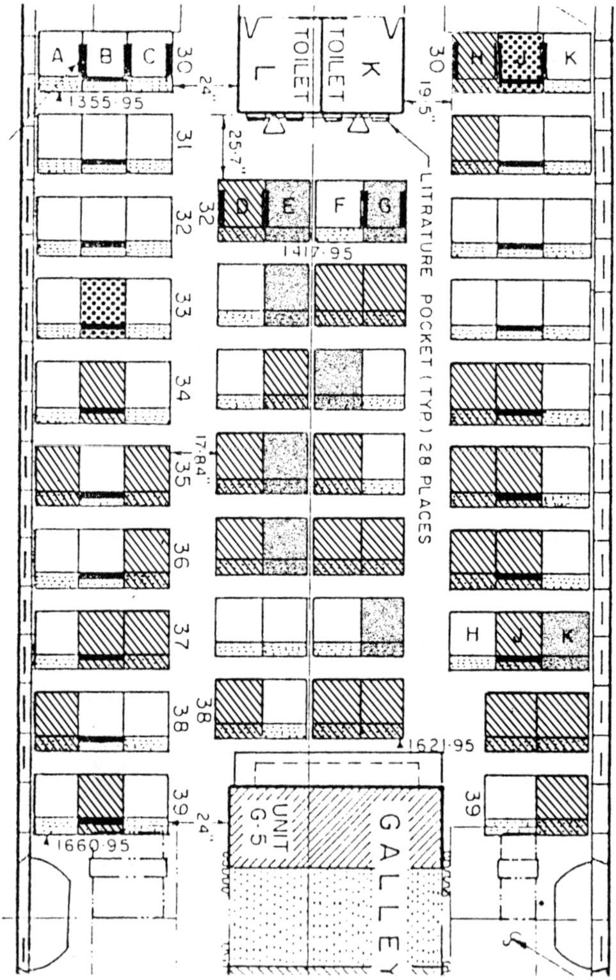

Zone E

123 ECONOMY AT 34" PITCH

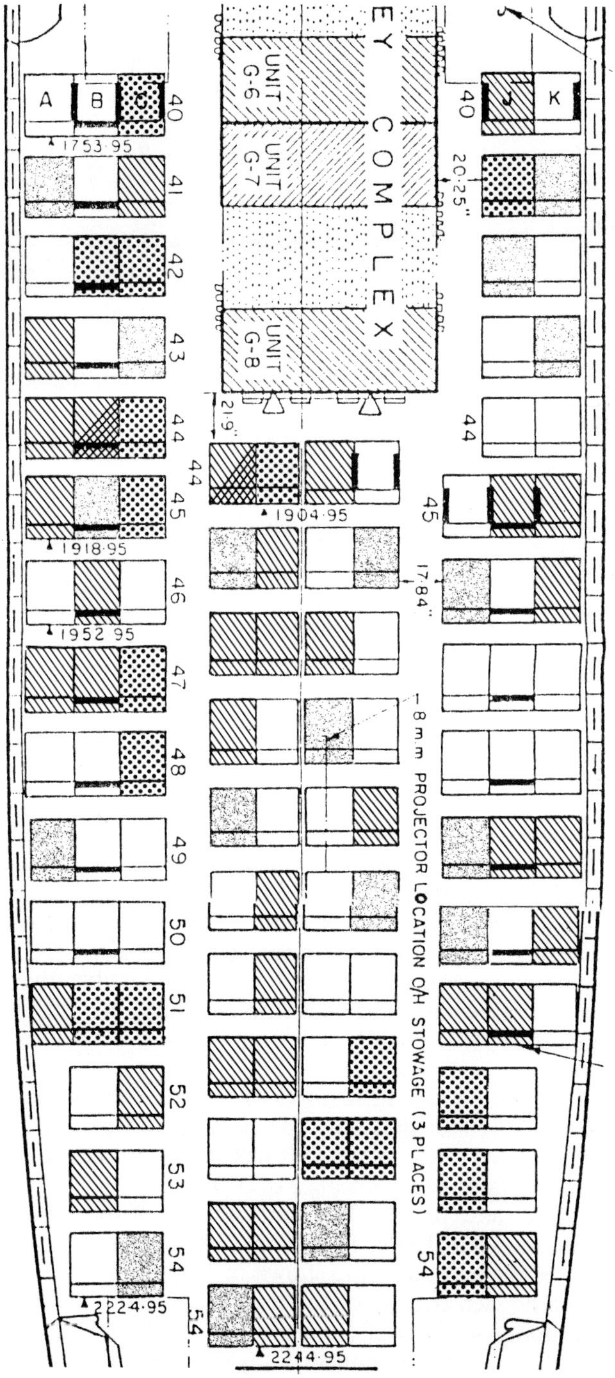

The significance test used depends on the standard deviation of sample means being normally distributed. This test is used because it is easy to calculate. There are others, such as the students t-test, which give approximately the same results, but depend on tables of probabilities and are not convenient.

$$\text{Standard deviation of mean} = \frac{\sigma}{\sqrt{n}}$$

So, if the population mean $= \bar{X}$

and the sample mean $= \bar{x}$

and the sample frequency $= n$

$$\frac{(\bar{X} - \bar{x})\sqrt{n}}{\sigma} \text{ is a normal distribution.}$$

The standard deviations and means are calculated in the normal way,

$$\bar{x} = \frac{\Sigma Px}{n}$$

$$\sigma = \sqrt{\frac{\Sigma(x - \bar{x})^2}{n}}.$$

The standard deviation and means for sex (male) are calculated assuming a binomial (two value) distribution,

$$\bar{x} = np$$

$$\sigma = \sqrt{npq}$$

Results

Inevitably with such a large number of victims, many of whom sustained a large number of injuries, a large volume of data was generated. This has been summarised and is presented in Tables 2 to 10.

Assuming that the maximum severity of injury was sustained in each section of each region, then the maximum scores possible are as shown in Table 8. To achieve the maximum total body score possible, the whole body would have had to have sustained catastrophic injury. In practice it has been found that a score of 150+ usually suffices to indicate such a gross severity of injury.

One of the most important features of this accident, when considering what happened, is the fact that only 131 bodies (39·8 per cent of the total number of victims) were recove This has an important bearing upon the conclusions drawn, and the significance of this is illustrated when we look at the distribution of these people. The configuration of the aeroplane and its complement are shown in Tables 11 and 12. The numbers recovered in the C, D and E zones of the aeroplane are shown in Table 13.

Thus it can be seen that all of the recovered victims were seated in the main part (economy section) of the aeroplane, and that the recovery rate increases towards the rear. Consequently any statement about the injuries and

TABLE 2

Average Scores and Range in the various groups of the victims recovered

	Number	*Percentage*	*Average Score*	*Range*
Adult Males	14	10·7	83	35–146
Adult Females	79	61·1	80	26–153
Cabin Crew	5	3·8	87	28–140
Infants (0–5 yrs)	7	5·3	32	16– 40
Children (6–12 yrs)	26	19·1	56	30–115
TOTAL	131	100		

TABLE 3

Average regional and total body scores for adults, excluding crew members as their seating positions were unknown. Seats A–C are on the left side of the aeroplane

	Seats A–C		
Bodily Region	*Zone C*	*Zone D*	*Zone E*
Head	14·8	18·0	18·5
Face	9·9	3·3	12·6
Neck	2·0	1·5	1·4
Upper limb	6·8	4·6	6·4
Chest	18·8	29·0	21·3
Abdomen	7·4	10·9	11·1
Pelvis	0·5	5·0	3·7
Lower limb	6·4	6·8	8·1
TOTAL	66·4	78·4	83

TABLE 4

Average regional and total body scores for adults, excluding crew members as their seating positions were unknown. Seats D–G are in the middle of the aeroplane

	Seats D–G		
Bodily Region	*Zone C*	*Zone D*	*Zone E*
Head	9·5	22·0	19·6
Face	2·8	11·8	8·3
Neck	—	2·4	1·9
Upper limb	4·7	5·5	6·4
Chest	15·7	25·8	26·7
Abdomen	9·2	12·6	13·8
Pelvis	1·7	3·4	7·1
Lower limb	6·4	5·3	8·4
TOTAL	49·6	89·1	92·1

TABLE 5

Average regional and total body scores for adults, excluding crew members as their seating positions were unknown. Seats H–K are on the right side of the aeroplane

	Seats H–K		
Bodily Region	*Zone C*	*Zone D*	*Zone E*
Head	16·1	22·0	17·5
Face	8·9	11·3	9·6
Neck	2·9	1·3	2·5
Upper limb	4·8	4·3	5·6
Chest	18·9	27·0	27·1
Abdomen	5·1	13·6	14·1
Pelvis	3·0	3·4	6·6
Lower limb	4·6	5·0	7·3
TOTAL	64·3	82·6	90·3

TABLE 6

Average score of all victims in each group expressed as a percentage of the total possible score for each bodily region

	Infants	*Children*	*Adults*	*Cabin Crew*	*MEAN*
Head	40	38.5	44	36·5	39·75
Face	2·9	6·6	16·4	14·3	10·1
Neck	4·4	5·0	5·9	5·6	5·2
Upper limbs	3·3	4·9	6·9	8·3	5·6
Chest	4·0	15·1	22·2	26·9	17·1
Abdomen	1·7	7·1	9·1	9·7	6·9
Pelvis	—	4·4	12·5	2·0	9·2
Lower limbs	3·6	6·3	8·1	11	7·3
TOTAL	5·7	10·2	14·5	15·8	11·6

TABLE 7

Average score of all victims sustaining an injury in each region (zero scores omitted), expressed as a percentage of the total body score

	Infants	*Children*	*Adults*	*Cabin Crew*	*MEAN*
Head	16	15·4	17·8	14·6	16
Face	1·8	3·7	9·8	8	5·8
Neck	3·3	3·8	3·4	3	3·4
Upper limbs	3	4·2	5·7	6·6	4·9
Chest	4·3	16·3	24	29	18·4
Abdomen	3·3	8·8	11·3	15	9·6
Pelvis	—	6·2	8·5	8	7·6
Lower limbs	3·3	5·2	6·6	8·8	6

TABLE 8

Percentage of Injury in the various regions of the body

	Infants		*Children*		*Adults*		*Cabin Crew*	
Head	7	100%	25	100%	92	98·9%	5	100%
Face	6	85·7%	26	100%	86	92·5%	5	100%
Neck	3	42·9%	11	42·3%	51	54·8%	3	60%
Upper limb	6	85·7%	25	92·3%	90	96·8%	5	100%
Chest	7	100%	26	100%	93	100%	5	100%
Abdomen	6	85·7%	26	100%	93	100%	4	80%
Pelvis	–	—	6	32·1%	49	47·3%	4	80%
Lower limb	6	85·7%	26	100%	90	96·8%	5	100%

TABLE 9

Maximum scores possible in each bodily region

Region	*Score*
Head	40
Face	56
Neck	32
Upper limb	80
Chest	108
Abdomen	124
Pelvis	32
Lower limb	80

TABLE 10

Frequency of Total body scores
(Note: Children here includes infants, and Adults includes crew—the numbers of whom are too small for individual analysis in this context)

	Frequency		
Body score	*All Victims*	*Adult*	*All Children*
0–9	0	0	0
10–19	1	0	1
20–29	4	3	1
30–39	19	10	9
40–49	19	9	10
50–59	14	13	1
60–69	18	14	4
70–79	7	3	4
80–89	8	6	2
90–99	8	8	0
100–109	6	6	0
110–119	9	8	1
120–129	8	8	0
130–139	3	3	0
140–149	6	6	0
150–159	1	1	0
	131	98	33

TABLE 11

Configuration of Flight AI–182 and occupancy

	No. of seats		*Seats occupied*
Zone A	16		1
B	22	(4 crew seats)	–
Upper Deck	18	(2 crew seats)	7
C	112		104
D	86		84
E	123		105
Total	377	(6 crew seats)	301
Configuration	16F	40C	321Y
Seats occupied	1F	7C	293Y
Seats vacant	15F	33C	28Y
6 infants on board			

TABLE 12

Breakdown of complement of Flight AI–182

	Adults		*Children*		
	Male	*Female*	*Male*	*Female*	*Total*
Passengers	95	136	34	42	307
Flight Crew	3	—	—	—	3
Cabin Crew	10	9	—	—	19
Total	108	145	34	42	329

TABLE 13

Recovery of victims

Zone	*Occupants Recovered*	*% of number in zone*
C	29	27·9
D	40	47·6
E	57	54·3
Sum	126	
Crew	5	
Total	131	

the events which may have caused them, can really only refer to that part of the aircraft. This is an important proviso, especially if and when inference, which it is considered may have a bearing upon the cause of the accident, are being made.

Discussion

Interest in and speculation concerning the postulated causes of this accident, combined with the facts that it occurred in international waters and the bodies were taken to a country different from the origins of the airline and the flight, posed particular problems for the investigators. The medical aspects of this investigation to which this paper is restricted were accomplished because of the high degree of co-operation and team work which existed. Moreover, the facilities provided by the Cork Regional Hospital Board were excellent — they included storage of bodies, temporary mortuaries, radiography, secretarial and rest rooms. Arrangements were also made for the reception and care of relatives, a vital and sometimes forgotten aspect of mass disaster investigations. It was particularly fortunate that the layout of the hospital was such that there was no interference with the normal day-to-day activities of the hospital and so patients were not inconvenienced. The mortuary site was also secure.

Arrangements such as these are important, because success in any investigation of this nature is to no small degree dependent upon their smoothness of running and the diversity of the available facilities. In this case, the fact that sabotage was mooted meant that the accident had to be treated as a suspicious death, which placed a greater strain on all of those involved. Whilst this did not by itself influence the approach used in the analysis of the post-mortem findings, it did provide an impetus for the use of numerical scoring of injuries.

Accident-injury analysis is a comparatively new, but well established procedure, which uses a variety of techniques to try and explain what happened in a crash, so that the causes of injuries might be elicited. Apart from possibly highlighting the causes of the accident, the analysis is done so that potentially hazardous designs of aircraft, and their fixtures and fittings, might be avoided in the future. The basic methods used have been tried and tested in many different types of transport accident. However, it is sometimes necessary to modify some of the tools used, especially in aircraft accidents, where there may be, for example, many fatal injuries.

The basic object is to look at the injuries sustained by the victim and to see how they compare with one another. Are all of the injuries the same or different, are they the same or different from those produced in other similar and different accidents? Occasionally, one victim may be found whose injuries are totally different from those seen in the other victims. This may be important, because it could give a clue as to how the crash occurred. Similarly, in an unexplained accident, the finding of a pattern of injuries which is known to occur in specific circumstances may well indicate how that crash occurred.

Injury scoring has been used for many years and a variety of different schemes have been devised, to try and meet the needs of all research workers and to obviate subjectivity. They nearly all use an assessment of the severity of injury as a basis for analysis. The desire to be able to express easily and accurately the severity of any injury has existed for very many years. Latterly this desire has become an urgent need, at least amongst research workers who are trying to express comparative risk to non-medical colleagues, and who have large amounts of information to process. Superficially this should not be a difficult task, but so far many systems have been tried, without achieving conspicuous success.

Because terms like minor, severe and fatal are thought to be inexact, a number of workers have tried to use numerical assessments of injuries. Some use 0 to mean no injury, others that it is a fatal lesion. The variability in their usage made them too hazardous and so attempts to remedy the situation were made. De Haven and his colleagues at Cornell (1) are widely credited with producing the first research-orientated scale, usage of which revealed imperfections culminating in a series of modifications. These did not obviate variation in the numerical values assigned to different injuries.

Towards the end of 1968, a committee was set up by the American Medical Association, whose aims were to review the problems of numerical injury severity assessment and to devise a universally acceptable method. They sought advice from a variety of medical specialists, engineers and others. All of the doctors invited were said to have special expertise in treating injuries in their respective fields of practice. They were asked to devise a scale of injury severity based upon energy dissipation, the threat-to-life, permanent impairment, treatment period and incidence.

The result of all this discussion was that two injury severity scales were put forward, the abbreviated and the comprehensive. In effect all the abbreviated scale did was to widen the scope of the earlier systems, providing specific examples of injury. Users compared the lesions found in the victims they were studying, with the description in the book and then placed them, hopefully, in the appropriate group. The body was split into five regions with scoring for unknown lesions and categories for different "degrees of fatality". Different degrees of fatality just means that more than one fatal lesion can be recorded.

There have been many reports stating that the abbreviated and comprehensive injury scales are valuable adjuncts to crash injury research (2, 3, 4). However, in a comparative study, designed to assess observer bias, codings by two observers were compared. This showed that 20 per cent of the scores given were incorrect (2). It is therefore apparent that subjectivity has not been eliminated. This is true even with the latest revision which was completed in 1980 at the request of a number of workers, who found that there were too many anomalies in the earlier formats.

Because of all of these difficulties, it was decided to use a simple 0–4 system (Table 1) of scaling injuries, which has proved successful in the past (1 and 5). Admittedly it does have the problem of subjectivity, but its ease of use does make it more attractive in sorting out injuries in this context. A score of nought is given if there is no recorded injury, 1 is equivalent to a small cut or bruise, 2 to a simple fracture or a large laceration. In both cases the injury would be assessed as being one which ought not to lead to death, or to serious complications which cannot be treated, nor should it, therefore, be the cause of permanent impairment. An injury which scores 3, on the other hand, will inevitably require much more force to produce it; it will probably lead to some later functional impairment, although this may be minimised by treatment. Such injuries pose a threat to life, and include compound fractures, severe lacerations of the viscera and widespread soft tissue disruption. Injuries which cause death are given a score of 4.

Since there were 131 victims, who sustained a multiplicity of injuries of varying severity, the volume of numbers created and the need for accurate, rapid statistical handling, posed problems. These were overcome by computer analysis, which generated a series of reports, which in turn had to be looked at from the point of view of the known causes of injuries in aircraft accidents.

There are, of course, many features of an aircraft accident which can affect what happens to an individual. The way in which the occupant moves in response to the force applied has a profound effect upon the nature and severity of the injury produced. This in turn is affected by the post-deceleration behaviour of the aircraft, restraint, position and posture as well as the intensity and direction of the forces produced.

The material impacted is of great importance. The degree of elasticity, or the lack of it, directly affects the deformation distance and thus the duration of the impact. The effect is not purely one of elasticity though, because the capacity to adapt to the body's contours is important, that is the plasticity of the substance.

Water has unique characteristics, since its relative deformation (the depth an individual goes to and the elastic properties) may vary considerably, depending upon the surface area of the body, its orientation and the surface condition of the water (e.g. rough or smooth), as well as the speed of any currents. Thus high divers attempt to cleave the surface of the water with their hands, consistently making dives of over 100 ft. into small pools of still water, without apparently sustaining any injury.

In the majority of aircraft accidents, the causation of injuries is a result of the reaction between the individual and the aeroplane. Pathologically the causes of injury are classified thus:

1. *Crushing within a collapsing airframe*
   Varying degrees of collapse can occur in any intensity of crash, but usually there has to be a substantial degree of damage, and that requires a moderately intense impact. The amount of airframe damage produced is of course variable. When substantial crushing occurs in a low velocity impact, it indicates that the structural strength of the airframe is inadequate.

   In its typical form, crushing is a feature of high velocity impacts, in which there is intense structural deformation. It is associated with severe injuries, notably amputations and crushing of the body between parts of the airframe. Perineal splitting, which is usually accompanied by varying degrees of sacro-iliac joint injury, with or without visceral herniation and damage thereto, indicates a high vertical loading.

2. *Entrapment within the wreckage*
   This occurs in two ways as a result of widely different circumstances. In a deforming, but not very intense impact, the hull may twist, making exits inoperable. This situation may be accompanied by fire, which can stop people using exits. In these circumstances traumatic injuries may be minimal, usually soft tissue bruising and at the most extreme limb fractures and concussion. Death results from the products and or the effects of fire, or in ditching accidents, drowning. Death may also be due to traumatic asphyxia, if the chest is compressed, for example.

   In more extreme accidents, because of structural collapse, which is less intense than that seen in the first category, victims are trapped directly by wreckage. They may be pinned in their seats, or in the aisles. As well as severe limb injuries, there are widespread limb lacerations, more severe injuries to the torso and there will almost certainly be severe head injuries. Death may occur because of the injuries themselves, because of complications resulting from the injuries either alone, or in part due to delay in rescue and treatment and because of fire or other environmental effects.

3. *The absence or failure of restraint*
   To a certain extent the injuries seen here may be similar, but they occur at different intensities of impact. Absence of restraint is associated with a high rate of ejection, through gaps in the aircraft. On the way out contact may produce severe lacerations and/or impact injuries. Further phases of injury may occur when the body lands and if it hits objects before doing so. Limbs may be torn off, long wide lacerations may be seen and typically there are severe head injuries. Ejection increases the mortality rate by as much as six times.

   Failure of restraint may occur in the harness itself, at its attachments, the seat, or the floor. Combinations of these may occur.

   Seat failure occurs either because the vertical load is too great, or because the horizontal forces overstress the mountings. The pattern of injuries produced is different in the two types of failure, although, because of the high forces involved, it may not be easy to distinguish them in some accidents.

If the vertical forces are high, then failure may occur just at the "seat legs", or there may be disruption of the floor. In each case the legs will be fractured, particularly the tibeae and fibulae and there may be ankle and foot injuries, partially as a result of entrapment, or by contact with aircraft structures, or also because of the transmission of impact forces through the foot. The actual pattern seen will depend upon the position of the limbs. If they are flat on the floor then, the appearances may simulate a hard landing on the feet, with calcaneal fractures. Entrapment of the foot will cause fracture and displacement of the more anterior parts of the foot. Breakage of the floor may be associated with lacerations caused by the jagged edges of metal. There may also be penetrations of the legs and the body by a displaced spar, for example. More intense forces can cause limb amputation.

When the seats collapse forwards, the appearances are similar to those seen when entrapment within the wreckage occurs.

In all of these situations, there is a high incidence of injuries to the head, thorax, pelvis and abdomen, in descending order of frequency. Visceral ruptures are frequently seen and they are commonly very severe, often amounting to total disruption of the organs.

4. *Being struck by loose objects*

When this occurs in low velocity impacts, it is a result of either carelessness or poor crashworthiness. The overhead racks in airliners should not be used for heavy hand baggage, nor should anything capable of causing injury be stored there. Passengers often fill them with bottles and other items, all of which may, if they do not kill in a crash, cause severe and possible incapacitating injury.

Usually it is only in very severe accidents that radios and other instruments break free, but even in turbulence, meal trays and other items can be thrown about the cabin. The heavier and the sharper these are, the more damage they will cause. Bruises, lacerations, fractures and penetrating injuries have all been seen.

5. *Injuries associated with escape*

Ejection at altitude may be associated with hypoxia and/or cold injuries, as well as those discussed earlier. In civilian aircraft, these are usually associated with falling from the aeroplane. Fractures, sprains and bruises, usually of the limbs, predominate. Lacerations may occur if there is any jagged metal in the vicinity. Flash burns and blast injuries are also seen. Occasionally aviation fuel and hydraulic fluid produce chemical burns. If the aircraft has ditched, then drowning may occur.

6. *Explosive decompression*

By itself this is seldom fatal, being well tolerated. The classical injury is rupture of the eardrum without fracture of the base of the skull. Emphysema is also a feature, or there may be other features of pressure wave injury.

In this accident the possibility of bomb blast was mooted, which presents a separate set of problems to the pathologist. It has long been recognised that people who are some distance from a blast source can be incapacitated and killed by it and that they may show either little or no sign of external injury. The diagnostic dilemma may be compounded by the victims being hit by displaced objects, and/or they themselves being thrown over and subsequently suddenly decelerating. Heat, hot gases, dust and ionising radiations may all complicate the pathological picture found. Thus blast injury is a complicated phenomenon, which, if it is not properly sought for, may, in appropriate circumstances, be missed.

There is general agreement (6) that the effects of blast waves may be divided into three groups:

(i) Primary blast injury is due to changes in environment pressure. Regions in which there are greatest variations in tissue density are most susceptible to injury at this stage. A fact which is borne out by the greater susceptibility of air-containing organs, such as the ear, the lungs and the gastro-intestinal tract.

(ii) Secondary blast damage occurs because the shock wave projects a variety of missiles about, principally in the main direction of the blast, but some may be dispersed erratically. When these hit the body they behave as any other missile does, tearing out lumps of flesh and embedding themselves in the tissues.

(iii) Tertiary effects are due to the sudden displacement of the individual, as a direct result of changes caused by blast waves. The injuries produced are caused by and are typical of accelerative/decelerative forces.

There are two impediments to the unqualified application of these principles to the analysis of the Air India accident. Firstly only 131 of the victims were recovered and secondly it cannot be guaranteed that they were actually in their seats at the material time. However, we do know from the wreckage that the zones of the aeroplane were separate and that the front and the rear were very badly damaged, the tail being totally separated from the remainder.

The absence of unequivocal signs of lap belt wearing indicates that there was no forewarning of the accident. As with other responsible airlines, Air India gives warning of turbulence and other emergencies, advising passengers to fasten their seat belts. Thus it would seem that the events were sudden and unanticipated.

It can be seen from the results quoted that the detailed data on the children and infants has been omitted. They are in small numbers, and spread throughout the three zones of recovery, thus they are statistically doubtful. Similarly the lack of seating position and the fact that only 5 cabin crew were recovered makes them statistically non-viable. Notwithstanding these comments, some review of their findings is necessary.

There is little difference in terms of severity between all of the adults. However, the children and infants (Table 2) do show a marked difference in average injury severity. The adults were on average 2·6 times more severely injured than the infants and 1·4 times more than the children. Even though these are small groups, the possibility of this finding being solely due to chance is remote, especially when it is acknowledged that most of the recovered children were in zone E. This was the most severely damaged part of the aircraft from which people were recovered.

As infants form a group which may not be given a seat, and they are likely to be sat on parents' knees, they ought, theoretically, to be more prone to sustain serious injury. That they did not suggests that some other factor was at play. It is widely held that this group of the population does not sustain the same severity of injury as do adults in similar circumstances. The findings here support that view.

When the accident is judged as an overall event, it can be seen that it was moderately severe (Tables 2–10). There is a great disparity between the actual and potential injury scores achieved (Tables 7 and 10), despite the fact that in most regions of the body there was a high incidence of injuries (Table 8).

Although caution must always be exercised when drawing conclusions from studies of seating patterns and injury severities, there is no doubt that some idea of the general picture can be obtained. The basic problem is that no one can, in all circumstances, be absolutely sure that the seating plan is accurate. People change places and mistakes occur in the records. Also people may be standing, in the lavatories or elsewhere at the moment an accident occurs. Moreover, we do know that variations in injury patterns can occur in people who are seated next to each other. Finally, individual tolerances to trauma do vary.

The adults confirm what can only be an impression from the children's figures, and that is that it was comparatively safer in the D–G region of zone C. If injury severity is regarded as being a function of the degree of damage to the airframe, from whatever cause — and there is ample evidence to support this view — then it would seem that the greatest amount of damage occurred towards the rear of the aeroplane, in particular in regions D–G of zones D and E and regions H–K of zone E. If the possible reasons why this was so and the mechanics of how it happened are to be explained, then the severities of the injuries sustained by the different parts of the body in the various zones and regions of the aeroplane have to be looked at in detail.

Head injury is depressingly common in all types of aircraft accident and either alone, or combined with damage elsewhere in the body, is a potent cause of mortality, both directly and indirectly. The mechanisms of head injury are complex; here we are not concerned with metabolic or pathophysiological causes, for the timescale is in all probability too short. Neveretheless the means whereby impact trauma actually causes injury to the brain are a source of considerable debate and the literature is an inconclusive as it is profuse.

All of the victims recovered were from the economy part of the aeroplane, where the pitch of the seats is said to be 34″. As the seats are only fitted with lap belts, this means that the majority of people will be able to make contact with the back of the seat in front. This is confirmed by the finding of a high incidence of cranial vault as well as brain injuries. Moreover many of the victims showed the typical fore-aft facial/cranial flattening which this type of contact produces. However, this is not the only way that intracranial or cranial injury can occur. Impact forces passing directly up the spine may be transmitted to the base of the skull and thence to the brain and the vault of the skull. A number of victims undoubtedly suffered this type of injury. Also injury to the brain can occur because of violent shaking of the head. This type of cause is seen most often in children, where the C7/T1 (neck/chest) linkage is said to be particularly mobile. Finally, lateral contact and other contacts with loose objects may occur.

Facial injury is not so common as head injury, at least as far as its reported incidence is concerned. Judging by the reported incidences of the various grades of injury, especially in respect of the more serious grades of head injury, facial lesions are under-reported. This is not so surprising as it might at first appear, because skeletal damage in this region of the body can be very difficult to diagnose, even with radiographs, because of the complexity of the skeleton.

As far as the adults are concerned, there is a paucity of recorded neck injury. As can be seen from Tables 7 and 8 the tendency is to minor injury. One interesting feature does emerge though, and that is that as far as the neck is concerned, the front part of the aeroplane, particularly the H–K region of zone C, appears to be the most dangerous. Slightly more adults (43 per cent — 42 out of 98) did not have recorded neck injuries.

The other interesting feature is that the middle of the economy area (zone C region D–G) is, as when the head and facial scores were being looked at, more dangerous than zone E. This is in contrast with the overall severity of injury. The pattern of injury recorded here and previously increasingly indicates that more than one phase of injury occurred in this accident, and that different forces were generated and transmitted to the various parts of the aeroplane.

As can be seen from Tables 3, 4 and 5 the severity of injuries varies in the different parts of the aeroplane. Statistically there is little to choose between the various regions in so far as the arms are concerned, though the left side of the aeroplane contained the highest scores.

Chest injury, which is a potent cause of death in all accidents, either alone, or in combination with head injury, was found in all of the recovered victims. Although everyone sustained some degree of abdominal injury it was relatively minor in degree.

Pelvic injuries are difficult to dissociate entirely from those in the lower limb and the abdomen, but because there are special features of them, particularly in their pathogenesis, they deserve special attention. Only 6 children out of a total of 33 sustained any pelvic injury, but the range of scores is wide, 2–18. The one child with a high score also had high scores in the head and chest, but not in the abdomen, or the lower limbs, which might have been expected.

The pattern of pelvic injuries in the adults is interesting, because there are so many victims who did not have recorded injuries in this region (Table 12). Theoretically, if they were subjected to the same forces then they should have had the same injuries, provided that they were in the same position. Most of those with severe pelvic injuries were to the rear of the aeroplane.

The interest in the post-mortem findings rests in two distinct but related areas: what do they mean in relation to the cause of the accident and, as part of this, how were they caused; and secondly, what do they mean as far as flight safety is concerned? These are not easy questions to answer fully, because we have only 39·8 per cent of the victims. Moreover, as none of the flight deck crew, nor any of those in zones A, B and the upper deck were recovered, no medical findings can be made, nor can any conclusions be made about what happened in this part of the aeroplane.

The reasons why people were not recovered has to be looked at, for it has some bearing upon what took place on Flight AI-182. If the bodies did not surface with an air bubble, then 10 per cent would float immediately, 10 per cent would hover between the surface and 20 feet for a variable time before surfacing, 20 per cent would sink to variable depths and surface later, and 60 per cent would sink to the bottom and surface later. The female to male floating ratio would be of the order of 4:1.

This of course assumes that no bodies are trapped within the wreckage. Here about 40 per cent of the bodies were recovered. The female to male ratio of 104:27 is as expected. As all of the bodies were recovered within 24 hours of the accident, and as only 2 have surfaced since, one of which floated away again (the results of the post-mortem examination are not known to me), this would suggest that some of the bodies may have surfaced in an air bubble having been trapped within the wreckage.

There is some evidence that this could have happened. As loss of clothing is associated with violent ejection from an aeroplane, then it is reasonable to propose that those still wearing it could have been retained within the wreckage, at least for a time, and then released more gently. The fact that 15 (51·7 per cent) of the occupants of zone C were fully clothed and that only 3 (10·3 per cent) were nude, lends credence to this view. Moreover, they tended to be seated to the front right of the aeroplane, and they were less seriously injured than the remaining victims.

In any aircraft accident, the mechanisms of injury production are complex and it can be extremely hard to decide how and when an individual injury occurred, especially when there is superimposition. Pattern analysis of injuries often helps, provided that the approach is logical. This implies that groups and sub-groups must be viewed as part of the whole pattern. One case which has at various stages in the investigation been looked at, and given overdue importance in relation to the remainder, is those with flailing injuries. Thus some commentators have tended to regard these as being diagnostic of the cause of the accident, rather than as being consistent with, but not diagnostic of, its effects upon the individuals.

Flailing occurs under two sets of circumstances. It can occur whilst the victim is seated, when the limbs are thrown about during impact. Here the injuries which are seen are usually due to contact with parts of the aircraft's structure. The second circumstance when this happens is in individuals who are thrown out of an aeroplane at altitude, where the cause of the injuries seen is windblast, and/or if they are thrown about within the cabin of the aeroplane, their limbs undergoing violent movements.

As the victims leave the aircraft they enter the air which may be stationary, at least in comparison with the forward speed of the aircraft. The result is that each victim is subjected to rapid deceleration due to wind drag. The extent of the deceleration depends upon the equivalent air speed of the mass and the effective cross-sectional area exposed. The higher the initial air speed, the greater will be the deceleration. Although the total linear deceleration produced is not affected by altitude, the rate is. At higher altitudes it takes longer to achieve total deceleration, because of the decreased air density. If the victim is stable and facing forwards, the forces thus generated will be along the

Gx axis and they will be directed against the back of the victim. This is obviously advantageous because they are dissipated over a wider area, therefore they are less dangerous. When the victims spin and tumble, they are multidirectional and are potentially much more dangerous.

It is convenient at this stage to look at injuries to the lower limb, especially as so much comment has been directed at flailing. The incidence of injuries here is the same as that in upper limb whilst in the infants the average severity of injury is comparable (Tables 6 and 7). In the others the lower limbs were more seriously injured than the upper limbs, yet they constituted a greater threat-to-life when viewed as a percentage of the total body score.

In seated individuals damage to the thigh, and the hip, can occur because the victim is jammed up against the seat in front. Thus the impact forces are transmitted back along the shaft of the femur. The low incidence of knee joint injuries suggests that this was not a common mechanism of injury.

Unlike the arm the majority of the injuries are to the upper part of the limb. Moreover, the incidence of compound fractures (grade 3) is far greater than it is in the upper limb (28·5 per cent and 16 per cent respectively). This also suggests that flailing of limbs occurred, but it has to be remembered that compound fractures do regularly occur in other circumstances. One of the interpretive problems concerns the mutilation of victims by sharks, which masks the impact damaged.

Amongst those with pelvic injuries there was a group of individuals who, at first sight, appeared to have severe pelvic injury of the type commonly seen when high vertical loads are applied to the pelvic region. There were 23 adult victims who fell into this category, 13 of whom had very little clothing and 3 were nude. Their seating positions show that they tended to be seated to the rear, right side of the aeroplane. They were older than the other victims. When the whole population was looked at, it was seen that they had much higher chest, abdominal, pelvic and lower limb injury totals, and were consequently more severely injured overall than the remainder of the victims.

There is an obvious problem in the interpretation of these findings. In particular there is the apparent paradox of no reported pelvic injury and the findings of severe pelvic injury in a victim sitting nearby. This may indicate that seating position was not relevant; however, it has long been established that there can be a wide variation in the severity of injury reported in the victims of aircraft accidents, even in those sitting in adjacent seats when the victim's seating position can be guaranteed. Here though, we cannot be absolutely certain of the exact position each individual was in at the time of the accident, as has been stated earlier.

In so far as the pelvic injuries in this sub-group are concerned, the question arises as to their possible cause. The nature and the appearance of the injuries arises as to their possible cause. The nature and the appearance of the injuries is consistent with a high vertical loading. The fact that 12 of these people were in the E zone of the aeroplane, 5 in D and 4 in C, suggests that the force must have been greatest, or at least more widespread in that zone of the aeroplane. It is, however, difficult to compare the various sub-divisions within this sub-group of victims who have been subjected to vertical impact forces, because of the small numbers within them. Unfortunately this is of great importance as far as causation is concerned.

If a vertical force did cause these injuries, when was this applied to the aeroplane — at altitude, during the fall or at impact with the sea? As 16 were either nude or had very little clothing on and, as is discussed below, this is indicative of being thrown out of the aeroplane at altitude, it also suggests that the force causing the injury in these people occurred whilst they were at altitude. It could be argued that the vertical loading resulted from impact with water, with the victim in a seated position. Had this been the case, it would have been expected that there would have been severe soft tissue injury; but as can be seen from Table 2, there was not a high percentage of perineal soft tissue injuries.

It is of course always possible that there was more than one phase of injury, and that those who were fully clad had, having remained in the aeroplane, received their injuries because of vertical loadings applied to the aeroplane at sea impact. The appearance of the wreckage, as described to me, suggests that a lot of force was applied to the airframe at this stage of the accident sequence. This does not negate the previous argument, but rather it reinforces the point made earlier, that this was a complicated accident in which the crash sequence was complex.

The overall appearances of all of the victims suggests that in addition to the above, there were a number of other sub-groups of victims, and that these were independent of age and whether or not those involved were members of the crew. An analysis of the severities of injury, seating positions and other relevant factors bore this out.

Arguably the most obvious difference between the victims was the degree of clothing which they were found to be wearing when examined in the mortuary. So far as is known none was removed prior to their examination. Indeed the Garda Siochana were particularly keen to preserve the clothing on each individual, because the accident was regarded as being a suspicious incident.

In all, 4 categories of clothing were identified. Those regarded as being moderately clad had at least one item of outer clothing, whilst those classified as having very little clothing had only undergarments on. The distribution of the various categories was fully clad 19 (22·1 per cent), moderately clad 38 (29 per cent), very little clothing 43 (32·8 per cent) and nude 21 (16 per cent). The seating position for the four categories of clothing in the victims is given in Table 14. Thus it can be seen that people at the back of the aircraft tended to lose their clothing, whilst those at the front retained it.

If the aeroplane did break up at altitude, then the occupants would have been exposed to an atmosphere which had a low oxygen content. When this occurs, then the oxygen masks are deployed. The evidence for this is equivocal, which indicates that either the mechanism failed, or that the time available for it to happen was too short. No conclusions can be made either way, because, so far as is known, too little of the wreckage was available for examination. Some evidence from the bodies is available though.

Signs of hypoxia, namely visceral patechial haemorrhages with and without pulmonary oedema, were found in 26 victims, all of whom had low total body scores. Half of these people were children of whom 40 per cent were male. If they are included, then the score for chest injuries is low. The highest incidence of children can be explained by the fact that they are more susceptible to hypoxia and, being smaller, they might have been trapped within the collapsing disintegrating aeroplane, without necessarily being grossly

TABLE 14

Number of adult victims without pelvic injury

	Region		
Zone	*A–C*	*D–G*	*N–K*
C	7 (87·5%)	3 (50%)	6 (60%)
D	5 (62·5%)	6 (50%)	7 (58·3%)
E	5 (45·5%)	7 (43·4%)	2 (20%)
	Overall	51·6%	

TABLE 15

Distribution of victims and degree of clothing

	Zone								
	C		*D*		*E*		*TOTAL*		
	No.	*%*	*No.*	*%*	*No.*	*%*	*Crew*	*No.*	*%*
Fully clothed	15	51·7	6	15	8	14	–	29	22·1
Moderately clad	6	20·7	12	30	18	31·6	2	38	29
Very little clothing	5	17·2	17	42·5	18	31·6	3	43	32·8
Nude	3	10·3	5	12·5	13	22·8	–	21	16
Total	29	22·1	40	30·5	57	43·5	5	131	99·9

damaged by it. In one case the autopsy appearances were strongly indicative of traumatic asphyxia.

Explosive decompression is always difficult to diagnose. When this occurs the risk of damage to the occupants of an aeroplane increases in proportion to the ratio of the area of the defect, to the volume of the cabin and the ratio of the pressure change. Normally aeroplanes do not sustain large defects, because large potential openings are designed so that they open inwards, therefore windows are the biggest such area. As a consequence, if a large defect did occur, then it must have resulted from some structural failure, of whatever cause, which may be consistent with destruction of the aeroplane. Gross failures of cabin walls are not likely, as metal fatigue is well recognised and accounted for in design. Recently, however, cracks have been found in some older Boeing 747s. However, corrosion has to be remembered, and the possibility of sabotage has also to be borne in mind.

Generally speaking, the larger the volume of the cabin, the slower will be the rate of decompression; and the larger the defect in the wall, the faster it will be. Initially the rate of fall is rapid, gradually tailing off as equilibrium is approached.

Decompression causes a sudden flow of air in the cabin, which is accompanied by dust and the condensation of water vapour, impairing visibility. The rate of flow of the air is greatest close to the defect, gradually decreasing as the distance away from it increases. The air blast created can blow loose articles, furnishings, and people in the immediate vicinity of the defect out of the aeroplane. If there is a major structural failure many and perhaps most, of the occupants nearby may be severely or even fatally injured by the airblast. The relevance of this lies in its relationship to the cause of death of the victims and the cause of the accident, especially when the decompression leads to the disintegration of the aircraft.

In this accident, where large numbers of the victims sustained severe injuries, the possibility of finding all of the classically described signs in all, or even a few of the victims, was remote. Typically, rupture of the eardrum is described, without associated skull fracture, but this can also occur in blast injury. Indeed the primary effects of blast are virtually the same as decompression injuries. Thus the lung is said to be the most vulnerable organ to injury, owing to the rapid expansion of gas within the alveoli, causing emphysematous bullae to be produced and, if air escaped, surgical emphysema.

There were 25 people on this aeroplane, who were recovered, and who had varying degrees of surgical emphysema and emphysematous bullae on the surface of the lungs. The latter can of course occur because of other causes. These people tended to be seated on the right of the aeroplane, they had a greater severity of right-sided injuries and increased chest injuries, though the latter was not so obvious when the children were removed.

Of these 25 people, 7 also showed signs of hypoxia, which is one of the features of decompression. This occurs because there is a decrease in the oxygen tension of the blood and an increase in the alveolar tension of carbon dioxide. As there is a decreased concentration of oxygen in the inspired air, then that of the alveolar air is lowered. At altitudes in excess of 30,000 ft. then, the pressure of the oxygen in the blood is greater than that in the air and therefore oxygen is given up to the air. At this height there are about 70 seconds of useful consciousness.

Conclusions

This was a complex accident, in which there were at least three phases of injury. The large number of victims recovered and the diversity of their injuries made injury scoring methods of analysis necessary. When combined with the circumstantial evidence and the appearances of the wreckage, this revealed that the aircraft broke up at altitude, but it did not give any idea as to the cause. The accident was sudden and unanticipated. Although only a moderately severe accident when judged in terms of the severity of injury sustained, it was made non-survivable by the circumstances. The success of the medical investigation is a direct result of the high degree of co-operation which was obtained amongst the members of the medical team.

Acknowledgement

The author is grateful to the Director, General Medical Services (RAF) for permission to publish this paper. The opinions expressed are those of the author and in no way reflect those of the Ministry of Defence (Air).

Grateful thanks are also offered to the Garda Giochana, the Coroner for Cork and colleagues Professor C. T. Doyle, Dr J. Harbison, Dr C. Keohane, Dr J. O'Hagen, Dr J. Lucey and Dr R. Taite with whom it was a privilege to work.

References

1. Hill, I. R. MD Thesis. Cambridge University, 1984.

2. States, J. D., Fenner, H. R., Flamboe, E. E., Nelson, W. H. and Hames, L. N. Field Application and Research Development of The Abbreviated Injury Scale. Proceedings of the 15th stapp car crash conference. Society of Automotive Engineers. New York, 1971.

3. Baker, S. P., O'Neill, B. W. and Long, W. B. The Injury Severity Score. *Journal of Trauma*, 1974; 14: 87–196.

4. Bull, J. P. The Injury Severity Score of Road Traffic Casualties in Relation to Mortality, Time of Death, Hospital Treatment Time and Disability. *Accident Annual of Prevention*, 1975; 7: 249–255.

5. Hill, I. R. *Injury Mechanism Analysis in Aircraft Accidents*, 1978; AGARD–Cp–255. Paris–France.

6. Marshall, T. K. Deaths from Explosive Devices. *Medicine, Science and Law*, 1976; 16 (4): 235–239.

HANDMAIDENS

W. D. S. MacLay

In the courses for police surgeons the clinical examination looms large, for everyone wants to be able to answer the two questions — "is she a virgin?" and "has she had intercourse?" I like to remind them that what is learned from such an examination is often no more important than the information to be gleaned by the forensic scientist whose concern is the trace evidence the doctors should be preserving. Deductions made by the scientists cannot be soundly based if the doctor has not performed his part of the task well. Needless to say the doctor must accept instruction from the forensic scientist, who must in turn be able to communicate what is likely to be of significance. In this sense, then, the doctor is acting as handmaiden to forensic science, a relationship which many of those attending this meeting will applaud. The gender implicit in the term has assumed greater prominence than formerly, but I shall return to that.

In the more usual clinical situation familiar to doctors when, for example, it is necessary for diagnostic purposes to take a sample of blood, the hospital laboratory staff will quite likely reject the sample if its accompanying form is not properly completed or if it is sent in a bottle of the wrong type, but such a high-handed response is not open to the forensic scientist — if it is found that trace evidence has not been properly packed and labelled it is simply not there to be procured a second time. It is essential that laboratory staff be appraised of its provenance, be made aware of any factors likely to influence its significance for the case under investigation.

In Strathclyde we have another sort of handmaiden. Almost three years ago we began to give to selected woman officers much more specialised instruction in aspects of sexual assault. These officers become involved immediately a complaint of sexual assault is made. The same officer, working under the supervision of a senior detective, provides both continuity and a point of contact with the complainer throughout the whole case, even after any trial. Her duties thus include investigation and support for the victim. Among other topics in their training, such as the relevant law and an understanding of the psychological impact of these offences on the victims, we include detailed accounts of the medical examination and of the requirements of the forensic scientist. Members of this unit — and I must emphasise that they are available at all hours throughout the Region — are aware of what is good practice for doctors to follow, they know what samples are needed, what information must be passed to the laboratory. There is a form which accompanies label products (anglice exhibits) to the laboratory; its proper completion is the responsibility jointly of doctor and policewoman. As information on the form includes matter which will not generally be admissible in court, it does not become one of the case papers. We believe it valuable in principle to have both doctor and policewoman consider each other part of the same team. "Team" does, of course, imply a sporting analogy and I wonder if that is not a danger. All of us have, I suppose, an underlying feeling that we work in the interests of justice. Our concept of this may be somewhat vague, perhaps idealistic. Probably only the legally qualified among us have given much thought to jurisprudence as an idea, or had the opportunity to study the theoretical basis of legal systems or to consider in depth the complexities of the rules of evidence.

Most of us here are more practical people or indeed we would not have come to look at the practical uses of the forensic sciences. Dr Rodger, in his capacity as President of the Forensic Science Society gave a paper last year (1) at the Society's Autumn Symposium in which he indulged in that time honoured activity of presidents, namely, the inspection of a collective navel, in his case, that of forensic science. Although my usual area of operations is some distance below the umbilicus I thought I might look rather at the navels of various others.

Let me start with the courts. Here in Glasgow we have a court usually described by the scribblers as the busiest in Europe. It is about to move into new premises where no expense has been spared in their embellishment. But, then, money is always available for law and order, is it not? Justice should be done in dignified surroundings, and why not its acolytes work in reasonable comfort?

Only a few days ago H.M. Chief Inspector of Constabulary was urging the police committee in Strathclyde to spend more money on policing the Region. He is reported as saying, "The cumulative effect of cutbacks over the past five years is that the effectiveness of the force in meeting its statutory obligations to the community, particularly regarding the more serious offences, is being greatly diminished."

It is not disputed, I think, that so long as they spend sufficient time in the one locality to be recognised and to get to know the inhabitants, the presence of officers on the street will act as a deterrent to the unlawful. How many more officers would be available if those in charge of administering courts were obliged to consider the waste of police manpower day in, day out, as they sit waiting to give evidence. The forensic scientists are better served, even although from the Strathclyde Laboratory they are cited to courts all over Scotland, yet in 1985 the 13 court-going scientists wasted 254 hours in fruitless attendance in 80 cases when they were not called to the witness box. This contrasts with 1170 hours when they did give evidence in 330 cases. Often many more cases are called than can be dealt with lest the calendar collapse and, horror of horrors, a judge might be kept waiting. Judges are, of course, awesome personages, but have they the least idea of the problems their attitude causes, or what is interpreted lower down the ranks as their attitude? When I first gave evidence as an expert in the High Court in Glasgow, cases were never heard in the months of April and August and seldom occupied more than the first two weeks of any month. My own holidays were always arranged to take account of this routine, but why, even then, there should have been a sitting in July, the month in which comes the main Glasgow holiday, was a mystery. Now the High Courts sit all over the Region, often in unsuitable accommodation. No doubt this should bring justice nearer the communities where crime is committed, but it involves professional witnesses in a great deal of travelling, taking them away from other work. It adds to the disruption of social as well as working routines. Who thinks of the difficulties of explaining to a wife and family when a well deserved holiday is ruined? My worst experience is travelling from a resort near Aberdeen to Glasgow three times within five days. I say this acknowledging that court officials have frequently gone to great lengths to manoeuvre me in and out at top speed. It cannot be beyond the wit of those civil servants who manage such matters to improve procedures, or do I misjudge the civil service?

Some twelve years ago, with the Assistant Chief Constable in charge of crime in Glasgow, I went to look at the forensic science facilities provided in the West Midlands and in the Metropolis, for we were unsure at that time what was the proper role of police laboratories. We were struck by the concern expressed in both laboratories that the court-going of scientists had been reduced to such an extent that few had sufficient experience of giving oral evidence.

In any trial, it is well understood that the evidence of a single witness is never enough to sustain a conviction (except in some statutory instances) but must be supported by at least one other. This doctrine of corroboration poses particular difficulties in sexual assault, for the victim's evidence must be corroborated by that of other witnesses. In many such cases sufficient evidence is not available, so conviction cannot be safe. Where the incident complained of is one of a series involving the same, or several victims, corroboration may be achieved under another doctrine known as Moorov. In Moorov (2), an employer was charged with a series of indecent assaults on female employees over a period of about four years. No single offence could be corroborated, but the course of conduct revealed by the individual events was sufficient to support conviction.

Again and again, where a single incident, usually against a child, has caused no physical injury, has left no trace, the difficulties of securing a conviction must be carefully explained to parents and, if possible, to the complainer also. That justice must remain even handed is hard for the wronged to accept, but I for one see no escape from this evidential cul-de-sac. Beltrami recounts (3) the case of a 25-year-old teacher falsely, indeed diabolically, accused by two of his pupils aged 13. He was charged that he had unlawful sexual intercourse with them both on two occasions and with one of them thrice. At first sight the evidence, though largely circumstantial, was damning. The author's forensic skill enabled him to destroy the girls' evidence, yet it took the jury two hours to acquit the panel. The medical evidence was so inconclusive on the state of virginity of the complainers that it was joshed in the pages of *Punch*. I dare to hope that similar circumstances investigated today, by police, doctors and the Crown, would be better elucidated. Despite the apparent lessons of that case, my own experience does not suggest that there are many totally false accusations of rape or indecent assault, but there are certainly some and some complainers do gild the lily.

Having mentioned a legal principle, it is perhaps apposite to make the point that statute enshrines the superiority of the police and forensic scientist in Scotland over those south of the border. Only a few weeks ago a particularly nasty crime in London attracted a great deal of publicity. In due course arrests were made. From this distance it seemed astonishing that prisoners could be held in custody for so many hours before being charged. Had the police been operating under the Criminal Justice (Scotland) Act, 1980 they would have been allowed to hold a suspect for questioning for a period of only six hours from the moment of detention. Thereafter, he must be formally arrested and charged, with all that that implies in the change of the prisoner's status. Thereafter prisoners must be released, or alternatively held in custody to appear on the next lawful day in court. If not arrested, they must be liberated and cannot again be detained on a matter arising from the same circumstances. Contrast that procedure with the 36 hours available under the Police and Criminal Evidence Act 1984. Furthermore, an indictment here must normally be served on an accused who is still in custody before the expiry of 60 days to allow his defence to be prepared. The trial must conclude within 110 days. The pressure of such a timetable on laboratory staff is enormous.

Violence has been implicated as the fundamental cause of rape. Locally, this view has been promoted by the husband and wife team of Dobash from Stirling University, it is repeated in publications of the Rape Crisis sorority and has become an assumption in articles in the ordinary press. To find support for this view the author has reviewed cases with which he has been concerned over the past year. It should be explained that the author seldom sees victims shortly after the complaint is made.

Particular cases may be referred because the police surgeon has doubts about the significance of his findings or the police feel the need for clarification of some aspect, often after further investigation, or the fiscal wishes his evidence to be strengthened. In every other clinical situation doctors of first instance have the right and the duty to seek a second opinion in appropriate circumstances. These circumstances arise for many reasons, perhaps because the doctor has not experienced the particular appearances before. In sexual assault cases nuances of history, variations in what may be considered normal anatomy, the effects of previous sexual activity, the complications of infection, poor hygiene, all of these may compound the police surgeon's problems. This is nothing we should be ashamed of. No one has a monopoly of wisdom, of infallible insight. The knowledge, too, that a second examination may take place could act as a cautionary influence on police surgeons. Over and above the further embarrassment to the victim, it has been objected that two examinations allow the defence to make hay with different reports, but appearances do alter with time and the skilled professional witness ought to be able to cope with counsel's attempts at obfuscation.

At any rate, all of these factors render the author's cases atypical but nevertheless worthy of some analysis. Over the 12 months, February 1985 to January 1986, were seen 61 female victims of rape, assault with intent to ravish, incest or the like, or at least where serious allegations had been made, almost all for the purpose of giving a second opinion. Again, to put these figures in context, rapes reported to the police in Strathclyde last year numbered 170. Their average age works out at $23\frac{3}{4}$ but the modal was 14. A quarter were aged 13, 14 and 15 with more than half in their second decade.

Of the nine who were 12 and under, three involved incestuous or near incestuous intercourse, with two others subjected to incestuous conduct not amounting to intercourse; three involved male baby-sitters (although it does not take hindsight to discern their individual unsuitability for such a task), two of whom had conducted themselves in a lewd and libidinous fashion, with one where there was almost certainly no sexual activity, but a fall, and the remaining "victim", a girl of 11, had been attempting intercourse with a boy who, having kissed, told, so that it came to attention, thereby necessitating some embroidery on her part.

In all there were 12 cases of incest, or attempts, or similar conduct, one coming to light only years later. She had had a child to one brother, although more than one had intercourse with her. Her child's father returned to the home after a long absence and tried to resume the practice; at first she tolerated it, possibly because a serious head injury sustained in a road traffic accident when one of her brothers was chasing her, had dulled her senses.

In only four instances did the complainer's history seem wholly or mainly fictitious, but two of these fall within the simple minded or educationally sub-normal category, numbering in total five. It may be objected that just such children, who require more care than most, most deserve to be believed. It must be said that their stories require not less, but possibly more investigation. Their often tragic lives, the handicaps they bear, induce in us a great measure of instant sympathy, but that should not cloud our minds to their powers of imagination. Alcohol was a significant factor, in a quarter of the cases, most strikingly in one girl of 13 and two of 14.

In most of 16 and over, only 7 experienced violence out of proportion to the immediate needs of the assailant, or had perverted acts performed upon them. It is not easy to accept, therefore, that violence or domination or sadism was the motive force behind many of these crimes.

That any male should commit opportunistic rape, as so many commit opportunistic theft, is heinous. Setting aside for the moment the many difficult aspects of consent (which is really at the heart of the matter) the criminology of rape is not at all clear. American experience cannot be extrapolated to this society. Ideally, we should have a properly constructed, disinterested investigation divorced from the prosecution process to elucidate why individuals have raped, whether and how they planned the attack, what emotions they experience, where (if at all) they find normal sexual satisfaction. Enquiry by interview, months after the event, depending on anecdote will not do. Our own emotions and prejudices vitiate retrospective studies, however controlled according to sociological tenets they may be. We are bedevilled by misunderstanding, by a lack of satisfactory definition. I have argued often that the very word rape is a hindrance; we should give serious thought to treating these crimes as a species of aggravated assault.

Another area of misunderstanding concerns that great public health problem of our time, the epidemic of hepatitis B and AIDS. This has been described (4) as generating "the latest manifestation of fear, prejudice, ignorance and professional disarray.... The high prevalence of the disease among homosexuals has caused an already suspect, heretical and despised minority to suffer greatly. For some religious fanatics, AIDS is the judgement of God on these flouters of his law; and among vindictive and self-righteous haters of homosexuals, great satisfaction is taken from this evidence of divine (or earthly) punishment."

The belief "that premarital sex causes venereal diseases, that homosexuality causes AIDS" may be denied (5) on the grounds that "infectious diseases are caused by an infective agent and not by sinful behaviour" but such an argument is sophism.

One does not need to be a religious fanatic, nor a self-righteous hater of homosexuals to see that a reduction in promiscuous behaviour will reduce the spread of the disease; were abusers of intravenous drugs to eschew the habit of sharing equipment (6) (to many a part of the ritual), the spread of AIDS and hepatitis would lessen. The compassion required of the medical profession in dealing with individual sufferers must not inhibit us from taking a moral stance, and it is a moral matter. These problems, and the drive to assault and terrorise women indicate the depths of spiritual poverty we in this society have reached.

Police officers participate in the fear engendered by this epidemic, for in the nature of things they deal with those most likely to be carriers. The author already quoted (4) comments in amazement that police officers should charge an AIDS patient with "assault with intent to murder" because he spat on them. We are fortunate here that the fiscal has secured a conviction on the basis that the spitting assailant knew he was a carrier of hepatitis B and knew the fear and alarm this would provoke. Twelve per cent of drug abusers attending for treatment in Glasgow have current hepatitis B infection and only 30 per cent show no evidence of past or current infection. About 5 per cent have proved positive for HTLV–III infection, over 90 per cent of whom in turn had markers of current or past hepatitis B infection. Sixty per cent of all acute cases of hepatitis B in the West of Scotland are related to drug abuse (7).

Police officers are not considered to fall within the high risk group of workers but it has been argued (8) that they should be protected by vaccination against hepatitis B. We in Strathclyde, with the willing cooperation of colleagues in the Blood Transfusion Service, have established the routine use of specific immunoglobulin on exposure to infection. Such injections give a fair degree of short-lived passive immunity to the disease. Regular assays of serum are made after the injection. We believe this, at the moment, to be a procedure which, if followed, will be effective. There is, not unnaturally, some confusion in the minds of officers about the difference between active and passive immunity, between hepatitis vaccination and injections of immunoglobulin. It is to be regretted that such confusion exists also in some areas of medical practice. The whole matter is subject to guidance from the Scottish Home and Health Department in a document (9) not characterised by clarity of thought and expression.

Confusion is compounded by journalists who ought to ensure that they are better informed. In one local newspaper an article based on the death of one of our officers began,

> "Scottish policemen are living in fear of contracting the deadly liver disease hepatitis B from infected drug addicts. In the last year 25 Scots police officers working in Glasgow, Edinburgh and Tayside have caught the disease after being either bitten, scratched or spat on by drug addicts. In 1984 there were only 4 cases. Some police officers, particularly in Edinburgh, have also been injured by addicts who were AIDS carriers."

The unfortunate officer had, indeed, been spat upon but this had not the slightest connection with his death. Moreover, it is quite untrue that 25 officers have contracted the disease. I have quoted one newspaper, but its contemporaries were no more careful in their statements.

What better is to be expected of hacks whose command of English is nowadays so poor that they cannot punctuate, cannot handle our few irregular verbs, cannot distinguish pairs of words such as appraise and apprise. Perhaps that may explain why 25 officers are said to have contracted a disease they may simply have contacted. In my persona of editor of the Journal of the Association of Police Surgeons of Great Britain, I despair of the many similar faults in manuscripts. How far we have sunk when the works of Richmal Crompton could recently be held up as examples of writing full of concepts, liberally sprinkled with polysyllables, clearly familiar to the boys who read of Just William's adventures when the books were published.

English is the greatest handmaiden of all, an abstraction with a soul. How we neglect our language! Listen to those who con'tribute to a dis'pute, who fail to alter emphasis in distinguishing nouns and verbs such as pro'test and prote'st, who try to make us say kilo'meter while treasonable clerks stand aside, telling us that dictionaries are descriptive, not normative. Why should anyone consult a dictionary, if not to confirm spelling and pronunciation? The purpose of speaking and writing, to communicate thought and opinions, is impeded by the lack of clarity which accompanies all these faults.

To descend, however, from a hobby horse, we must return to the first mentioned handmaidens. Is there still a job for police surgeons to do? Some years ago the author was asked to speak to a detective training course in Canada where police surgeons on our pattern are, or were then, unknown. Arrangements for clinical examinations were haphazard, depending largely on the goodwill of casualty officers. In this country police surgeons deal with sudden and suspicious deaths, they examine cases of physical and sexual assault, they still see some motorists to assess impairment due to drink or drugs, they are concerned in the large category of fitness for detention where doubts arise because of sickness, injury or mental illness. Most of this is trying work, involving decisions important for the police, the witness or prisoner, the prosecution. Over a period of years it is expected that police surgeons acquire knowledge based on experience as, for example, in non-accidental injury although, here again, their contribution is depreciated (10). Their use of this will depend on enthusiasm and on the stimulus of interest. Of all this work, none provides greater satisfaction than the investigation of sexual assault.

Figures (11) published in 1980 for a rural area suggested that loss of police surgeon income from RTA cases with the introduction of evidential breath machines might well make it not worthwhile for a doctor to make himself available for police calls. This factor must also apply in busier areas, if those doctors now experienced in examining victims of rape are to be deprived of such work on the grounds that examinations should be performed by women. That this is so has been made plain to the author by valued colleagues. In Strathclyde we are attempting to assess how much interest there is in helping us among the 450 female general practitioners. In the six weeks since letters were sent to these doctors we have received a reply from fewer than 5 per cent.

Far be it from me to give any impression that I am too concerned with motes to ignore the beams. Doctors, like other professional groups, must be aware of constructive criticism and, I hope, respond appropriately. Published guidance is available (12) on the contribution doctors should make to the investigation of rape. Its attitudinal aspects are freely discussed (13) by police surgeons. All the more reason, then, with the main body of police surgeons keen to act in the best interest of justice, for precipitate change not to be wrought.

References

1. Rodger, W. J. Forensic science — policy option? *Journal of the Forensic Science Society*, 1986; 24, 69–78.

2. Moorov, 1930, J.C. 68.

3. Beltrami, J. *The Defender*. Edinburgh: W. & R. Chambers Ltd., 1980; 138.

4. Silver, G. Collective madness. *Lancet*, 1986; i: 609.

5. Skrabenek, P. Preventive medicine and morality. *Lancet*, 1986; i: 144.

6. Mulleady, G. and Green, J. Syringe sharing among London drug abusers. *Lancet*, 1985; ii: 1425.

7. Follett, E. A. C., McIntyre, A., O'Donnell, B., Clements, G. B. and Desselberger, U. HTLV–III antibody in drug abusers in the West of Scotland: the Edinburgh connection. *Lancet*, 1986; i: 446.

8. Zuckerman, A. J. Who should be immunised against hepatitis B? *British Medical Journal*, 1984; 289: 1243–1244.

9. Police (CC) Circular 9/1985, Scotland Home and Health Department.

10. Shepherd, R. C. Child abuse inquiries. *Lancet*, 1985; i: 1511.

11. Keighley, B. D. The rural police surgeon — what future? *The Police Surgeon*, 1980; 18: 23–25.

12. The New Police Surgeon — Rape. MacLay, W. D. S. ed., *Association of Police Surgeons of Great Britain*, 1984.

13. Davis, N. The re-education of police personnel in the investigation of sexual offences. *The Police Surgeon*, 1985; 28: 8–14.

FORENSIC MEDICINE — HOW WILL IT DEVELOP?

A. A. Watson

Introduction

Two army officers were discussing battle strategy, in particular the Normandy Landings. One officer proposed that the correct approach should have been an "advance-slowly-and-annihilate" tactic. The other man, of equal military rank, supported the rapid sweep through the countryside forgetting the little pockets of resistance and moving into wide areas. On the one hand we had a slow, thorough advance; on the other hand an all-embracing movement but avoiding any impediment. In military terms, therefore, there was no single solution, and that is how some planners of undergraduate medical education seem to work. One wonders whether the battle planners of the past now sit on the curriculum committees of our medical schools. Sometimes the approaches to medical education seem like a slow but an inexorable advance, while at other times sweeping changes are made with an almost indecent haste.

To be fair to our medical planners, to some extent this is understandable; one would be surprised if recent advances in medicine were not reflected in an altered curriculum in the medical school. We find on the medical scene today such new advances as immunopathology, computerised medicine, community preventive medicine and advances in resuscitation and transplantation. All of these are outstripping the more traditional facets of medicine. The advances are amazing and exciting and quite naturally they attract young, keen and aggressive teachers to their ranks.

But there remain some subjects which cannot be overlooked nor simply swept aside just because their content is less attractive or their basic teaching remains almost unchanged. Returning to our example of military strategies, the entrenched, resistant and difficult areas must be dealt with at the same time and with the same enthusiasm as the rapid forward action into new branches of medicine. The dull areas, the difficult areas of medicine, must be dealt with and must not simply be bypassed and forgotten.

Forensic Medicine is just such an example of a difficult area of medicine. Towards the end of the last century in Scotland, the need for instruction in medico-legal matters was widely acclaimed. Compulsory examinations were established, Chairs were present in the four medical schools. In England, too, the subject of Forensic Medicine held a place of respect and was taught as an important, if not indeed a major subject. But look at it now — since the Second World War the teaching of Forensic Medicine throughout the entire country, with a few notable exceptions, has been in a state of decline. In some medical schools it is not much more than an apology for the subject. In some places the students receive just a few perfunctory lectures and what is worse still, the planners of the medical curricula seem to be disinterested or unconcerned about the state of the subject.

Let us return to the subject itself — What is the problem? When a doctor accepts a request to treat a patient a contractual relationship is established; there is a legal duty of care and this creates rights and obligations between the doctor and his patient; but does the medical student know that? Does he also know that when a doctor neglects to honour his contractual obligations towards his patient, the aggrieved party, namely the patient himself has now accrued rights — rights of action against the doctor? Has anybody told the medical student that? Does he know what it involves?

Another effect of the demotion of Forensic Medicine becomes apparent when one discovers that a young hospital doctor is almost ignorant of the circumstances which require him to notify a death to the legal authorities; occasionally he is almost unsure of how to complete satisfactorily death and cremation certificates. Sometimes one hears almost in quaint naïvety, about a doctor who seems to take upon himself decisions which very properly should be taken by the Coroner or the Procurator Fiscal. Some years ago a young resident surgical officer attempted to give to the relatives a death certificate written in the following terms: (1a) Hypovolaemic shock, due to (1b) Stab wound of the heart (operation) due to (1c) Murder. All of which goes to underline the fact that insufficient instruction in legal medicine had been given to him as an undergraduate.

One other problem, and that concerns the literature on Forensic Medicine. As recently as 15 years ago most of our textbooks laid great emphasis on crimes and accidents involving violence; in fact one could almost say that the textbook was a textbook of "traumatology"; injuries from firearms and all the physical agents were studied in great depth by anecdotes and crime case reports. Nowhere was it stressed that these injuries are relatively rare, or at least uncommon, nor was the fact stressed that the study of such is the prerogative of the forensic medical experts. In summary, the textbooks became studies in forensic pathology to the almost total exclusion of subjects which are necessary to the everyday practising doctor. It is therefore not surprising that as we look back over our shoulder we see that mainly macabre and spectacular cases have been taught to the students, and, in my view, this was probably the main reason for the demotion of Forensic Medicine as a major academic subject.

With hindsight it looks as if the baby just escaped being thrown out with the bathwater, for there was a real danger that the very important subject of doctor–patient relationships, with its emphasis on the teaching of Medical Ethics and Professionalism, was to have been jettisoned along with all the other so-called unnecessary parts of Forensic Medicine. It is not really surprising, therefore, that many medical schools decided to do away with it altogether, or as far as they could within the restrictive limits of the General Medical Council. There is therefore a need to re-examine the subject of Forensic Medicine. From the standpoint of the emerging young doctor, he is the man that we should be considering before we advance into more exciting areas.

Which are the areas of resistance and difficulty? Can the doctor sign a Death Certificate? Can he write a medical report? Does he know how to present himself before lawyers and the Court? Does he understand the problems of medical negligence, consent to treatment and confidentiality? If insufficient instruction is given in these areas it can only be to the detriment of medicine as a whole and to the individual doctor in particular.

The Present Situation

Let us review the status of Forensic Medicine as it stands today in Scotland. The subject is taught in the four medical schools. The oldest department was headed by a Regius Professorship established in Edinburgh. However, the present incumbent has retired and there appear to be no plans at the moment for re-advertising the post for at least several years. This, I find deplorable. The reasons for this are not clear and must be found within the internal workings of Edinburgh University. The situation in Dundee and Aberdeen is more healthy in that there are lecturers in post who have responsibility for regular lecturing to the students. However, there is no compulsory examination and the students attend very much on a voluntary basis.

The situation in Glasgow is much more healthy; there has been, since 1839, an unbroken succession of Regius Professors and the eighth is now in post. Formal didactic teaching over two terms is given in the fourth year of the medical course followed by a compulsory written examination. Prizes are awarded and these include a Gold Medal and monetary prizes from a number of sources. There is therefore an incentive to the medical student to do well. Similarly, lectures are given to dental, legal and nursing students, as well as to a number of non-academic bodies. The situation in the Law Faculty is most interesting. The law students choose many of their subjects for their law degree, there being no set course for any particular student. Therefore, it is interesting to note that nearly 90 per cent of the students choose to take Forensic Medicine as part of their Ordinary course in their second year at Law School. Many of the students proceed to the Advanced or Junior honours course in their third year and probably 20–25 per cent go on further to take their LLB honours course in Forensic Medicine each year. They therefore graduate LLB honours in Forensic Medicine, with considerable knowledge, far and above that given to any other undergraduate in the University. It is a popular course, indeed the most popular Honours course in the Law Faculty and it augurs well for the future of the subject, although whether it augurs well for the young doctor who finds himself in front of one of these lawyers with a greater knowledge of the subject than himself, is debatable.

The Future

Where do we plan to go in the future? There was a Wise Man who, nearly two thousand years ago told a very simple story and was well known to children. It concerns two men who built their houses. One man built his house on the rock, the other built it on the sand. The result was that when the houses were exposed to the difficulties of the sea and the vicissitudes of the weather, the one that had a sandy, unstable foundation tumbled. A really simple illustration, but quite profound. Leaving aside the theological content I think there is a lot to be learned by all of us whether our subjects be Forensic Science or Forensic Medicine. It teaches us that we need, at all times, to check the educational foundations of our taught courses and the general teaching techniques in our departments. Have we based them on solid teaching? Has the structure grown up slowly and has it been consolidated at each stage of its growth? This is one thing that is clearly brought home to us when we lecture to the law students. In a forensic medicine class of nearly 90 law students each year there are probably 60–70 students who have never had a biological lesson at school in their lives! Without wishing to criticise the educational system in our schools, it can easily be seen that to teach matters of science and medicine — in particular medicine — when there is no biological foundation, is fraught with a degree of danger. They may absorb the subject as a subject with the trimmings and all the anecdotal illustrations which are given, but do they really understand the subject? In the case of the heart and coronary arteries, do they really understand the basic physiology, the general anatomy and therefore the principles of pathology, because this is essential if they are to understand a medico-legal problem involving a man suffering from chronic heart disease who suddenly dies on some form of an altercation. The question that must be answered is who or what was responsible for the man's death? It is incumbent on us as teachers to inculcate as much of the patho-physiological background as we can, so that the lawyer can have a reasonable chance to understand our explanation when we discuss the case either in open court or by means of a medical report. We are just as concerned that all our medical, dental and nursing students follow these academic and legal lines of thought just as closely as the law students.

Forensic Medicine — How will it Develop?

1. *Having Regard to our Foundations*

As we look forward into new medical problems and scientific research and at advancing techniques we must also look back. It is like the Roman god Janus worshipped at the beginning of the year. He had two heads: for looking forward and looking back. There is little point in having postgraduate examinations and postgraduate students doing research if their very basis is shaky. So in answering the question "Where are we going?" firstly we are going backwards to make sure that our foundations of medicine, pathology and the simple rules of evidence and procedure are thoroughly understood, and taught. It is essential that we teach our students a close examination of small points of detail. We need to stress the importance of taking time to examine a body to exclude criminality as far as it is possible. We must teach the need for close and careful thought in completing a simple medical report such as a Death Certificate. At all times, we must make our doctors safe doctors. It is only when we have the foundation correct; when our lecture notes are checked year by year for accuracy, not only in the content but with regard to recent legislation and recent developments, that our lectures can be said to be good and therefore useful in establishing good foundations. What I have said about teaching in medicine applies equally to teaching in toxicology and the forensic services and I imagine too, each reader who has responsibilities in teaching will agree that this is an important step. We must look back before we look forward. The god Janus had two heads; we only have one head, but we must keep it swivelling backwards and forwards. Only when we are satisfied that our background knowledge, both personal and departmental is satisfactory, and we are content that we can hold our heads high in regard to our own particular subjects, are we then in a position to look for developments in the future.

2. *Under the Wing of a Larger Authority*

In Scotland we are fortunate in having had published the Bowen-McCluskey report (1). This has now brought under the aegis of the Crown

Office in Edinburgh, the four medical schools teaching Forensic Medicine. I can only speak for Glasgow, although I have some idea of how it works in the three other schools.

In Glasgow, much of the day-to-day routine work is handled by three senior pathologists. We have the assistance of National Health Service doctors when the workload becomes just too great. We are therefore relieved of the burden to try and do every case that presents itself. In some parts of the U.K. the pathologist is out all day and almost every day doing nothing else than routine service work. That cannot be good for the pathologist nor for his department. We provide a service not only for the areas supplied by the Fiscals in Glasgow, Airdrie, Hamilton and Dumbarton, but we have a watching brief for Paisley, Greenock and elsewhere in the south and south-west of the country. To a lesser extent we are also invited to oversee the work of some of the other Fiscals in the west and north of Scotland. All of this work is done under the direction and control of the Crown Office in Edinburgh.

3. *By a closer Cooperation with Scientists, Police, Prosecution and Defence Lawyers and with other Interested Bodies*

We have developed under our wing a good toxicological sub-department. This is highly essential, to have the toxicology department working as close as possible to forensic pathology. Experiences of this in England where material was posted some distance away and from which a factual report was received without comment and without identification of the operator showed that it was almost impossible to have a meaningful discussion over the results. In Glasgow, we are blessed with a scheme whereby the toxicologist and the pathologist are in the same building, and the scientists are not far away. This enables a dialogue to take place and encourages understanding and a respect for one another so that the agreed laboratory result has a degree of meaning which otherwise would not be present in the post-mortem or medical report.

This may not always be possible, but it is essential to encourage a closer cooperation between forensic toxicology and, indeed, all branches of forensic science and the medical people. Remember that scientists and medical practitioners speak two different languages. Our thought processes are different, and as we must write our reports for the understanding of lawyers, closer cooperation between scientists, doctors and lawyers, each trying to learn the other's language, can only be for the good of forensic sciences and forensic medicine. In summary, development comes from teamwork between the interested parties.

4. *In the Area of Postgraduate Education*

In Glasgow we have a Master of Science Degree for forensic pathology and a similar degree, together with a Diploma, for forensic toxicology. We have had our first graduates successfully pass these examinations. These are taught courses with dissertations. We have now PhD students in medicine and science amd LLM students in law, all within the department. Within the last few weeks, we have broken new ground in that we will be able to offer a Diploma in Forensic Medicine which I think is unique in that it will be open to graduates of medicine, science, law and social sciences. The object is to have a postgraduate Diploma which is orientated around the court room. It is in this area that the greatest ignorance is displayed between the three disciplines.

It is often displayed in front of the general public and the press. We believe in Glasgow that a Diploma aimed at all three disciplines, each being taught within the same course framework, with a common examination and a common Diploma to be gained, would be to the advantage of the Court.

5. *In Scientific Research*

There are many areas of medical research to be explored. For example, we do not understand why the chronic alcoholic should suddenly drop dead. We do not really understand the process of drowning. We do not really understand the problems of electrocution and why some die at a lower voltage than others and why some do not die until after a long period, once the electric current has been switched off. These are just a few examples from many areas to be explored. We are still remarkably ignorant on the effects of drugs on different anatomical systems. In this respect we would welcome manufacturers of scientific materials to show an interest in the special needs of the forensic pathologists as well as the scientists.

Forensic Medicine has been a subject to which many people have turned in their plight and almost in desperation. Over the last 15 years many problems have been sent to us after having been sent first to other areas of research and study, rather like the patient who has been seen by the general practitioner, then sent to the hospital, and having been passed from one specialist to another, all in vain, finally ends up on the psychiatrist's couch. Many medical problems seen by the forensic pathologist have been sent to us not as a first-line of attack but often accompanied by a despairing comment "let us try Forensic and see if they can come up with anything". In some ways this can be flattering that we are considered at all, but I would like it to be seen that Forensic Medicine can offer something to our clinical and pathological colleagues much earlier in their investigations.

Our way forward is to work closer with all the other disciplines. In the past we have held ourselves aloof, distancing ourselves from colleagues. There has been the feeling that we have somehow got the ear of the lawyer, that we seem to be the guardian of the mores of medicine. To some, we have given the impression of being unapproachable because of the way that we can speak in court and the lawyers accept our dicta. This has to stop. We must be seen to be part not only of a medical team but equally part of the whole investigation of the case which has a medico-legal content.

In conclusion, we look back to our basic roots, to check that everything is in order, and we also look to the development of the subject which I think now has a healthy future. What is being done in Glasgow I believe can be done elsewhere. But we need a fair share of wisdom and understanding to do it. Perhaps we should reflect on that well-known prayer which goes "Lord, give me the courage to change the things that I can, the serenity to accept the things that I cannot change and the wisdom to know the difference."

References

1. A Joint Scottish Home and Health Department and Crown Office Report of Forensic Pathology Services in Scotland. Edinburgh, 1982.

POLICE

INTERPOL TODAY

R. G. Kendall

Experience dictates that for most audiences, even those consisting of professional police officers, it is necessary to describe the Organisation and its functions as there are often many misconceptions, not helped by an exaggerated image which would have us be international agents involved in James Bond type activity. For this reason it becomes necessary to review Interpol yesterday.

The Organisation's origin is credited to Prince Albert I of Monaco, a researcher of considerable foresight and scientific ability who, as you are no doubt aware, founded the most famous Oceanographic Institute of Capitaine Cousteau fame. In April 1914 he called an international conference on crime which was attended by police officials and lawyers from some two dozen countries. Discussions were centred on observations that criminals were able to move easily from one country to another, thus evading arrest and prosecution because legal authority in no way extended beyond national borders. The then new means of transport, railways and motor cars, were making it possible for criminals to leave police disarmed to a large extent in the face of this new mobility. International co-operation and extradition were discussed as well as the possibility of setting up an international criminal records system.

A second meeting was planned but the outbreak of war in 1914 temporarily put an end to any further development.

The break-up of the Austro-Hungarian Empire in 1919 as well as certain political instability following the war years engendered the continuing evolution and growth of crime of an international nature. In 1923 the then Commissioner of Police of Vienna, Dr Johan Schober, revived the idea behind the 1914 Monaco Conference and called a meeting of some twenty countries with a view to setting up an International Police Organisation. The International Criminal Police Commission was born and a small headquarters was set up in Vienna under the presidency of Dr Schober, and General Assemblies were held. The general assembly agendas did not differ to a great extent from those of today in that the subject matter was very similar: how to control such international types of crime as illicit drug trafficking, and theft, economic crimes and currency counterfeiting.

It was the involvement concerning currency counterfeiting which first gave Interpol true international recognition. In 1929, as a result of initiatives taken in the then newly formed League of Nations, the 1929 Geneva Convention on the suppression of Counterfeit Currency was adopted.

It provided that currency counterfeiting be regarded as both a national and an international crime, irrespective of the country's money which was being counterfeited. More importantly it provided for the centralisation and co-ordination of law enforcement activity in this domain by the International Criminal Police Commission. Interpol carries on this 1929 Convention role to this day.

In 1939 Nazi Germany invaded Austria and took over the Commission's headquarters. The headquarters was transferred to Berlin by a constitutional subterfuge and the Organisation seems to have continued to function throughout the war years, notably within the occupied countries. This fact and the effect that it may have had on the Organisation's reputation in the years following the Second World War merit discussion but space does not permit this interesting subject to be developed.

In 1946 some senior police officers who had been members of the Commission before the war met in Brussels and the Organisation was reborn. Its headquarters was established in Paris (there was a choice between Paris, The Hague and Prague) first in the national police headquarters and finally, in 1966, in a specially constructed building in the suburb of St Cloud which is where it is housed today.

So much briefly for yesterday. What about today?

Firstly some brief facts. There are now 138 Member Countries and two more have applied to join in 1986. The Headquarters in Paris has a staff of some 270 of which there are 60 or more police officers from countries all over the world. Since 1985, for the first time in its post-war history, it is under the direction of a non-French Secretary General. Interpol is undergoing a complete modernisation of its telecommunications facilities as well as of its internal electronic data processing possibilities. It will move to a new custom-built headquarters in the central French town of Lyons in 1988. The Organisation is at a new turning point in its history. It does, however, have to come to terms with a multiplicity of mainly political initiatives over which it has little control. This is particularly so since the creation of such political entities as the European Economic Community. There is an increased emphasis on the development of regional activities which, whilst they are a necessity, may to a certain degree hinder or slow down a global approach to dealing with certain types of criminality.

The old expression "long arm of the law" takes on a new meaning in the context of the possibilities offered by Interpol. The "arm" can now circle the world with minor exceptions. The police resources of 138 nations are available to the investigator who finds himself confronted, as he more and more frequently does, with a crime with international implications. Interpol provides the only practical means by which many law enforcement authorities can follow up a criminal matter beyond their national boundary. They have at their disposal a telecommunications network which handles hundreds of telegrams a day; a headquarters which is gradually becoming an efficient crime information system; the possibility to have published international preventive and wanted notices on individuals as well as information concerning particular types of crime. To do this without Interpol, a national police department would need personnel with foreign language capabilities, with a knowledge of other countries' criminal codes and justice procedures, a personnel with sufficient contacts to establish credibility with the appropriate authorities in other countries. A considerable budget for travel and communications would also be required.

The value of the international notice can be illustrated by the fact that the Italian police were quickly able to identify Ali Agca as the would-be assassin of the Pope by virtue of the fact that his fingerprints were in their records having appeared on an Interpol wanted notice for murders committed in

Turkey. The communications network enabled them to establish that the automatic weapon used had been manufactured in Belgium, legitimately exported to Switzerland, legally exported again to Austria where it was illegally delivered by a shady arms dealer who was identified.

In terms of budget, the Organisation is financed by contributions from its Member States. The present annual budget voted and approved by the General Assembly which meets once a year is in the region of 16,000,000 Swiss francs (our predecessors wisely established the budget in this currency) or approximately £5,000,000. For the services rendered this sum is very small and represents less than one per cent of the total budget which most countries contribute to all international organisations. It is derisory when compared to national expenditure on law enforcement. The growing significance of international crime will necessarily require a change of attitude in relation to budgetary matters where, as you can imagine, restriction and constraint are the watchwords.

It would be remiss of any recent article about Interpol not to mention what is considered to be a major international crime problem today — terrorism.

Interpol has in its constitution, adopted in 1956, an article which forbids it from dealing with matters of a racial, religious, political or military nature. There was a mistaken idea when terrorism, as we know it today, began to manifest itself in the early 1970s that because it was generally politically motivated it could not be the subject of international co-operation through Interpol channels. Nothing could be further from the truth. Terrorist acts are examined in the context of the circumstances in which they take place, as ordinary law serious crimes, the motivation taking second place. It is clear that an international police organisation could not ignore such offences as aircraft hijacking, hostagetaking and bomb attacks, simply because the perpetrators claim political motivation. The Organisation has clearly established its guidelines and doctrine for dealing with such offences in a series of general assembly resolutions over the last few years which have translated themselves into a practical reality by the creation within the General Secretariat since January this year, of a specialist group to deal with terrorist matters. The development of activity in this domain is already necessitating a re-enforcement of personnel in this area. This activity takes place in the context of the Police Division of the Secretariat but there are other secretariat activities which are more closely akin to your own areas of interest.

Over the past fifteen years there have been seven international forensic science symposia held at the General Secretariat, the last being in December 1983 and the next planned for December 1986. Lists of reference collections established by forensic science laboratories throughout the world, are published periodically, the last list being published in 1980 and no doubt in need of updating. In recent years a proposal has been examined to establish an international institute of criminalistics and forensic science. This proposal is now being examined more particularly in relation to cost and viability. We are being pressed, notably by certain European countries to carry out a more important co-ordinating role in relation to activity in the forensic science area. I personally have mixed feelings about this and feel that this is more a matter for the professionals themselves in this field who already seem to be relatively well organised. It would be interesting to receive views as to the usefulness of the Interpol forum for the development of Forensic Science activities at an international level.

Interpol does have one excellent example of a multi-disciplinary approach to dealing with a common international problem and that is in the area of disaster victim identification. A permanent working group on this subject has produced an internationally accepted disaster victim identification form and this has been used in incidents recently. The same group has also prepared a disaster victim identification manual which is in the course of publication.

Interpol has its critics, particularly in times when the management efficiency and effectiveness of some major international organisations have recently come under scrutiny. Some of the criticisms are justified, particularly in relation to the response to modern technology. The governing bodies of the organisation, the General Assembly and the Executive Committee under the guidance of its President, John Simpson, Head of the United States Secret Service, have addressed this issue and as mentioned previously, considerable investment has been approved for modernisation. This is important for a police organisation which has a semi-operational role.

Free progress will not, however, be achieved unless there is a political will to do so. There are increasing indications of interest in Interpol at government level. Many of our smallest meetings now take place under the patronage of senior government officials. A recent drugs meeting in Pakistan was hosted by President Zia himself, a counterfeit currency course in Peru was held under the direct patronage of the Minister of the Interior and perhaps more importantly the General Assembly in Washington last October was addressed by President Reagan. The principle of universality practised by the Organisation offers interesting possibilities in a world where political differences are accorded exaggerated significance. At the same meeting, mentioned previously on drugs, representatives of two countries at war, Iraq and Iran, sat at the same table to discuss a mutual law enforcement problem. Likewise Israeli and Arab representatives will meet together in two weeks time at an Asian Regional Conference where general crime problems will be discussed. This means that the Organisation provides a possibility of international concourse which transcends to a large extent political interests and which, by its professional approach to important human problems of a global nature, can achieve positive results.

CAN TECHNOLOGY REPLACE DETECTIVE SKILLS?

B. D. K. Price

A Professor of Chemistry at the University College, Hull, in an essay entitled "Scientific Aids in Criminal Investigation" published 50 years ago (1) had this to say, "It has been said that the three qualities which make a successful detective are Tact, Patience and Perseverance and it is owing to the possession or cultivation of these qualities by most members of detective forces that the incidence of crime in this country has been kept within reasonable limits." He went on to say, "Other countries in which serious crimes were more numerous and varied found it necessary, as long ago as the last quarter of the last century, to resort to means other than the natural gifts of their police officers to maintain the upper hand in the perpetual struggle of society against the criminal. Austria, Germany and France, among others, recognised the help that science is able to give a detective officer in his work and each, in various ways and in different degrees, built up in the early years of the present century, organisations in which, by co-operation between their police force and workers skilled in chemistry, biology and other sciences, the maximum efficiency was secured for their forces in the fight against crime. Great Britain has lagged behind in this progress of police organisation."

He reasoned that there was a reluctance to submit to a criminal court, evidence based on scientific observations of a type with which the man in the street is unfamiliar because in some way it breached our proudly proclaimed principle of a fair trial for those accused of crime.

His essay, of course, was written some 50 years ago and those of you with a better knowledge of the history of forensic science may rightly claim that Tryhorn was exaggerating when claiming we were lagging behind in the 1930s and you will point to the many celebrated cases, some still quoted today, where scientific evidence was a significant factor in bringing the offender to justice. But looking at the general availability of this type of evidence in other parts of Europe in the 1930s, we were very much the backmarkers in the United Kingdom.

What cannot be challenged, and what must be emphasised, is the manner in which forensic science in the United Kingdom, particularly post-war, has moved forward and in consequence has pushed back the boundaries of knowledge of forensic evidence so that we are now rightly acknowledged as leaders of the world in many fields. Even so, in the wider context of using this scientific knowledge as compelling evidence in our courts, we are still lagging behind. Unfortunately there is in some quarters still a reluctance to acknowledge that such evidence is necessary in crimes other than those that are labelled "serious".

Perhaps doubts still linger as to whether it is morally just to bring forward evidence that cannot be understood by a jury let alone an accused. It is the author's belief that the next few years will prove to be a watershed for the forensic science service as currently organised in England and Wales.

In our system of law it has always been a matter of great difficulty to furnish legal proof of guilt in a criminal trial. It is natural, therefore, that any system of acquiring evidence, which places a suspect at the scene of a crime, is highly prized among investigators and, of course, a major bench mark in this aspect of investigation was the eventual acceptance that Sir William Herschel and Dr Henry Faulds had something, when they asserted that each of us is possessed of a unique arrangement of ridge patterns on our fingers. This acceptance was late in coming.

A committee appointed by Asquith in 1894 to report on "the identification of habitual criminals" was not greatly impressed by the evidence presented to it, even though a system of identification based on the same principles was already in being in parts of India and proving a great success.

It was not until 1903, following two further high-powered committees, that the principle was adopted in Britain and evidence of fingerprint identification was allowed in court.

The first case in which it was used was one of burglary at Windsor, where a mark was discovered on a lantern used during the commission of the offence. It was identified as coming from an old lag named Wilson and it is amusing to recall that he challenged the validity of this evidence claiming that it was, "a hazy and fallacious method imported from France where many innocent men had been condemned by it". What has happened to this most singularly effective weapon in the armoury of detectives since those early days?

The obvious response has been that persistent offenders have, over the years, taken much care to ensure they do not leave their marks behind. Even so, they still make occasional mistakes. However, the real blunting of the weapon has occurred through our increasing inability to compare marks found at the scenes of crime with the total or major part of the collection held at the National Identification Bureau. This collection houses in excess of 3·7 million. Because of these numbers, there now has to be a most compelling case arising from the most notorious of crimes, before a full search of the main collection can be justified. It is rarely done in practice, the majority of manual searching of this nature being carried out in the various local bureaus containing local collections; even then the search is restricted.

The mobility of criminals and their ability to switch from one type of crime to another has made a nonsense of these localised and restricted arrangements and whilst unexpected hits do occur it must be said that the identification of offenders by fingerprints without other indicators as to their identity are now relatively uncommon.

Of course, it must be acknowledged that the collection of millions of sets of fingerprints in the National Identification Bureau (N.I.B.) is aimed at establishing the previous criminal records of persons arrested for crime and this is of vital importance to the criminal justice process, but with such a massive collection of data, a case has long since been made that it should be better used on the investigative side of crimes. This is not a criticism of the N.I.B. or local fingerprint bureaus, as the circumstances which have brought about the present restrictions are well known and fully understood. It was as long ago as 1967 that the police service and various departments of the Home Office joined forces to explore ways in which developing technology could be used to improve the existing methods. This programme is now known as A.F.R. — Automatic Fingerprint Recognition. Through the joint efforts of the Home Office and the police we are on the verge of an exciting breakthrough. At the risk of boring those already familiar with these developments the A.F.R. system may be summarised as follows: A fingerprint or mark submitted for search against the main collection is first scanned by a TV camera. Its image is processed by computer and automatically coded and searched against previously encoded fingerprints. The coding method is based on fingerprint ridge characteristics. The system is able to rank the collection in order of the most likely match to the least likely, thus focusing the fingerprint officer's attention on the most productive areas of the collection.

The matching techniques of A.F.R. are so accurate that when searching the fingerprints of an arrested person, or an unidentified dead body, it will only be necessary for the fingerprint officer to look at one or two forms in the collection to confirm identity; that is, providing the subject's fingerprints have previously been taken.

In a "scene of crime mark search" under this system, examination of only about ten fingerprint forms will be necessary. The advantages are obvious and there will be greater productivity and return for the heavy investment currently committed to the present system on fingerprinting.

Searching undertaken by A.F.R. is rapid, resulting in earlier identification which will mean swifter intervention by investigators with the added benefits of preserving further evidence of the type often lost with the passage of time, and better opportunity to recover stolen property. Some systems which search on a complete set of fingerprints are already commercially available and offer a performance of several hundred comparisons a second. The real breakthrough will come with the availability of systems providing the single mark searching facility. Major advances in computer technology will enable us to reach this goal in the very near future. It can be confidently forecast that in the 1990s there will be a resurgence of fingerprint evidence in criminal trials. Whilst its impact will be greater in the areas of lesser crime such as house breakings, motor vehicle crime, violence and malicious damage, etc., it must be right that the main thrust of new technology and investigative technique should be directed at those areas of crime which, according to Home Office Crime surveys, cause the most anxiety, irritation, and dissatisfaction to the majority of the populace.

In highlighting the existing development, it is not suggested that the science of fingerprints has stood still. Far from it. Marks can now be lifted and developed or photographed on the most unlikely surfaces but such advances do beg the question — If you cannot now process all the marks found at scenes of crime, is there much point in discovering new methods of developing marks on surfaces that would previously have been ignored? A negative question perhaps but there is a corollary with the problem that now faces the Forensic Science Service. When police demands on existing skills and technology are greater than ever before and cannot be fully met, is it right to continually titillate the police with your newest discoveries when, in fact, in percentage terms of the overall crime rate, we are obliged to use you less and less?

The consequence of this diminishing availability of using fingerprint and scientific evidence in the lesser crimes, is that young detectives and young police officers no longer think "forensic" or think "fingerprints" and no matter now much instruction they might receive on the various training courses it is the use of such sciences at first hand which develops the sense of its proper use and the understanding of its real worth in evidential terms.

Let us move onto another method of identification, that is the practice of photographing convicted persons. For almost every set of fingerprints held in the National Identification Bureau there is a photograph of its maker either held centrally or regionally. Certain sections of this library are replicated at force and even station level. Millions of photographs, the majority of them rarely used, require administrative arrangements ensuring security and swift access. Valuable space to store such large libraries is consumed.

Having admitted that the majority are rarely used, when they are required they are of considerable value. As a service we could not contemplate discarding this facility.

In 1981 the Home Office scientific research and development branch commenced a project based on photographic retrieval from optical disc (PROD for short). This project is now well advanced and we will shortly be able to retain our libraries in a form which takes no more space than an ordinary desk and in a manner ensuring fast retrieval of high-quality images that can be produced in hard copy with no loss of definition.

In the fullness of time as forces take on this system networking will develop, providing a speedy transmission of images throughout the United Kingdom. But in terms of today's technology this is relatively old hat. The exciting prospect in store for "Fastfoto", as it is called, is that it may be possible, in the future, to equip the system with an electronic photofit module. This would enable the construction of a likeness on the screen using witness recall, which the computer can compare with all the images in its memory — another good example of how the Home Office and police service have collaborated to modernise an existing investigative tool but also to take it forward with a keener cutting edge.

There are many other examples where valuable evidence and intelligence is being acquired by using technology, some of it no longer considered new in the rapidly changing world of electronics — closed circuit television, for example, where the latest camera can be less than two inches square but yet produce high-quality pictures, giving a wider choice of options where it may be concealed.

When coupled to video recorders that are only activated when there is movement, increased light, or heat in a room, physical surveillance of premises in which theft is a regular occurrence or subject to repeated attacks from burglars, is greatly reduced as is the cost of such police operations. Electronic footpads in such vulnerable premises as schools are being increasingly used to great effect and, when activated, alert the local police control room who dispatch the necessary resource.

Video enhancement is a recent development which is proving particularly effective now that most major football grounds have closed circuit television (C.C.T.V.). To develop photographs of evidential value from a video recording was not possible until a couple years ago and a good example of its use was during the enquiries made by Merseyside police when trying to identify participants in the violence which occurred at the Heysel Stadium in 1985 and which led to so many deaths.

The enhancement of blurred photographs is also achievable and where a photograph is taken from an oblique angle it can be readjusted as though the photograph had been taken head on. Thermal images, infra-red photographs, explosive sniffing devices, fibre optic endoscopes are just a few of the further examples where developments in fields unrelated to law enforcement have been adapted for use by investigators of crime.

In reminding you of these relatively new advances we are in danger of painting too rosy a picture of the police service as a modern forward-thinking organisation hand in hand with an enlightened Home Office. Some less complimentary observations on our ability to identify a developing problem and fashion a solution will redress this imbalance. The management of major complex criminal investigations is one of these areas. In the past decade several notorious cases highlighted some deficiencies in our systems but we did not properly acknowledge these difficulties. Paradoxically the fault probably lay in our own success in major crime investigations.

Our detection rate in murder and terrorist atrocities has always been high and ranks amongst the highest in the world. The warning bells were doubtless muffled by this impressive record. But an in-depth examination into one particular series of murders identified the need for some radical rethinking and was the driving force behind the changes that were to follow and are still in being.

The Home Secretary of the day, in addressing the House, said of this particular series of crimes that it was necessary to respond constructively to the experience gained. He went on to list the specific areas requiring close examination:

1. The management requirement of the investigation of a series of major crimes — this has been taken on by the police staff college who now train officers at chief officer level who might be called upon as officers in overall command.
2. The training of senior detectives and personnel working in major incident rooms.
3. The command of investigations involving a number of crimes which cross force boundaries.
4. The harnessing for such investigations of the best detective and forensic science skills in the country.
5. The use of computers.

A working group, chaired by the author, was set up in June 1983 to look specifically at all these areas with the exception of the first. The brief was much wider but for the purposes of discussion will be confined to observations where technology was used to achieve some of our objectives.

The first requirement was to convince the service that a standardised major incident room procedure and standardised documentation was essential and achievable. It had to be a manual system even though a computer project code named Miriam was well advanced in its development stage. No computerised system was then available in spite of noises to the contrary from the computer industry and the media.

Each function in the incident room was subjected to detailed analysis and documented. The flow of information through the system was designed so that the indices were as up to date as was humanly possible in a manual system and that priorities were identified for early action. The life blood of any investigation is information from whatever source. Hitherto we have not been properly geared to handling the floods that occur at various stages of any enquiry particularly following media coverage, especially the electronic media. As an example, in a recent murder enquiry in my county, we were able to secure a 30-second commentary about our case at the commencement of the television "Crime Watch" programme which showed a photograph of a man we wanted to interview. This resulted in a team of ten telephonists being kept very busy for an hour and a half. The result was staggering in that it not only resulted in the man coming forward with his solicitor but some very valuable evidence and new lines of enquiry were established. Such is the power of the box.

To return to the endeavours of the working group, many of our recommendations were made with the knowledge that the transition into computerised handling of some of the data was not far away. If that transition was to be successful, the initial adjustment to accommodate the system should be minimal. The manual system was designed with that objective very much in mind.

The first stage of computerisation was labelled the "Interim Solution" and enabled all the indices currently held in card systems to be computerised. Where the manual system demanded that, in certain circumstances, as many as five cards needed to be handwritten for just one item of information in order that they could be placed in relevant indices, one entry to the computer was sufficient to ensure the information was stored in all the relevant sections. This was a considerable step forward and attracted the interest and favourable comment from the most doubting of Thomas's.

The next stage, known as Holmes, is now well advanced. It is a modular approach with forces able to make their choice on the basis of what their need is perceived to be and what their police authorities will permit them to spend. The modules in simple terms are: Module 1, Indexing; Module 2, Action and Document Management; Module 3, Word Processing and Free Text Retrieval (the most expensive but most attractive). The indications are that by the turn of the decade the vast majority of forces will have acquired the full system. Such is the acceptance of computer technology, even by the long in the tooth and large in the belly elder statesmen of the detective fraternity.

That, however, is not the end of the story. There is still a requirement for some upward growth path and a central facility for merging enquiries when a positive link has been established. The technology is there but some funding principles and suitable locations have yet to be finalised.

In the early days of the working group, criticisms were being voiced that we had gone systems crazy and had produced a labour-intensive administration with some strange belief that, at some stage in its machination, bells would ring to announce the identity of the perpetrator of the crime under investigation. However, we all acknowledged that outside investigators, directed by a well-informed senior investigating officer, held the key to any successful investigation. In a complex and protracted enquiry a properly constructed system of management of information is essential. The credibility of this information base is paramount because if shortcomings exist they will soon be apparent to the outside enquiry officers and once that happens it's a slippery slope leading to casual, half-hearted enquiries, short-cutting and even deceit.

We vowed, as a group, that if it was possible we would ensure that no outside enquiry officer would embark on an enquiry into an individual or other subject without being in possession of all the information contained in the system appertaining to that subject. To the uninitiated this does not sound a daunting task but let me give you some facts and figures relating to a murder enquiry that has recently been concluded. At the time the arrest was made the following items of information were contained in the system: 21,500 nominals, 5,300 vehicles, 4,250 statements, 6,350 actions, 6,800 messages. This volume of information, not uncommon today, helps to put our task in some sort of perspective. To be able to do this without causing inordinate delays we had to be sure that our system catered for a fast flow of information through the incident room.

To meet this requirement both in the manual and computerised systems, personnel are required in greater numbers than ever before but it is an investment that pays handsome dividends. Firstly, the cutting edge of the job, the outside investigator, is more efficient and effective. We must not forget that the positive elimination of a person from an enquiry is an advancement of the investigation. To do that speedily adds to the impetus of the enquiry. More importantly the detective's skill, his flair, his sixth sense, call it what you will, is always heightened when he is confident that he has the best information available.

The manual system was adopted throughout the mainland on the 1st January, 1984 and the "interim solution" of computerised indices has rapidly spread since then. In addition a few forces already possess the "all singing, all dancing" system of Holmes I, II and III.

There have been several cases since 1984 where the detective's flair, enhanced by the full information then available, has led to an arrest bringing to an end a complex and costly enquiry.

Subsequent examination of other lines of enquiry suggest that the culprit would have come under the strong light of suspicion later in the investigation but the earlier arrest saved many thousands of man-hours which of course means money. Unfortunately, the best examples are cases yet to come to trial and it would be unwise to comment further on them — but the details would have made the point for me, that heavy investment in personnel in the incident room does pay dividends and secondly they would also have gone some way to answering the question posed in the title of this discourse. In these cases technology enhanced but certainly did not replace detective skills.

Another feature which has escalated in recent years is the need to set up satellite incident rooms. For example, a child is abducted in one force area and the body found later in another force area, sometimes hundreds of miles away. This creates two major areas of enquiry. These need to be linked so that outside investigators in either area have full access to the same data base. Sadly, we have had several cases of this nature recently but this has given us experience in using and developing the necessary communication link and also enabled us to test modern facsimile equipment under operational conditions.

I referred earlier to the Home Secretary's list of areas requiring close examination which included the management requirement of the investigation of a series of major crimes. Before you can talk of managing a series of crimes they have to be identified.

To enhance our ability to do this several measures have been taken. Firstly, Criminal Intelligence Offices have been set up on a regional basis. Superimposed on this structure is a computerised system of crime pattern analysis. The data base consists of certain categories of crime (in some categories we covered a ten-year period in the back record conversion programme). Some success has already been recorded, but I believe it is a tool the full potential of which has yet to be realised. Some adjustments to the quality of input and a greater understanding of its use and benefits is still needed by some middle and senior detectives in the service. Of particular disappointment to members of the working group is the delay that has occurred in getting pathological and forensic items of intelligence on to the system. Agreement was reached with both branches of science, the format was designed and agreement reached with the police national computer unit. We were geared up to go live on 1st January, 1985 but implementation is still some months away. In the longer term we hope to be able to explore with the forensic service how other types of criminal intelligence, lying dormant in laboratories, can be extracted and used to assist the process of linking crimes and identify series more rapidly than we are currently able to.

The technology we now have to aid us has been briefly outlined and the benefits are obvious. There are, however, some disadvantages. When such computer assistance is available and known to the media and public at large as being available, excuses from a chief constable that he was unable to afford it sound hollow when his organisation is accused of being slow to apprehend a killer who has struck again; or he has failed to respond to intelligence of likely terrorist activity and been unable to prevent the mayhem, destruction and death that such people intend. Remember it is not just the cost of purchasing such machinery but also the resource consequences of the personnel required to operate it.

As a recent example, in the summer of 1985 hard intelligence, supported by evidence, indicated that a bombing campaign at seaside resorts throughout England was likely. In the Devon and Cornwall police area there were many vulnerable resorts. Every hotel had to be checked out. The force possessed computer technology to assist in handling large quantities of information in a complex enquiry. The Chief Constable therefore *had* to use it. He was not permitted the luxury of making a decision in terms of cost effectiveness or resource consequences. Time was also of the essence. This was the result. Forty-six people in two twelve-hour shifts drove the machines, handling and processing information derived from a large team of outside investigators; whereas elsewhere, another force, who shall be nameless, who did not possess computer facilities, could only do as much as was within their capabilities. In the outcome, nothing of consequence was found in either area but in financial terms the Devon and Cornwall operation severely dented the budget — in the other area it was only bruised.

In spite of the hiccups and occasional disadvantages that have resulted, the service can claim it has responded positively to the lessons learned from the investigation that the Home Secretary was obliged to comment on in the House of Commons. It may have been noticed neither the case nor the force involved has been mentioned by name. This is not a desire to be coy or to seek to avoid embarrassment to those concerned. It was a conscious decision. The deficiencies that then existed, particularly in the availability of technology, existed elsewhere, and if blame is to be apportioned it must be shared by us all including some sections at the Home Office who had the responsibility for the development of the technology that would have been of immense value in such a complex enquiry.

Let us direct our thoughts to the forensic science sevice and remind ourselves of the title of this article. In terms of electronic gadgetry, some ambiguous answers to that question have been proffered — in some cases it has heightened detective skills while in others it has replaced certain aspects of it. It has also created a requirement for new skills; the detective officer is not yet defunct.

In relation to some areas of forensic science (as with fingerprint evidence) it could be a much more positive answer in the affirmative.

Let me remind ourselves of the three qualities Tryhorn (1) identified as making a successful detective, Tact, Patience and Perseverance. The modern vogue of defending advocates is to invite juries to interpret tact as deviousness and unfair practice. Patience is interpreted as lengthy aggressive interviews with suspects locked up in cells until they confess. Perseverance is "get a confession at all costs". Acquittal rates demonstrate the success of such tactics.

Ironically, the police service today is more honest, professional and less aggressive than ever before. One cannot but escape the fact that today, evidence of confession and of damaging police interviews seem to carry little weight with juries. Perhaps tape recording of interviews will reverse this trend.

In the history of organised criminal investigation there has never been a greater need for forensic evidence to counter the present imbalance in the scales of justice, whether it directly links the accused with the crime, or is just circumstantial.

Huxley got it absolutely right when he referred to "that ugly fact which destroys even the most beautiful hypothesis". As a service we are anxious to have more of these ugly facts. But what is the reality? Let me pose some questions. If we have a 20 per cent increase in crime, can we also anticipate 20 per cent more cases being handled by our local laboratory? If a murder suspect has been detained and he declines to answer any questions on the advice of his freely provided lawyer, could a rapid examination be carried out at the local laboratory on relevant material in order to give some circumstantial evidence justifying an application to the magistrates' court for a further period of detention under the new procedures of the Police and Criminal Evidence Act? For that matter, is anyone in the forensic science service interested in the impact on police procedures of this new legislation? Can an officer realistically expect the director of his local laboratory to be interested in assisting him in dealing with an outbreak of vandalism, or house-breaking on a council estate, where the loss to the victim is in tens of pounds, rather than thousands?

When a major crime comes along, can a policemen always rely on a good service from his laboratory? Most policemen share the same concern at what is, in relative terms, a shrinking service. Blame does not lie with those who are working within the system.

In a country where crime and disorder is causing such concern it seems strange that we are only prepared to pay something of the order of £13 million a year (for England and Wales) for the provision of a service which could have a much greater impact on the problem. If more forensic evidence was available there would be less room for pleas of not guilty and less resources spent in the trial processes of our judicial system.

There seems some inconsistency here, when the Law Society decided that it was not prepared to take part in the Police and Criminal Evidence Act procedures whereby a detained person could have legal advice at short notice throughout 24 hours of the day, somebody in the corridors of power in Whitehall found 16 million pounds overnight.

If that money could be found to protect the interests of a suspect or accused person, why are we so parsimonious with some of the other services needed to support law and order?

How can we hope to attract suitably qualified scientists to join our laboratories when their skills and talents attract greater rewards in almost every other area? A £12,500 salary for a Senior Scientific Officer is ludicrous in this day and age.

How can we hope to retain such people and maintain our position in producing leading authorities in certain areas of forensic science at that level of remuneration? A reassessment of the role of the service is urgently needed. The service has been subjected to a number of reviews and the results of some of them have been demoralising. But change is needed if we are to avoid being the backmarkers we were 50 years ago.

If it makes you feel any better, from a policeman's point of view, we value you. We need you and we wish to support you in obtaining better conditions, more attractive career structure and more resources.

References

1. Tryhorn, J. Scientific Aids in Criminal Investigation. *Police Journal*, 1936; 33–41.

"FIRST CATCH YOUR HARE"

A. K. Sloan

Most people will be aware of the well-known Victorian cookery expert Mrs Beaton, who in her recipe for hare soup included the words "first catch your hare".

This excellent advice can be readily transferred to the forensic science and crime investigation scene where "evidence" only becomes relevant when the culprit is identified. It is a discussion of this aspect of the investigation of serious and series crime which follows since in recent years there appears to have been a swing towards a laboratory-centred service to the courts at the expense of giving the first priority to assisting the investigator to identify the suspect. Having secured a suspect it is then necessary to concentrate on the evidence to prove the case or otherwise before a court. These two demands are not independent but move in converging lines, meeting when the suspect has been arrested and is available for tests.

It is easy to trace the causes of the retreat of the forensic scientist from the investigative process. Nostalgia with its rose-coloured spectacles makes us remember a past when crime, scientists and policemen were in lesser numbers. In England and Wales the judicial system demanded frequent visits to court and, in general, conditions were such that the scientist, the policeman and the pathologist as well as the lawyer were well known to each other, understood each other's problems and harboured no doubts about the integrity of each discipline.

From the mid 1960s matters began to deteriorate. Forces amalgamated and by 1974 they had reduced from 128 to 43 in England and Wales and from 20 to 8 in Scotland.

At the same time new laboratories were built in England, staffs were consolidated and a psychological and geographical distancing occurred. Recruitment direct from university to laboratory with no outside experience, little or no contact with the investigator other than through the liaison officer, all led to a belief that servicing the needs of the courts was the prime function.

The larger police forces now in existence suffered a surfeit of arrogance and formed bigger and better Scenes of Crime units lavishly equipped, better trained and more than ready to fill the space being vacated by the Scientist. Inclination, isolation, economics and over-confidence formed an unholy alliance resulting in the steady erosion of the Scientists' attendance at scenes and a willingness on the part of the Scenes of Crime Officer to replace him. The scientist was replaced by the technician by mutual consent.

The effect on crime investigation was similar to that of the panda car on uniform beat patrolling. The economies of larger units and technology were used to paper over the gaps in investment and resources. Instead of the panda car being an additional layer of response policing based firmly on foot patrols, public assistance and crime intelligence, a lack of manpower, increased workloads and scarce resources meant that the panda only remained to offer the public a "fire brigade" service. A good scheme was corrupted by a failure to commit adequate resources.

Similarly the emergence of the new laboratories, the isolation of staff, the lack of resources to attend scenes or examine larger numbers of exhibits contributed to a decline in the service offered to the police in the investigation of crime. Forensic science sulked in its tent while a police service, partly as a result of its failure to complain early enough about the lack of scientific resources and partly by its own arrogance in assuming that it could more than adequately fill the gap, began to experience great difficulties as serious and series crime escalated.

Homer — like the lawyers stood firmly aside and applauded the separation forced on the two services in the interests of economy and integrity and indeed suggested that the isolation of the Scientist should be reinforced. We saw edicts such as the 1981 prohibition on the scientist reading the statement of the rape victim (1). No other scientists are expected to work in such glorious seclusion and deny themselves information which may or may not suggest profitable lines of investigation or areas where further effort would be negative. How does this compare with Home Office Circular No. 114/83 (2) and Scottish Home and Health Circular No. 3/1984 (3) on the efficient use of resources? Integrity is a vital part of the criminal justice system and no participant has a prerogative in this.

The result of these decisions was that one of the major contributions to the successful detection of crime was greatly diminished. The ideal of the scene visit by the investigator, the pathologist, the forensic scientist and the scenes of crime officer was almost never achieved. This not only prevented the acquisition of the maximum amount of "evidence" from the scene but it obstructed the early communication and exchange of ideas that is vital to a successful investigation.

During the time all this was happening, crime grew at an exceptional rate. The days when the Head of CID investigated all murders quickly passed and this important role is now often carried out by Detective Chief Inspectors to a very high standard. The proliferation of important investigations has of itself created communication problems as well as to greatly increase the demand for resources devoted to scene examination.

This can be illustrated by using the serious crime figures for England and Wales over a 20-year period (4, 5).

In 1961 there were 261 Homicides which increased to 459 in 1971 and grew to 559 by 1981. Similar figures for Scotland are 57, 72 and 89.

All crime grew during this period and one has only to think of the more recent phenomena of terrorism, hostage and kidnapping, poisoning of foodstuffs and other products in supermarkets as well as in armed robberies and arson to realise the immense demands being made on both services. The crime of arson illustrates this growth (4, 5). Again in England and Wales in 1961 there were 1,115 cases which increased to 3,562 in 1971 and grew in 1981 to 15,116. Similar figures for Scotland are 158,771 and 3,037.

The problem was further complicated by the emergence of series crime on a regular basis which not only consumed resources as never before, but created public anxiety and tremendous pressures on the investigator. These are factors which are frequently overlooked by those responsible for the provision of the means of efficiently investigating major crime under the full glare of publicity, media interest, public concern and political pressure. This has created a tremendous pressure on the investigator, who is faced with three priorities, successful investigation, public reassurance and a need to prevent the next crime in the series. The sensitivity of the public in these incidents, whipped up by media pressure and the gratuitous advice of experts ranging from old war horses to instant pundits concentrates the mind of the investigator wonderfully. What he requires is help in catching the perpetrator — there can be no other priority. If a criminal is systematically killing members of the public, the police or anyone else, there can be no other objective than to effect his arrest.

It would be appropriate at this stage to examine these pressures in real life and to do this it is necessary to refer to two cases:

The Case of Barry Peter Prudom

On 17th June 1982, Barry Peter Edwards or Prudom shot dead a police officer at Harrogate, North Yorkshire; three days later he committed an offence of robbery in Lincolnshire. On the 22nd June he shot dead a male person near Newark in Nottinghamshire and shot and seriously injured his wife. On the 24th June he attempted to murder a police officer in Bickley Forest, North Yorkshire, by shooting at him and on the 24th June 1982, he shot and killed a police sergeant at Malton, North Yorkshire. On the 3rd July he took three persons hostage but fortunately left before discovery by the police. This scenario contains all the pressures previously mentioned and emphasises the need for an arrest as soon as possible because of the continuing dangers to the public. The enquiry took place in three police areas only two of which were contiguous. The investigators knew that any contact between Prudom and the police, or a member of the public showing resistance, would result in a further shooting and probably death.

One factor on the positive side was that the identity of the probable offender became known early in the enquiry. Prudom was known to be an expert shot, to have practised survival skills and to be used to living off the country. The search in the Malton area, between the 28th June and the 4th July 1982, required a total of 3,331 police officers; an average of 475 officers per day being deployed composed of armed officers, dog handlers, technical support personnel and a large number of patrol officers. These figures do not include the investigators. The cost in salaries, overtime, transportation, and subsistence was obviously very high.

There were 399 reported sightings of the suspect, each of which had to be checked out by a seven-man response team. Statements were taken from 1,043 people and there were 3,982 actions. The cost of the operation and the pressures on the police were horrendous.

The early identification of a probable suspect did simplify matters but there remained two vital tasks for the forensic scientists involved:

(a) To assess all available scientific evidence to confirm or deny that the suspect was Prudom. If he gave himself up freshly showered and with a change of clothing, accompanied by a solicitor could we confirm he was the culprit? If he was not, we would have to continue the search.
(b) To examine "hides" and other places suspected to have been used by Prudom in order to confirm that he was in a particular locality.

Anyone who knows the North Yorkshire area will realise the difficulties in cornering a suspect and systematically searching for him. This was a tremendous task and the possibility that the suspect might kill again or depart to other similar areas of the country which he knew well was always present.

One other task of the scientist was of course the examination of all scientific evidence for use by the court. With the benefit of recent experience in the police service, the decision to fully involve the scientist was made early. The services of Stuart Stanley Kind to coordinate this side of the enquiry was acquired from the 1st July 1982. Circumstances dictated that three Forensic Scientists from two Forensic Science Laboratories were involved in the five reported incidents.

Similarly two pathologists were each involved in one incident and one pathologist in two, including the death of the suspect Prudom. Of the two investigators involved one had responsibility for one offence and the other for three, plus the death of Prudom.

A coordinator was appointed on the 22nd June and an officer in overall command on the 1st July 1982.

A computer was used, albeit in a crude form, to successfully link all four incident rooms.

After the death of Prudom on the 4th July 1982 forensic examination proved that all the shootings had been carried out with the same 0·22 pistol. A bloodstain found in the car used in the Harrogate shooting, a hair found at the Lincolnshire robbery and a number of other factors were also shown to be important in the forensic evidence. These findings were corroborated by items found in Prudom's possession arising from different scenes.

The Case of Malcolm Fairley

The "Fox" case, as it was dubbed by the media, started with a petty burglar and thief Malcolm Fairley breaking into a house in Leighton Buzzard, Bedfordshire, on the 11th April 1984. He surprised the 70-year-old female householder in bed and indecently assaulted her. He committed further burglaries and on the 10th May, hooded and armed with a shotgun, he broke into a house and awaited the return of the male householder who was then subjected to indecent assault and sexual perversion. Offences continued and a further shotgun was stolen and shortened. Fairley, hooded and carrying the shotgun, then embarked on a series of raids on houses. On one occasion he made a "hide" of armchairs and a bedspread while he watched video films and this created his "Fox" image. He then broke into a nearby house where he surprised and shot the male householder at point-blank range causing serious hand and arm injuries. Further offences of burglary, rape, indecent assault on males and females occurred in the area. On the 17th August 1984 he hid his car near a motorway junction in the Rotherham area of South Yorkshire while he broke into a house nearby and raped a woman. The scene where the car was hidden was discovered later and a shotgun recovered. Of great significance was a small sample of paint removed from the scene and which was identified as having arisen from a British Leyland motor vehicle of a bronze yellow colour. Further offences were committed in Durham and in the Thames Valley prior to Fairley's arrest on the 11th September 1984.

Throughout this time the pressure by the media, public concern and political interest and demands, were tremendous. Each incident triggered off further waves of hysteria and the need of the police to make an arrest grew correspondingly. Here the assailant was not known and all resources were diverted to identifying him.

Lessons of the past demonstrated the advantages of the early appointment of an Officer in Overall Command (OIOC), the complete integration of the investigation teams from all forces and the early appointment of a senior forensic scientist to the management team.

The terms of reference of the scientist, Mr J. G. Craddock, Head of Biology at the Home Office Forensic Science Laboratory at Huntingdon, were to generate in the police forces such an awareness as to make the most effective use of the investigation role of the Forensic Science Service in these offences, as well as in the subsequent work normally undertaken by a Forensic Science Laboratory once a suspect has been found; in addition, to provide an input from a different (non-police) discipline into the normal processes of the police investigation.

He was provided with an office at the main enquiry centre at Dunstable, given copies of all statements and had unfettered access to all information and facilities. He attended relevant management meetings at the request of the Officer in Overall Command.

He sought to improve the flow of information to and from the Home Office Forensic Science and the Metropolitan Police Laboratories and other scientific agencies. He regularly reported his assessments of forensic science findings and sought to make clear what information was conclusive and what was only tentative. In the early stages, "scene intelligence" was vital to identifying all previously reported offences thought to be connected so that the maximum amount of information could be gleaned. A draft proforma was prepared for these. His normal working day always exceeded twelve hours. The laboratory director, Ronald Outeridge, took a personal interest in the enquiry and covered for the assigned scientist when he was away. An example of the value of their work was that when the "hide" near Rotherham was discovered and a surveillance set up, they convinced the Officer in Overall Command that they should be allowed to make a discreet but thorough scene search. This established the colour, shape and approximate size of the motor vehicle used.

While a number of Forensic Science Laboratories were utilised, the bulk of the work was carried out at Huntingdon utilising some 25 staff in Biology, Chemistry and Firearms Departments. This represents more than a third of the total staff. At times the whole of the Biology and Chemistry staffs were exclusively assigned to the investigation and when one bears in mind that the laboratory had to service ten police forces, not only were resources stretched but there was a need to persuade other forces to allow priority and to farm out work to other laboratories.

Altogether, 730 items were examined in connection with six serious sexual offences, several other assaults and numerous minor burglaries. The amount of work involved, however, was vastly greater than would have been the case if the offences could have been treated separately. For example, a burglary case might involve a single comparison between an instrument mark and a suspect instrument. In this investigation, however, it was necesary to compare each instrument mark with others found at the various scenes since at the "scene intelligence" phase of the work, there were no suspect instruments available. The problem was one of determining which offences could be attributable to the series. Moreover, while it is often possible to show that two people have been in physical contact because fibres have been transferred from one to the other, in this investigation, the problem was to show that each of a number of individuals had been in contact with a single assailant without information about the constituent fibres of his clothing.

Following the Rayner Report (6) ordinary burglary cases would not normally have been examined by the laboratory but for the "Fox" investigation this was essential because of the pressing need to establish a pattern.

The equipment used during this investigation was that available throughout the Home Office Forensic Science Service and included isoelectric focussing electrophoresis for the grouping of semen, light and scanning microscopy for the characterisation of debris, hairs and paint; comparison microscopy, infra-red spectrophotometry and microspectrometry for the characterisation of fibres, and pyrolysis gas chromatography for identifying paint.

It is clear that the early involvement of the Home Office Forensic Science Service and the close liaison between the police and the Forensic Science Laboratory at Huntingdon produced useful results quickly. This was a big advance on previous experience when priorities were not so clearly established.

On the 10th September 1984 two young detectives, provided with all the information currently available, interviewed the suspect in London. By the use of this information, particularly the colour and shape of the car, they identified a vehicle nearby which Fairley admitted was his. Good detective work did the rest. The enquiry incurred extra costs in excess of £1,500,000. At one stage there were 150 officers enquiring into these crimes and over 300 officers engaged on public protection duties.

The lessons to be learned from these two enquiries are, I hope, self-evident. When serious crimes are committed and, even more so, when there is a strong likelihood of them being continued to be committed, it is imperative to use all available resources and effect arrests as early as possible. Every day that passes increases the cost of the investigation and increases the risks to the public. Nothing is more important to the police in their duty to protect life and property.

It should not be forgotten that senior Forensic Scientists have considerable experience of major crime investigation and their attachment to an enquiry makes that experience directly available to the police. It provides an additional input from a non-police discipline that is varied and unique, giving the officer in command and the management team a different perception of problems concerning the overall investigation.

There must be continual and total close cooperation between the police and the Forensic Science services. It must be considered the norm and should start with opportunities being afforded to young scientists to regularly visit the scenes of serious crime, even if they are domestic murders with the suspect in custody. It is only by this close early association between the investigator and the expert that mutual confidence and professional skills will develop. The young scientist, the Scenes of Crimes Officer and the young investigator are the people who in later years will be called upon to investigate major series crime. They must be trained to have the confidence to withstand the pressures of media, politicians and public alike and apply themselves to effecting the arrest of those responsible and maintaining public safety and tranquillity.

In these days of efficiency and effectiveness, priorities and value for money, it is not easy to obtain the resources that would be necessary to promote such an increase in joint scene investigation. It is therefore all the more important not to allow this desirable end to be forgotten or the progress of recent years to be impeded. It may be that by piecemeal efforts we will achieve our aims but we must ensure that we use our current resources to the maximum of efficiency. We must then make our case for improvements on this basis so that early joint cooperation in crime investigation can be demonstrated to pay for itself by a greater likelihood of detection and an earlier conclusion of the investigation. Each day saved has a marked effect on the budget.

Questions will be raised on the propriety of the investigator and the scientist working so closely together with doubts being expressed on their objectivity. This is nothing new and in 1968 Sir Richard Ormrod said "A more ambitious reform — which would have the most far reaching effect would be the detachment of the Forensic Science Laboratories from the Home Office and their attachment to a body analogous to the Medical Research Council. The staffs of these laboratories are invaluable and their evidence usually of the highest quality but their connection with the Home Office inevitably leads to their identification in the mind of the ordinary man and of many lawyers, with the Police and the prosecution and so induces a sense of mistrust of their independence *which is unjustified*" (7). There follows a homily on justice being seen to be done.

There can be no justice in court unless there is a prisoner at the bar. It is up to the Police Service to investigate and as Dr W. J. Rodgers says (8) "they should make use of all legitimate means to pursue that end, including the best scientific assistance available" and further "The function of the forensic scientist is to assist in the investigation of crime which is carried out primarily by police officers. The forensic scientist, therefore, assists police officers. To state this is in no way to state that the integrity of the forensic scientist is suspect." No discipline has a special claim to integrity and it should be assumed that all disciplines involved in justice maintain the highest standards. Failures, when they occur, are no respecters of demarcation lines. We all have an interest in justice, for the accused, for the victim and for the community at large.

As far as resources permit there should be a steady expansion of the forensic science service in the United Kingdom. Whether it is Home Office controlled as in England and Wales or more directly associated with the police as in Scotland is immaterial. The service must be available to the investigator to assist him in the detection of offences particularly those relating to murder, terrorism, serious assaults, rape and the misuse of drugs. The early solution of an enquiry can effectively save large sums of money which can be better spent on improving the quality of life for the community.

It is the duty of the Universities first of all to produce the students who will step into the role of forensic scientist, lawyer or policeman with the requisite skills, understanding and a comprehension that only by joint endeavours can crime be solved and justice done. The University must also pioneer the new techniques which are invaluable to scientist and investigator alike and to provide a back-up service for the more difficult and obscure problems. They can also provide a validation of techniques and a compendium of knowledge. Above all they can teach an open-minded search for the truth for that, above all, is the target and it is from this that justice flows.

Any moves to separate the police investigator from the forensic scientist or any other experts is a measure we can ill afford and the hard work of the last few years to re-establish this well-tried and effective cooperation must continue. Any moves to the contrary will see a split in the forensic science service as the police will demand the operational involvement of the scientist and the courts can go their own way.

References

1. Instruction from the Director of Public Prosecutions for England and Wales, 1981.

2. Home Office Circular No. 114/83.

3. Scottish Home and Health Police Circular No. 3/83.

4. Her Majesty's Chief Inspector of Constabulary for England and Wales Annual Reports for 1961, 1971 and 1981: Crime Statistics.

5. Scottish Home and Health Department Criminal Statistics, Scotland 1961, 1971 and 1980–82.

6. The Rayner Scrutiny Programme, 1981. Home Office Project. The Forensic Science Service.

7. Ormrod, R. Scientific Evidence in Court. *Criminal Law Review*, 1968: 240–247.

8. Rodger, W. J. Does Forensic Science Have a Future? *Journal of the Forensic Science Society*, 1984; 24: 549–551.